Bilingualism across the lifespan

BILINGUALISM ACROSS THE LIFESPAN

Aspects of acquisition, maturity, and loss

Edited by

KENNETH HYLTENSTAM
Stockholm University

and

LORAINE K. OBLER
City University of New York

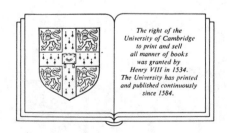

The right of the
University of Cambridge
to print and sell
all manner of books
was granted by
Henry VIII in 1534.
The University has printed
and published continuously
since 1584.

CAMBRIDGE UNIVERSITY PRESS

CAMBRIDGE

NEW YORK   PORT CHESTER   MELBOURNE   SYDNEY

Published by the Press Syndicate of the University of Cambridge
The Pitt Building, Trumpington Street, Cambridge CB2 1RP
40 West 20th Street, New York, NY 10011, USA
10 Stamford Road, Oakleigh, Melbourne 3166, Australia

© Cambridge University Press 1989

First published 1989

Printed in Great Britain by the University Press, Cambridge

British Library cataloguing in publication data

Bilingualism across the lifespan: aspects of
acquisition, maturity and loss.
1. Man. Bilingualism. Neuropsychological
aspects.
I. Hyltenstam, Kenneth, *1945*–
II. Obler, Loraine K.
401′.9

Library of Congress cataloguing in publication data

Bilingualism across the lifespan: aspects of acquisition, maturity,
and loss/edited by Kenneth Hyltenstam and Loraine K. Obler.
  p. cm.
Includes index
ISBN 0 521 35225 8.   ISBN 0 521 35998 8 (pbk)
1. Bilingualism. 2. Language acquisition. I. Hyltenstam,
Kenneth. II. Obler, Loraine K.
P115.B5428 1989
404′.2–dc19   88–31178   CIP

ISBN 0 521 35225 8 hard covers
ISBN 0 521 35998 8 paperback

This book is dedicated to all who value diversity
Among them Carlos Yorio, in memoriam

Contents

Contributors

Maria Bolander
Department of Scandinavian
Languages
University of Umeå

Suzanne Flynn
Department of Foreign Languages and
Literatures
Massachusetts Institute of Technology

Margaret Humes-Bartlo
Cognitive Neurosciences Program
City College
City University of New York

Kenneth Hyltenstam
Center for Research on Bilingualism
Stockholm University

Eric Kellerman
English Department and Department
of Applied Linguistics
Nijmegen University

Jürgen M. Meisel
Department of Romance Languages
University of Hamburg

Loraine K. Obler
Speech and Hearing Sciences Program
Graduate School
City University of New York

Ellen Perecman
Department of Neurology
New York University School of
Medicine

Shana Poplack
Department of Linguistics
University of Ottawa

Herbert Seliger
Department of Linguistics
Queens College and Graduate School
City University of New York

Michael A. Sharwood Smith
Department of English
University of Utrecht

Christopher Stroud
Center for Research on Bilingualism
Stockholm University

Susan Wheeler
Department of Linguistics
University of Ottawa

Anneli Westwood
Department of Linguistics
University of Ottawa

†Carlos A. Yorio
Lehman College and Graduate School
City University of New York

Preface

Over the years our interests in bilingualism have interwoven with our interests in the language changes of healthy aging and the language changes of dementia. Our training as linguists has been complemented by the study of brain-damaged patients of various ages. As neurolinguists today, our theoretical approach strives to elucidate the underlying brain bases for language; our teaching and involvement with training foreign and second language instructors encourage us to consider applied aspects of bilingualism research as well.

Thus we took the opportunity to bring together a diverse group of researchers to a conference entitled "Bilingualism Across the Lifespan" held at the Linguistic Society of America Summer Institute in 1986. Not only did the conference papers prove of interest; discussion in both public and informal environments was stimulating. Therefore we determined to put together this book which includes revisions of a number of papers given at the conference, and others invited afterwards. Our thanks to all who participated in that conference.

We are grateful also to teachers, colleagues, and students who have enabled us to advance our thinking over the years of our work in disciplines related to bilingualism. For KH these include Maria Bolander, Pit Corder, Björn Hammarberg, Inger Lindberg, Eva Magnusson, Bertil Malmberg, Manfred Pienemann, Christopher Stroud, Åke Viberg, and Maria Wingstedt. For LKO they include Martin Albert, Eva Baharav, Meg Humes-Bartlo, Nancy Mahecha, Margaret Fearey, Eta Schneiderman, Michel Paradis, Jyotsna Vaid, Shoshana Blum-Kulka, Andrew Cohen, and Elite Olshtain.

We thank also those institutions that have enabled us to work on this project: Stockholm University, the City University of New York Graduate School, the Aphasia Research Center, and the Hebrew University where LKO spent a brief Visiting Professorship 1987–8.

Most particularly we thank our contributors whose careful and thoughtful and generally prompt work has enabled us to fulfill our original vision of providing a varied and comprehensive approach to considering what the study of bilingualism from diverse perspectives can tell us about language performance and the brain.

Kenneth Hyltenstam and Loraine K. Obler
Stockholm
New York and Boston
July 1988

1. Bilingualism across the lifespan: an introduction

KENNETH HYLTENSTAM AND LORAINE K. OBLER

The large variety of questions dealt with in current research on bilingualism provides a rich potential for insights into human language processing. Research within the field has created a number of subdisciplines taking as their core specific issues, such as "early bilingual development", "code-switching", "second language acquisition" etc., with a broad range of methodologies and a diversity of assumptions and theories. The picture we get of bilingualism is thus one of a dynamic, rapidly developing field. No single researcher can hope to encompass more than a few aspects of bilingualism, leading to the necessity for specialization and concentration.

Thus, as usual, the other side of specialization is increasing isolation between those who work in different subdisciplines; cross-reference between the different fields is relatively rare. Therefore, a moment for reflection on the interrelationships between these subdisciplines would seem desirable at this point, stimulating researchers to pool their specialist knowledge on points of common interest. Ultimately, this should lead to a cross-fertilization of the whole field and new perspectives on specific topics.

The primary impetus for this book – and for the conference that motivated it – was a long-felt need to gauge how newer developments in bilingual research bear on the classical questions of how the bilingual's two (or more) language systems interact with each other and with other higher cognitive systems, neurological substrata and the social environment. Furthermore, we were curious as to how the frontier of research was being moved forward, how new theoretical frameworks were being applied to questions of long-standing interest, whether new questions were being formulated and whether alternative methodologies were being made available. We therefore invited researchers with various theoretical and disciplinary backgrounds to focus on central topics in their respective fields of expertise. Our purpose was to provide a comprehensive overview of the diversity of the field and stimulate researchers to extend their thinking beyond their own specialities.

Three dimensions, which we consider especially pertinent, were used to structure the discussion of the book:

(1) bilingualism at the various phases of the lifespan
(2) bilingualism under healthy and pathological conditions, and
(3) the development and loss of bilingualism.

Language across the lifespan

Firstly, then, we believe a fruitful approach to the issues involved in bilingualism might be to consider them in the context of research on language across the lifespan generally. Research on age-related variation in adult language behavior is a comparatively recent endeavor (see Obler, 1985), and the resources that have been expended on this topic are minimal in comparison with the massive work that has been carried out on early child language. The implicit assumption seems to have been that nothing of particular interest happens with an individual's language once it has been "fully" acquired, and thus nothing of interest for linguistic theory would be gained from studies of linguistic change in the adult individual. Considering the fact that linguistic changes in the earliest phases of childhood are so dramatic that no one can avoid observing them, while changes in later phases of childhood and in the adult are much less apparent, it is only natural that researchers have focused their endeavors on uncovering patterning in the child's early language acquisition. Pedagogical and clinical needs for information on normal and abnormal language development have likewise been an important incentive for this research.

The earlier research neglect of later lifespan language change has recently turned into a decisive interest in this question. In particular, there have been strong practical and theoretical motives behind the investigation of linguistic characteristics of the latest phase of life. The practical need for knowledge of what is normal language behavior in old age is evident in clinical diagnostic and therapeutic work with patients suffering from the various kinds of diseases that affect neurological functioning such as dementia, strokes, tumors, or head trauma. Theoretically, new knowledge about human linguistic capacity and its interaction with other cognitive capabilities can be gained from the results pointing to quantitative and qualitative differences in language between older and younger speakers (Obler and Albert, 1980).

In particular, differences have been documented between younger and older healthy monolinguals in their performance on naming and comprehension tasks, which declines with increasing age, and (arguably) on oral discourse, which may become less complex with extremely advanced age (Obler, 1980; Kemper, 1987) No age-related changes, however, are seen for automatic language tasks, and metalinguistic tasks. On written discourse an increased elaborateness with increasing age has been recorded (Obler, 1980), although there are possible social explanations. It would seem that brain changes associated with aging, even healthy aging, can be linked to the language changes of age. Such changes are even more striking, of course, and even qualitatively different, in the language and communication changes associated with strokes and dementia in late adulthood.

In the case of bilingual speakers, the lifespan variation in linguistic behavior is, of course, often quite spectacular. A large number of factors surrounding the acquisition and use of each language and the interplay between them at various phases of the individual bilingual's life conspire to determine the individual's linguistic "status" at any given point in time. Of obvious importance in this respect is, for example, whether both languages initially developed simultaneously, or whether one was acquired prior to the other, whether both languages were used throughout the lifespan, or whether there were periods when there was no need for one of them or no possibility of using it – or its use was socially problematic. Further important factors are whether the second language was learned in a formal classroom setting or acquired in an informal communicative situation, whether one of the languages was eventually lost or retained in modality or domain specific uses. (See Vaid, 1983, for a review of these factors as they affect lateral brain organization for the bilingual's languages.)

Language in health and pathology

The healthy–pathological dimension has a long tradition in research on bilingualism. To mention but one aspect of this multifaceted research tradition, cases of bilingual aphasia have contributed substantial data relevant to earlier and current hypotheses on cerebral organization in bilinguals, in particular on lateralization patterns (see Paradis, 1977 and Vaid, 1983). As regards other pathologies affecting language, these have hitherto not been systematically investigated with respect to bilinguals, although there is a large body of results from monolingual schizophrenics (e.g. Andreasen, 1979; Rochester and Martin, 1979; Chaika, 1982; and Schwartz, 1982) and demented patients (e.g. Irigaray, 1973 and Obler, 1983). Studies of the various language disabilities in children (see Ingram, 1976 and Crystal, 1982), likewise, constitute an area of intense research in monolinguals. The clinical diagnostic and therapeutic issues related to language disorders and bilingualism, such as whether an aberrant item in a bilingual's production is a second language feature or a pathological deficit, have lately been discussed in the literature, for example in Miller, 1984.

As in all behavioral research, the exceptional cases of bilingual behavior help us see the general patterns in bilingualism, and ultimately in language as such. In this respect, the healthy-pathological comparison seems to have much to offer for future research. This book aims to contribute to the expansion of the systematic investigation of this area.

The methodological and practical difficulties inherent in the study of pathologically related language variation – as well as the variation we find across the lifespan – are manifold. The most striking of these, perhaps, is the fact that the researcher generally has no knowledge of his/her subjects' premorbid – or earlier – linguistic functioning. Our current knowledge does not allow us to make conclusive judgments about the previous behavior from what we see in the present. Similarly, we are not very good at predicting plausible future linguistic fates from what we know about a person's present linguistic behavior and his/her linguistic history. Given such individual differences in language as can be seen in talkative as compared to uncommunicative normal speakers, in speakers who exhibit different degrees of communicative empathy with their interlocutors, and in speakers who are more and less sensitive to linguistic form, one would expect to find that these variables, among others, would have an influence on the individual's language development and on what happens in the case of damage to their linguistic capacities.

Language acquisition, maturity and loss

In the field of second language acquisition, empirical research on learner language has generated a large body of results during the past fifteen years or so (see, for example, the work discussed in McLaughlin, 1987). These results concern such things as how the learner's system for the target language – or subsystems of this – unfolds, and how learners solve communicative tasks in a language where they have fewer expressive resources than in their native language. In other words, the results are concerned with matters such as which communicative strategies they use, what role is played by simplified and/or finely tuned input, what the reasons are for the non-nativeness of the ultimate state of second language acquisition, or what the influence is of various situational and socio-psychological factors in the learner's environment.

Studies of mature stage bilinguals have to date not constituted a subfield within bilingualism on a par with, for example, second language acquisition. Although we do find a plethora of studies on mature bilinguals in neuro-, psycho- and sociolinguistics (for example studies on code-switching by

Poplack, 1980; Perecman, 1984; and articles in Vaid, 1986), little work has actually focused on the characteristics of "steady state" bilingualism as such. Recent studies that would fall within this area can be found in research that has uncovered differences between bilinguals' and monolinguals' processing of the same language at various levels – differences that are imperceptible for native speakers but which come to light after close scrutiny. Topics that have been considered in such studies are perception/production of phonemes (Obler, 1982), intuitional judgments of grammaticality (Coppetiers, 1987), lexical decision latencies (Mägiste, 1986), distribution of error types (Hyltenstam, 1988), and narrative and pragmatic structuring (Stroud, forthcoming).

One reason why mature bilinguals have not received the research attention they deserve is in line with the lack of interest in adult language skills generally: linguistic characteristics that are not readily apparent are likely to be ignored.

In contradistinction to this, the investigation of language loss has developed into a recognized subfield of bilingualism during the last ten years. This is evident from the flow of articles and state of the art collections that have made their entrance on the linguistic scene during the 1980s (Lambert and Freed, 1982; Veltens, De Bot & Van Els, 1986; and Berko Gleason's *Applied Psycholinguistics*, vol 7, no. 3, 1986). In this development we find various approaches to the study of language loss, from psycho- and neuro-linguistic studies of individuals (Sharwood Smith, 1983), to sociolinguistic studies of the extinction of whole speech communities (Dorian, 1981), and typological linguistic studies of language attrition (Schmidt, 1985).

Among questions treated in the language loss area that are especially relevant for the present volume, are those dealing with possible parallels between healthy language loss ("forgetting") and pathological linguistic breakdown. The questions are concerned with the quality of language loss, as evidenced by errors and avoidance of certain structures and items.

Overview of papers

It has not been possible to structure the book rigidly along our three dimensions of lifespan, health-pathology, and acquisition-maturity-loss, as three-dimensional work does not lend itself to linear ordering, and the different chapters intersect in various ways. Therefore, we have chosen to place those studies that deal with "becoming bilingual", that is with acquisition, in the initial part of the volume and those dealing with loss at the end. In between these two blocks we have arranged the chapters dealing with mature "steady state" bilingualism. (Poplack, Wheeler and Westwood on a healthy population and Obler on developmental dyslexia studied in adulthood.)

Naturally enough those studies considering acquisition focus on the earlier part of the lifespan and deal with non-pathological conditions. They do range, however, from pre- to post-puberty, although there is little focus on the topic of critical age, which is well-documented elsewhere. There is some analogous correspondence between those studies dealing with linguistic loss and later phases of life or pathology. Because there is still so little work on the complementary topics, we find no study in this volume dealing with language acquisition in elderly speakers, interesting as this would undoubtedly be, and only one (Obler) deals indirectly with acquisition of two languages under pathological conditions. (We have recently learned of an autistic adult who was exposed to German in his grandparents' store when he was a child, and had no other contact with German. His development of English was appropriately slow for an autistic child, and as an adult he produces little speech. The family was shocked to discover that when he met a German speaker, his German was markedly more fluent than his English.) One chapter that clearly goes beyond this general convergence of research topic and choice of subject category is the chapter on first language loss in childhood (Seliger), especially since he investigates non-pathological circumstances for this loss.

The first two chapters consider bilingual development in children. Meisel treats the interaction/independence of cognitive and linguistic systems in the early development of children through a longitudinal study of their simultaneous acquisition of French and German. Meisel concludes, in contrast to other current views, that the children have developed a separate syntactic system for each language from the very earliest phases of language development and that a specific linguistic component – separate from the general cognitive system – needs to be postulated to account for the acquisition of functionally unmotivated parts of each language.

Humes-Bartlo compares unsuccessful and successful child L2 learners via a neuropsychological approach, using Geschwind and Galaburda's model of unusual brain organization (Geschwind and Galaburda, 1985) for individuals with especially good or especially poor skills. She reports that poor child L2 learners in fact show mild deficits in their L1, despite the fact that only those within the normal range for L1 were selected for this study, and are markedly better as a group on mathematical and visuo-spatial skills. More specific measures of the Geschwind and Galaburda hypothesis, however, were not borne out in her sample.

With Yorio's chapter, we move from early school years to late adolescent acquisition. Yorio reports on the use of conventionalized language among a variety of college students, demonstrating that even fairly proficient writers make grammatical errors when using conventionalized language. The term "idiomaticity" here goes beyond idiom *per se* to include appreciation of the appropriateness of collocations and sentence stems. The high correlation Yorio finds between good use of conventionalized language and linguistic proficiency indicates that at this stage of language learning his subjects are using more patterns, in apparent contradiction to the Bolander chapter. In her chapter, error and frequency data from adult Swedish L2 learners, at both low and high proficiency levels, indicate the employment of specific word collocations as well as specific sentence frames in the incipient learners. We suspect that both Yorio and Bolander are correct in that subjects *will* indeed employ patterns learned or acquired as such, but in the course of advancing and acquiring more propositional language forms, will lose some of the apparent skills as they try to abstract the syntactic rules implicit in conventionalized language and sometimes make errors in their abstractions (so called U-shaped learning processes, Kellerman, 1985).

In his contribution to this volume, Kellerman focuses on advanced Dutch learners of English, to determine what motivates their incorrect usage of the *if–then* English conditional, which seems to be a candidate for fossilization with these learners. He demonstrates that learners have a strategy of preferring to disambiguate tenses, and to create a symmetrical morphology in the verb forms of both *if* and *then* clauses. This results in their lack of appreciation of the subtle differences between Dutch and English conditionals, although, interestingly from a typological point of view, it makes their English interlanguage parallel in structure with what is preferred in several natural languages.

As has been done in the previous two chapters, Flynn performs an error analysis on a specific linguistic structure, in this case restrictive relative clauses. Her frame for explanation is Universal Grammar, and it is L2 parameter setting in particular that interests her. Her three groups of language learners (Spanish, Japanese, and Chinese) are matched with each other for overall English proficiency. They differ in terms of the match, or lack thereof, of head direction as compared to English, which is head-initial. Quantitative and qualitative analysis of learners with low, middle, and high proficiency in English all point to the facilitation of language acquisition when parametric values are the same in L1 and L2, and the difficulty in assigning a new value to the parameter when L2 differs from L1.

With the chapter by Poplack, Wheeler and Westwood we move on to study mature language use in bilinguals. Poplack's chapter and that of Obler deal with adult language use. While Poplack's chapter studies speakers of Finnish and English, Obler's chapter is concerned with a dyslexic adult speaker of Hebrew and English.

Poplack, Wheeler and Westwood address the question of language contact phenomena, specifically code-switching and borrowing, in a language pair as typologically distant as Finnish and English. They are led to conclude that the grammatical incompatibility between the two languages (Finnish being a postpositional and English a prepositional language) makes code-switching unproductive. Instead, nonce borrowing, i.e. a speaker's casual and adapted use of a word from the other language, becomes more prevalent. Poplack's general hypothesis, then, is that the grammatical constraints on language-mixing predict that bilingual speakers of typologically proximate languages have code-switching available to them, while speakers of typologically distant languages must employ different means if they wish to use the resources from both languages in one discourse, namely nonce borrowing. Whether speakers will use these possibilities or not depends on the social value that is given to language mixing generally in the community.

Obler studies the steady-state reading abilities of a single case, a 42-year-old Hebrew–English dyslexic. Most striking is the contrast between her reading error types in English, where inflexional endings are substituted for, added, or omitted, as compared to Hebrew, where although such errors are structurally possible, they are in fact rare. These cases are evaluated in the light of the literature on Hebrew–English bilingual reading as laterality tests have studied it, and in the few other cases of adult onset reading disturbance in Hebrew. It would appear that characteristics of the Hebrew orthography – among them the fact that it is read from right to left, as compared to English – influence the modes of processing in brain-damaged as well as in healthy readers.

The section on language loss opens with the case study by Seliger on a child who emigrated from an English-speaking environment to Israel at the age of six (her seventh year). She was studied longitudinally, starting two years later, for a period of three years. Relative clauses provide the most striking evidence that the subject, S, simplifies the English relative marker *that*, and transfers the rule of pronominal copy. Seliger concludes that sociolinguistic and functional variables cannot explain why some elements of a first language are more liable to be lost than others. Rather, it would appear that subjects unconsciously employ a strategy which replaces L1 rules that serve a similar semantic function across the languages but are linguistically more complex, with simpler L2 rules.

Sharwood Smith builds a complementary theoretical model in considering cross-linguistic influence in language loss. He treats both competence and processing control, and compares his framework with that of Andersen (1982) and Preston (1982). For Sharwood Smith a conspiracy of factors, including, most prominently, typological proximity, structural similarity, and crosslinguistic support, influence the transfer of structures or representations from the L2 to the L1 during attrition, a point in accord with Seliger's analysis of L1 attrition in the case of S. A twelve-feature model like that of Sharwood Smith clearly indicates the complexity of factors involved in attrition since it includes not only linguistic structural comparability but also a number of processing features such as coding efficiency and comprehensibility as well as, perhaps more strictly, psycholinguistic features such as familiarity and iconicity.

Language loss through brain damage rather than non-use is considered in the final two chapters, those of Hyltenstam and Stroud, and Perecman. Hyltenstam and Stroud report two cases of language loss among demented patients. Both subjects, reported to be premorbidly high proficiency bilinguals (German–Swedish and Swedish–Finnish), showed significantly altered patterns of language behavior in dementia. Interestingly, the subjects also differed between themselves with regard to patterns of code-switching, language choice and availability of each language. On the basis of their results, the authors hypothesize that the differences observed result from conspiring factors such as age of L2 acquisition, stage of dementia, and the typological relationship between the language pairs. Furthermore, the fact that code-switching, when it occurred, followed regularities proposed for normal populations by other researchers, leads Hyltenstam and Stroud to point to the essential automaticity and integrity of code-switching skills as a consequence of competence in each grammatical system. Also, language choice and code-switching may be subserved by separate neuropsychological systems.

Converging evidence on system mixing among bilinguals is brought to bear in developing a neurolinguistic model of language processing in the bilingual by Perecman. Various mixing phenomena from a series of cases in the aphasia literature are reviewed, and mixing in normals is considered as well. Perecman assumes on the basis of much of the literature that in healthy individuals it is never the case that one language is entirely "turned off". Changes in threshold influence whether languages will be mixed or not, and in the brain-damaged patient these thresholds may be permanently altered.

Methodologies and theoretical frameworks

As the reader will see, in addition to the diversity of languages covered across the chapters of this book, and the variety of linguistic structures treated in some detail, there is also a diversity of methods employed to study the bilingual processes in question. These range from case studies, as in the chapters by Meisel, Yorio, Hyltenstam and Stroud, Obler, and Seliger, to group studies, as in the work by Poplack, Wheeler and Westwood, Flynn,

Bolander and again Yorio. They include techniques of linguistic error analysis, both quantitative and qualitative, as well as arguments from a neuropsychological battery as in the chapter by Humes-Bartlo. Data of course came from brain-damaged as well as normal subjects, as was the intent for the entire book; Perecman incorporates both sources of data to build her arguments. Techniques involve the study of both learners and acquirers, with the somewhat different methods associated for studying each group. (In certain cases, of course, this distinction is hard to make, as in the case Obler reports, because in the real world people may be both learners and acquirers during the same period of their life, alternatively across periods.) Different modalities are treated, as when Yorio treats the writing modality, and Obler that of reading. Flynn discusses comprehension as well as production, but the majority of studies cover production in various ways.

Furthermore, various theoretical frameworks serve the authors. Seliger, Sharwood Smith, and Kellerman use a framework incorporating the notions of transfer and linguistic universals whereas Flynn specifically discusses these notions in the terminology of the Universal Grammar model. Bolander uses the notion of hemisphericity, while Humes-Bartlo speaks of neurocognitive style. Perecman incorporates the microgenetic model developed by J. Brown.

Running through the diversity of methodology which we included in the book to illustrate the various ways related questions can be addressed, there are certain common features that can be extracted from groups of chapters even when the chapters are not contiguous. Both Bolander and Yorio treat related questions of idiomaticity and formulae. Several chapters (those of Meisel, Poplack, Perecman, and Hyltenstam and Stroud) deal with phenomena of language-mixing under different conditions. The language-typological approach is also included across a number of studies, in particular those of Seliger, Sharwood Smith, Kellerman, and Obler.

The diversity we have deliberately included in methodology and theory is also reflected in a greater than usual variety of terminology. Rather than impose a fixed terminology on our contributors, we decided to include the rather broad variety that currently exists to discuss the issues of acquisition, mature proficiency, and language loss. Indeed, we spent many months debating exactly how to term the subtitle of the book. Should acquisition include learning? Should loss be considered as deterioration, or worse, pathology or deviance? Indeed, would our use of the triad "acquisition", "maturity", and "loss", cutting across the lifespan as we emphasize that they do, be considered to imply an inevitability of loss and deterioration that we do not subscribe to? We determined, as the reader will no doubt note, that rather than attempt to resolve fully all these terminological issues now, we would encourage a certain variety in usage to mirror the wide range of the field.

References

Andersen, R. W. (1982), Determining the linguistic attributes of language attrition. In: Lambert, R. and Freed, B. (eds.), *The Loss of Language Skills*. Rowley, MA: Newbury House.

Andreasen, N. C. (1979), Thought, language, and communication disorders. *Arch. Gen. Psychiatry* **36**. 1315–1330.

Chaika, E. (1982), A unified explanation for the diverse structural deviations reported for adult schizophrenics with disrupted speech. *J. Communication Disorders* **15**. 167–189.

Coppieters, R. (1987), Competence differences between native and fluent non-native speakers. *Language* **63**. 544–573.

Crystal, D. (1982), *Profiling linguistic disability*. London: Edward Arnold.

Dorian, N. C. (1981), *Language Death. The Life Cycle of a Scottish Gaelic Dialect*. Philadelphia: University of Pennsylvania Press.

Geschwind, N. and Galaburda, A. (1985), Cerebral lateralization. Biological mechanisms, associations, and pathology. I, II, III. *Arch. of Neurology* **42**. 428–459, 521–552, 634–654.

Hyltenstam, K. (1988), Lexical characteristics of near-native second language learners of Swedish. *J. of Multilingual and Multicultural Development* **9**. 67–84.

Ingram, D. (1976), *Phonological Disability in Children*. London: Edward Arnold.

Irigaray, L. (1973), *Le langage des déments*. The Hague: Mouton.

Kellerman, E. (1985), If at first you *do* succeed ... In Gass, S. and Madden, C. (eds.), *Input in Second Language Acquisition*. Rowley, MA: Newbury House.

Kemper, S. (1987), Syntactic complexity and the recall of prose by middle-aged and elderly adults. *Experimental Aging Research* **13**. 47–52.

Lambert, R. and Freed, B. (1982) (eds.), *The Loss of Language Skills*. Rowley, MA.: Newbury House.

McLaughlin, B. (1987), *Theories of Second-Language Learning*. London: Edward Arnold.

Mägiste, E. (1986), Selected issues in second and third language learning. In: Vaid, J. (ed.), *Language Processing in Bilinguals. Psycholinguistic and Neuropsychological Perspectives*. Hillsdale, New Jersey: Erlbaum.

Miller, N. (1984) (ed.), *Bilingualism and Language Disability*. Beckenham: Croom Helm.

Obler, L. (1980), Narrative discourse style in the elderly. In Obler, L. and Albert, M. (eds.), *Language and Communication in the Elderly*. Lexington, MA: D. C. Heath Co.

(1982), The parsimonious bilingual. In Obler, L. and Menn, L. (eds.) *Exceptional Language and Linguistics*. New York: Academic Press.

(1983), Language dysfunction and brain organization in dementia. In Segalowitz, S. (ed.), *Language Functions and Brain Organization*. New York: Academic Press.

(1985), Language through the life-span. In: Berko-Gleason, J. (ed.), *Language Development*. Columbus, Ohio: Charles Merrill.

Obler, L. and Albert, M. (1980) (eds.), *Language and Communication in the Elderly*. Lexington, MA.: D. C. Heath Co.

Paradis, M. (1977), Bilingualism and aphasia. In Whitaker, H. A. and Whitaker, H. (eds.), *Studies in Neurolinguistics*, vol 3. New York: Academic Press.

Perecman, E. (1984), Spontaneous translation and language mixing in a polyglot aphasic. *Brain and Language* **23**. 43–63.

Poplack, S. (1980), Sometimes I'll start a sentence in Spanish y termino en Español: Towards a typology of code-switching. *Linguistics* **18**. 581–618.

Preston, D. (1982), How to lose a language. *Interlanguage Studies Bulletin* **6:2**. 68–87.

Rochester, S. and Martin, J. R. (1979), *Crazy Talk: A Study of the Discourse of Schizophrenic Speakers*. New York: Plenum Press.

Schmidt, A. (1985), *Young People's Dyirbal. An Example of Language Death from Australia*. Cambridge University Press.

Schwartz, S. (1982), Is there a schizophrenic language? *The Behavioral and Brain Sciences* **5**. 579–626.

Sharwood Smith, M. (1983), On explaining language loss. In Felix, S. and Wode, H. (eds.), *Language Development at the Crossroads*. Tübingen: Narr.

Stroud, C. (forthcoming), Literacy in a second language. A study of text construction in near-native speakers of Swedish. In: Holmen, A. (ed.), *Bilingualism and the Individual. Copenhagen Studies in Bilingualism* **4**. Avon: Multilingual Matters.

Vaid, J. (1983), Bilingualism and brain lateralization. In: Segalowitz, S. (ed.), *Language Functions and Brain Organization*. New York: Academic Press.

(1986) (ed.) *Language Processing in Bilinguals. Psycholinguistic and Neuropsychological Perspectives*. Hillsdale, New Jersey: Erlbaum.

Veltens, B., De Bot, K. and Van Els, T. (1986), *Language Attrition in Progress*. Dordrecht: Foris.

2. Early differentiation of languages in bilingual children

JÜRGEN M. MEISEL

Introduction

The simultaneous acquisition of two (or more) "first languages" can be of particular interest for language acquisition studies. By analyzing the development of two linguistic competences in one individual, we may be capable of sorting out more easily to what extent the underlying logic of development is determined by the grammatical system to be acquired, or the particular way of human language processing as opposed to properties of the individual or of the communicative situation. There is, in fact, a steadily increasing amount of research in this area (see McLaughlin, 1984 or Taeschner, 1983 for fairly comprehensive overviews including more recent studies).

Much of this work is largely descriptive in its orientation, and theoretical questions are not always discussed explicitly. One question which is, however, pursued very frequently is whether bilinguals are able to "differentiate their two linguistic systems" (Lindholm and Padilla, 1978:334). (See, for example, Volterra and Taeschner, 1978, Redlinger and Park, 1980, and Vihman, 1982, 1985, and forthcoming, for some recent contributions to this discussion.)

The emerging picture is somewhat flawed by terminological confusions, especially with respect to those concepts underlying the terms "language mixing" and "code-switching". To avoid problems of this kind, I will use *code-switching* to describe the bilingual's ability to select the language according to the interlocutor, the situational context, etc. This choice is constrained by the properties of the linguistic system, among other things, much in the same way as with adults (compare Pfaff, 1979 and Poplack, 1980). *Language mixing*, on the other hand, will be used to designate a bilingual's "indiscriminate combinations of elements from each language" (Redlinger and Park, 1980:337), not being able to differentiate the two languages. In my conclusions (see page 36), I will suggest some modifications to this terminology.

13

With this terminological distinction in mind, one may try to summarize[1] very briefly the large body of research available as follows:

(1) Code-switching is a common phenomenon, among young bilinguals as well as among adults. Bilingual children often appear to use it as a kind of "relief strategy" when the necessary linguistic material is more easily available in the other language, e.g. when the topic of conversation normally falls within the domain of the other language. Children frequently seem to be aware of the fact that they are switching languages, and they tend to correct themselves in situations of this kind. Normally, however, when switching is used not only as a relief strategy, it becomes more frequent as the child acquires more proficiency in *both* languages, i.e. its use increases with age and with developing competence in the two languages. Code-switching, in other words, is thus regarded as part of the bilingual's pragmatic competence.

(2) Mixing seems to occur most frequently in the lexicon whereas it is most unlikely to happen in the sound system. As for morphological and syntactic mixing, the reports given in the available literature are contradictory. This is partly due to theoretical and methodological differences. It is not even possible to distinguish, in all cases, between switching and mixing if the authors themselves do not make this distinction nor give the necessary information. At any rate, mixing is most likely to occur if (a) one of the two languages is very dominant in the child's competence, and if (b) the adults in the child's environment mix or switch quite freely in their own speech. As McLaughlin (1984:95) phrases it: "interference ... can be held to a minimum if the domains are clearly defined and if the two languages are maintained somewhat in balance."

(3) Assuming the developmental perspective, we may summarize that mixing is reported to happen most frequently during a very early phase of language acquisition, before or around age 2;0 (years;months), whereas later on, bilingual children easily separate the two linguistic systems.

Findings of this kind have led Volterra and Taeschner (1978) to propose a three-stage model for early phases of language development in bilingual children. These stages can be characterized in the following way:

(I) the child has only one lexical system comprising words from both languages
(II) development of two distinct lexical systems although the child applies "the same syntactic rules to both languages" (Volterra and Taeschner, 1978:311)
(III) differentiation of two linguistic systems, lexical as well as syntactic.

In this chapter, I merely discuss the alleged stage II, focusing on syntactic and morphological aspects. For reasons of space, lexical development is not discussed, although it should be noted that the claim that bilingual children initially use only one lexicon is by no means non-controversial, as can be seen when looking at the data presented by Ronjat (1913), Pavlovitch (1920), Leopold (1939) and others. (For a more detailed discussion I refer to Jekat, 1985.)

With regard to a possible phase characterized by a single syntactic system underlying performance in both languages, the issue is even more controversial, as has been mentioned above. (See also Mikès, 1967, Bergman, 1976, Lindholm and Padilla, 1978, and Hoffmann, 1985.) Nevertheless, the three-stage model appears to have been widely accepted. In discussing its stage II, I will assume that certain factors (e.g. mixing in the linguistic environment, dominance of one language, social-psychological biases in favor of one language, etc.) may indeed lead to mixing and will certainly render language differentiation more difficult.

In my opinion, however, the theoretically more interesting question is whether the human "language making capacity" (Slobin, 1985) could allow the bilingual individual, in principle, to separate the two simultaneously acquired grammatical systems from early on, without even going through a phase of confusion.

Discussion of the theoretical issues involved

Before turning to empirical data in an attempt to answer this research question, it is necessary to examine a number of problems related to the following three issues: (1) the definition of stage II, as suggested by Volterra and Taeschner (1978); (2) the kind of empirical evidence necessary to support or refute claims connected with the alleged stages I–III; (3) theoretical assumptions about whether language processing in young children is grammatical (or "syntactic") in nature. A clarification of these issues should help to avoid the currently common confusion whereby authors arrive at contradictory conclusions about language differentiation and mixing – as a result of using apparently similar terms which are, in fact, defined quite differently.

1. The *definition of the three stages*, especially that of stage II, as proposed by Volterra and Taeschner (1978), is surprisingly vague. In fact, concerning stage II, one does not learn any more than the above quoted claim that the child "applies the same syntactic rules to both languages" (Volterra and Taeschner, 1978:312). No independent criterion is mentioned, like age, mean length of utterances (MLU), or any other feature which is not itself part of the definition of this stage. Note that not even for the children studied by Volterra and Taeschner themselves (children acquiring Italian and German simultaneously) are we given precise indications delimitating these stages. There exists only one remark[2] to the effect that "until the age of 2;9 she (Lisa, JMM) appears

to have acquired only one syntactic system" (p. 322). If, however, age, MLU, etc. are considered to be unreliable indicators of stage, other defining criteria could have been found. The most likely candidates would be syntactic phenomena, especially since stage II is defined in terms of syntactic features. Use of syntactic criteria is common practice in language acquisition studies, both for natural second language acquisition (see Meisel, Clahsen, Pienemann, 1981) as well as for first language acquisition (see Clahsen, 1982). The case for "stage II" would be much stronger if it could be stated that syntactic mixing occurred during developmental phases, for instance independent of age and MLU, when word order phenomenon X has already been acquired but phenomenon Y has not yet been acquired. (See Clahsen, 1986 for a convincing example using verb placement as an independent variable in assessing the order of acquisition of case markings.)

This is not to say, however, that using instances of "mixing" to define a stage of mixing must necessarily lead to circularity in the argument. But it may be – and in fact is, I will claim – a non-sufficient definition. For one thing, if one does not find such mixing, one may simply have overlooked it, it may not yet have begun or already be abandoned by the child – or it may not exist at all. More seriously, Volterra and Taeschner (1978) themselves show, in the course of their discussion, that instances of mixing do not constitute evidence in favor of the stages under discussion. They found (p. 319) that children at stage II "keep mixing words of the two languages" (Lisa at age 2;5). If, however, mixing of words may still occur after "the child distinguishes two different lexicons" (p. 312), how do we know s/he has already reached stage II; and vice versa, if this can be accounted for, how can we make sure that similar examples at stage I do indeed indicate that the child operates with only one lexical system for both languages? Even more intriguingly, would we have to allow for the possibility that the three stages need not be ordered chronologically? In that case, they would merely represent logical entities which need not appear in reality as discrete phases. Note that Vihman (1985), who adopts the three-stage model, concludes that these "stages" may surface in a parallel fashion.

All this is far from being clear and things become no clearer even after looking at the empirical evidence given by Volterra and Taeschner (1978). Examples quoted from the speech of Lisa, one of the children studied, fall into the following age ranges:

> stage I: 1;6 – 1;11
> stage II: 2;5 – 3;3
> stage III: 2;9 – 3;11

Bearing in mind that stage II is said elsewhere in their text to last until age 2;9 (see quote above), it seems that stage I ends around 2;0 and stage II lasts from

2;5 to 2;9, allowing, however, for features of stage I to appear at II, and features characteristic of II to be used at III.

Another fact is still more confusing: the tables given by Volterra and Taeschner (1978:321ff.) indicate that for at least one of the three syntactic constructions discussed (i.e. placement of adjectives), the Italian examples, which apparently indicate the use of one syntax for both languages, occur without exception at age 2;9 or later, and the German examples are all modeled on the adult norm. How could these speech samples then be used as evidence in favor of a developmental phase which is said to end at about 2;9? In addition, all constructions but one quoted from German utterances that look like "Italian syntax" appear at 2;9 or later. Whatever the explanation of this phenomenon may be, it certainly cannot be used as evidence in favor of stage II, since this child is said to have achieved the differentiation of the two systems at this point of development.

To sum up, I do not believe that the empirical evidence and/or the theoretical justification given is sufficient to support the hypothesized phase II of the three-stage model. One might add that the arguments given by Volterra and Taeschner (1978) in favor of a stage at which a single syntactic system is used, are based on data from only one child, Lisa. It appears that she was the only one of the children studied to use constructions which could be interpreted in this fashion. Yet, as becomes evident from what we are told about her, Italian is clearly Lisa's dominant language. In fact, Taeschner (1983:102, 107) mentions that Lisa strongly preferred Italian and had less contact with German for a considerable period of time. This happened at exactly the same time when she was said to be at stage II, namely from (at least) age 2;6 until 3;0.

In other words, these facts suggest that social-psychological factors may lead to language mixing or code-switching, as has been mentioned above. They do not, however, represent convincing evidence in favor of an early phase of mixing through which all children would have to go. One might add that Redlinger and Park (1980) also offer – although unwillingly – good evidence against "an initial mixed stage in language production" (p. 337). They studied the speech of four bilingual children (two German–French, one German–Spanish, and one German–English), who were between the ages 2;0 and 2;8 and with MLU of 1.39 to 2.66 at the onset of the investigation. They conclude that "the children whose language was more advanced produced fewer mixed utterances than the children at earlier stages of development," but they also admit that "Various linguistic and sociolinguistic factors seem to have influenced the degree of mixing" (p. 340). In fact, only one boy in their sample, Marc, used practically no mixed utterances; and this was also the only child for whom two languages were clearly separated in the environment, the mother speaking French with the boy, the father using German (adhering to the well-known principle "one person – one language"). Unfortunately, this boy's linguistic development was already fairly advanced (MLU 2.66) at the beginning of the study. In spite of claims made by Redlinger and Park (1980), however, language development does not explain what they call "mixing".[3] First, for each individual, it is not true that the percentage of mixes would decrease parallel to increasing MLU values. For Marc, no such correlation exists; his "mixes" even drop to zero at a point where his MLU also drops. Second, interpersonal comparison does not support the hypothesis by Redlinger and Park (1980). In other words, MLU values do not allow one to make predictions about frequency of "mixing". For example, at MLU 3.3, one child, Danny, uses 14.6 percent of mixed utterances, whereas Marc uses 2.1 percent. Thirdly, the nature of the input (i.e. separation of the two languages, dominance of one language, etc.) *does* make it possible to predict occurrence or non-occurrence of mixing. In other words, what Redlinger and Park (1980:340) call "sociolinguistic factors" seem to be the crucial ones. And I would like to emphasize their conclusion – which they limit to only one child (*sic!*) – that "the lack of strict language separation by person in Marc's linguistic environment may have had an effect on his overall high rate of mixing" (p. 341).

To conclude, I want to claim that the evidence offered by Volterra and Taeschner (1978), Redlinger and Park (1980), and others is not sufficient to support the hypothesis that bilingual children must pass through an initial stage of syntactic mixing which, in turn, would have to be explained as a result of their processing both languages as a single system.

2. The question which then arises is what *kinds of empirical evidence* could be accepted as instances of syntactic mixing or of differentiation between syntactic systems. Volterra and Taeschner, quite correctly, remark that the "mixed system" may be different from each of the two adult monolingual systems involved.

This should, indeed, be interpreted as a necessary condition: one should only consider those aspects of grammar where the two *adult target systems differ*. If, for example, both languages acquired by the child allow for SVO (subject–verb–object) ordering (as is the case in Italian–French–German), SVO sequences in the speech of bilinguals do not support one or the other claim. In fact, I would even like to suggest that one should try to find evidence in favor of, or against, a "common, non-differentiated" syntax in structural areas where language *uses of monolingual children* acquiring each of the languages under consideration also *differ*. Otherwise, one has two separate systems to consider which do, however, overlap with regard to just these structural properties, rather than one common system. As far as I can see, an empirically based method of deciding which of the two hypotheses is the correct one does not exist. The placement of negators (NEG), to give one example, proceeds through what may well be universally similar or identical phases (see Wode, 1977, 1981); preverbal placement of NEG is common even for languages where the adult norm allows only for postverbal position. If, therefore, German–Italian or German–French bilinguals use preverbal negation in both languages, there is no way of deciding whether they are processing both languages as one system or whether the two systems underlying this kind of language use merely overlap in this structural domain at the given point of linguistic development.

A different problem arises if the supposed common system is identical to one of the two adult systems in a given structural area. Even if the two target languages do differ in this respect, it is difficult to decide whether one really has only one underlying grammar. Instead, the commonalities in the use of the two languages may be the result of transfer from the dominant language. If one system interferes with the other, this is, by definition, not the same as when only a single grammar exists. To give another example, Lisa, the child studied by Volterra and Taeschner (1978) and by Taeschner (1983), initially seems to prefer what looks like "German syntax" in all three structural domains analyzed (possessor + possession (N + N) patterns, adjective + noun sequences,[4] and placement of negators in final position) in German and in Italian. This does not imply that these structures must always correspond to the German adult norm, as was observed by Volterra and Taeschner (1978:324). Later on, at approximately age 2;9 (*sic!*), Lisa apparently uses "Italian" surface structures more frequently. This shift corresponds to changes in the linguistic environment of the child where Italian strongly prevails after 2;6.

Note that I do not want to claim that whenever a structural pattern appears in both languages spoken by the bilingual, but only in one of the corresponding target languages, that this should necessarily be interpreted as evidence for transfer processes. In fact, I would argue that transfer occurs much less frequently than is commonly assumed (see Meisel, 1983). But I do want to claim that such phenomena cannot easily be interpreted as evidence in favor of the "one common system" hypothesis; especially not if sociolinguistic factors indicate that the language from which the "common" structures are taken appears to be dominant in the child's language environment.

3. In view of the methodological problems, which make it very difficult to find positive evidence in support of the one-system stage, it appears to be more promising to look for evidence in favor of the hypothesis that bilinguals do differentiate between the two grammatical systems from early on. If it can be shown that they use structures in which the two target systems (including

the respective child languages) differ, then this obviously also constitutes evidence against the alternative one-system hypothesis. Yet, whatever the empirical evidence may look like, it can only be interpreted if a crucial theoretical question is answered first, a question which, amazingly enough, is not even asked, let alone answered, in the literature on bilingual first language acquisition: at what point of language development may one reasonably assume that the child is *able to use syntactic* (or, more generally *grammatical*) *modes* of language processing?

In (monolingual) child language research, this is one of the most crucial theoretical questions. It suffices to look at recent collections of papers dealing with child language and theories of language development, e.g. Fletcher and Garman (1979), Wanner and Gleitman (1982), or Slobin (1985) to come up with a picture which can roughly be sketched as follows. It is generally assumed that child language is initially organized according to semantic–pragmatic principles. Only through a gradual process of "syntactiza-tion" will grammatical ways of processing come in. In other words, it is believed that after a period of semantic–pragmatic primacy, syntactic categories and relations develop which resemble (or are identical with) those in mature grammars. Givón (1979, 1985), for example, suggests a distinction between a "pragmatic" and a "syntactic" mode of language processing, and he furthermore claims that the former chronologically precedes (in ontogenesis as well as in phylogenesis) the latter. In fact, some authors would not even exclude the possibility that mature language competence, as well, could be described in terms of semantic–pragmatic principles without the use of specific grammatical categories or rules, e.g. Bates and MacWhinney (1982).

In the light of these discussions, at least two possible interpretations of the single-system hypothesis exist. First, during this developmental phase the bilingual children do not (yet?) have access to grammatical categories and principles. Rather, they rely entirely on semantic–pragmatic strategies of language use. This "pragmatic mode" of language processing would operate in exactly the same way for both languages of the bilingual and thus account for the structural similarities which are claimed to exist in their speech.

However, this interpretation is evidently not the one intended by those who defend the three-stage model since they clearly refer to *syntactic categories* and *rules, grammatical systems*, and so forth (see Volterra and Taeschner, 1978, Redlinger and Park, 1980, among others). To speak of syntactic rules, etc. obviously only makes sense if one presupposes that the child is capable, at this particular point in time, of returning to a syntactic mode of processing. Note that this first version of the model would also be neutral with regard to the current discussion since it does not imply any prediction or claim specific to bilingual language acquisition. Nor could it answer our initial question as to whether the language-making-capacity of humans allows for the simultaneous acquisition of two grammatical systems. It would merely state that monolinguals and bilinguals alike start out with a mode of processing which follows general pragmatic principles, rather than more language-specific grammatical ones.

We may thus take it for granted that the second possible interpretation is the one assumed by those researchers who support the single-system hypothesis: once the child has begun to use the grammatical (or syntactic) mode of language processing, s/he will initially develop only one syntax which is used to process both languages.[5]

From these considerations it follows that we cannot separate our initial question from a second one concerning the onset of grammatical processing. The answers given to this second question vary enormously if one looks at monolingual child language research. Maratsos (1982), for example, summarizes relevant findings and concludes that syntactic categories may not be acquired until the end of the preschool years, while Valian (1986) presents good evidence that this may actually happen much earlier, namely at approximately age 2;6 (MLU 3.0–4.0). Garman (1979) views the period around age 3;0 as the crucial one for grammatical developments. This is only to mention some reports which are, I believe, based on broad and reliable empirical research. We need not try to solve this problem, however, before addressing our initial question. Neither need we take a stand on the issue of whether grammatical processing is indeed preceded by a phase of pragmatic primacy. Instead, we may search for evidence in favor of *syntactic* categories and rules – and then work our way back into earlier developmental phases. In fact, if one can show that a bilingual child uses different grammatical means for expressing the same or similar semantic–pragmatic functions in both languages, this not only indicates that s/he is indeed differentiating the two grammatical systems, but also constitutes what I believe to be the clearest evidence that one can and, indeed, must attribute to the child – the ability to use the *grammatical mode*.

Subjects and data collection methods

In what follows, I will present some results from a study analyzing the acquisition of French and German by children of preschool age. The present analysis focuses on the speech of two children who were 12 months of age (1;0,0 – years; months, days) at the beginning of the data collection period and includes the period from age 1;0,0 until 4;0,0. One child (C) is a girl, the other (P) is a boy. So far, from 1980 to 1986, a total of eight children have been studied longitudinally by our research group DUFDE;[6] currently (1986 to 88), three children are being recorded and studied. The children are videotaped every second week while interacting with adults and occasionally with other children. The recordings consist mainly of free interactions in play situations; they last for approximately 50–60 minutes each, half in German and half in French. The well-known principle of "une personne, une langue" is observed. At least one recording per month is transcribed and analyzed.

Both children are growing up in middle-class families. The native language of the mothers is French while the fathers' first language is German. Each person uses his/her respective native tongue with the children; the language of communication between father and mother is German.

C is her parents' only child. At the age of 9 months, she started going to a German day-care center. She is, thus, exposed to German more often than to French, the language primarily spoken with her mother and with some French friends. The family usually spend their holidays in France, where French is then spoken almost exclusively. On average, this happens three times a year. During a period of several months, beginning at the age of about three years, C stopped speaking French. Even when communicating with her mother, she would respond in German. The recording sessions with C were stopped when she was 5;0,6.

P, the second child, usually speaks French with his sister who is three years older. At the age of 2;8 he started going to a French kindergarten. Since their mother works, a young person frequently takes care of the children in the afternoons. P and his sister speak German with their sitter as with their father, and French with their mother and in the kindergarten. Every year, the family spends approximately six or seven weeks in a French-speaking country. During these weeks, the children speak French almost exclusively. P was recorded twice per month until he was 6;6; since then, he is part of a group which is videotaped every three months.

It should be added that P's linguistic development is very slow, as compared to many other children who are described in language acquisition studies. Contrasting his development with C's, one finds that he is about six months behind, although he catches up after the period under investigation. This can already be noted towards the end of the investigation period. For both children, French initially appears to be the dominant input language and it is also the language preferred by the children at this time. This preference is clearly changing for C between 2;6 and 3;0, when she begins to favor German. As for P, his bilingualism seems to be fairly balanced.

To give an approximate idea of the degree and rate of development in both languages, MLUs are given in table 2.1. In spite of the well-known shortcomings of this type of measurement, it should at least allow for comparison of our results with those from other studies. By and large, we are

Table 2.1. *Age and MLU of the children.*

C: Age	German	French	P: Age	German	French
2;01,13	1.93	2.09	2;03,16	1.19	1.31
2;03,11	2.30	2.50	2;07,06	1.43	1.86
2;04,08	2.12	3.23	2;09,02	2.06	2.30
2;07,20	3.08	3.16	2;11,10	2.17	3.00
2;10,28	3.62	3.68	3;01,09	3.37	3.59
3;00,02	3.96	—	3;02,23	2.57	3.00
3;02,10	3.65	4.08	3;05,03	4.13	4.32
3;03,10	4.30	3.78	3;06,14	3.59	4.34
3;06,11	4.86	—	3;11,02	4.60	5.90
3;10,20	5.99	5.61			

using procedures to establish MLU values that are suggested by Brown (1973) and Bloom and Lahey (1978). Unlike many other child language studies, we do in fact count morphemes, not words, as soon as we have evidence that the child uses a certain morpheme productively. In the case of plurifunctional morphemes, each form is only counted once; that is, a flexive is not counted three times for case, number, and gender.

Discussion and results

In this section, I will try to test the research guidelines developed above empirically. I will thus examine some linguistic phenomena which are sufficiently distinct in French and German, to serve as test cases for the problem of language differentiation. If possible, they should also be distinguishable in French and German monolinguals' linguistic development. It will furthermore be necessary to investigate whether these phenomena may rightly be regarded as syntactic in nature.

Word order phenomena

Word order is a grammatical area which does, in fact, fulfill all the requirements mentioned. German word order, as compared to French, is rather variable. There is even disagreement as to whether German is an SOV or an SVO language. Unmarked order in main clauses is SVO, whereas the canonical order in subordinate clauses is SOV. Nonfinite verbal elements, however, always appear in final position: in main clauses at the very end, in subordinate clauses followed by the finite part of the verb phrase. This is the case with auxiliary (Aux + Past Participle) and with modal (Modal + Infinitive) constructions, but also with compound verbs (Particle + V). Some examples are:

(1) (i) Ich schrieb einen Brief   I wrote a letter
 (ii) dass ich einen Brief schrieb that I wrote a letter
 (iii) Ich habe einen Brief geschrieben I have written a letter
 (iv) dass ich einen Brief geschrieben habe that I have written a letter

The finite verb obligatorily assumes the second position of a main clause, as in (iii). Placement of the finite verb in second position is also required if some other element (NP, Adverbial, WH-word, embedded S, etc.) is fronted. Compare the examples in

(2) (i) Heute schrieb ich einen Brief Today I wrote a letter
 (ii) Einen Brief schrieb ich heute A letter I wrote today

In other words, verb placement is specifically interesting. It depends on whether the verb is finite or not, and on whether it appears in an embedded clause or not.

French word order, on the other hand, is almost strictly SVO. Problems arise with clitic object pronouns which are placed in preverbal position, resulting in SoV sequences. This type of construction, however, does not yet appear during very early phases of child language. Another phenomenon is also quite important for it is rather frequent in spoken colloquial French, i.e. *dislocation* of subjects and objects. Reliable quantitative evidence is not available, but it may be taken for granted that dislocation of subjects is far more frequent than dislocation of objects. As for the latter, placement to the left is more common than to the right, and direct objects are more likely to be dislocated than indirect ones. In any case, a pronominal copy must be left standing.

(3) (i) Il a tout bu, notre chat   He has drunk all of it, our cat
 (ii) Notre chat, il a tout bu   Our cat, he has drunk all of it
 (iii) Ce livre, je l'ai lu il y a   This book, I read it a long time ago
   longtemps

Furthermore, very specific situational conditions allow for placement of objects in initial position without leaving a pronominal copy behind. But this is a marginal case which is apparently not reflected in child language. Finally, it should be kept in mind that subject-verb INVERSION, a very frequent phenomenon in German, has virtually disappeared in spoken French, although it does exist in the grammar of the standard language.

To summarize these remarks: French is a fairly strict SVO language but other sequences are possible and appear in the child's linguistic environment, especially "double subjects" in dislocated constructions such as sVOS, but also those with cliticized objects (SoV).

Let us now look very briefly at monolingual acquisition of German and

French. Clahsen (1982, 1984) and Mills (1985) give evidence of the following developmental pattern in German. During phase 1 – roughly equivalent to Brown's (1973) stages I–II – word order is highly variable, but final position of the verb is preferred, and children soon begin to front objects and adverbials. During phase 2 – approximately stage III suggested by Brown – copula and modal constructions appear and the non-finite verbal element is regularly placed in final position, as required by the target grammar. Finite verbs, however, continue to be used in second as well as in final position. During phase 3 (Brown's stage IV), child word order follows largely the same regularities as the language use of adults. Subordinate clauses, however, do not show up until phase 4 (stage V). Interestingly enough, this is a case of error free acquisition: the verb is always placed correctly in final position, right from the beginning. In contrast to this apparent ease of acquisition of verb placement in embedded clauses, second position placement of verbs in main clauses represents a major acquisitional difficulty. Thus, in utterances with an initialized interrogative pronoun, or those with a topicalized complement, the verb sometimes appears in third position.

As for monolingual acquisition of French, we unfortunately lack information on some crucial aspects. Following the state-of-the-art paper by E. Clark (1985), one may nevertheless draw the following picture. During the two- and three-word phases, word order is fairly variable, but V(O)S sequences seem to be preferred. Some authors claim that children prefer SV(O) rather early. At any rate, this becomes the predominant pattern later on. Left and right dislocation of subjects appears quite early, and at least some children tend to use such sequences in the majority of their utterances.

Let us now turn to the development of word order phenomena in bilingual children, using data obtained from C and P (see (2) above). Some of the results of these analyses are summarized in Figures 2.1 and 2.2. (For more details see Meisel, 1986:143ff.) The analysis begins with what Brown characterized as stage II, having an MLU around 1.75, since it is during this period that children start using a larger number of multi-word utterances. Only declarative sentences are considered here, leaving aside the peculiarities of imperative and interrogative sentences.

First of all, one can observe that SVO is largely predominant in both languages, from the beginning of the multi-word phase through all of the period investigated. Word order is thus markedly less variable than in the speech of monolingual French and German children. There is, however, a difference between French and German for both bilingual children which reflects properties of the two target languages. In French, frequency values for SV(O) order rarely drop below 0.8, and they often reach 1.0. Word order use in German is more variable, although SV(O) is also clearly dominant during

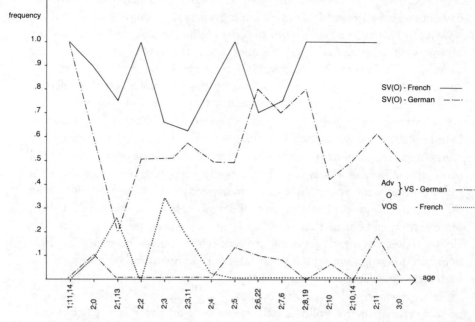

Figure 2.1. Word order C

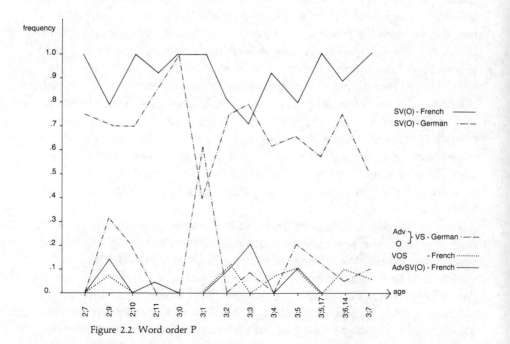

Figure 2.2. Word order P

the entire period. Note that SOV patterns, the preferred order in monolingual German child language, are not used except with the non-finite verb in final position, as required by the target norm. It goes without saying that this does not appear in French either with finite or with non-finite verbs. We thus find less variability in bilinguals as compared to monolinguals and, more interestingly, a quantitative difference between French and German for each bilingual child in the use of SV(O) sequences.

Another difference between French and German in bilingual language use results from the dislocation of subjects to the right in French. Since children during these developmental phases tend to omit subject pronouns, such uses may surface as VOS patterns. They only exist in French and never in German. In addition, the subject in French is also dislocated to the left occasionally; this is not shown in the figures, since these uses are rather infrequent.

Whereas so far the differences between the uses of the two languages have only been quantitative in nature, or resulted from the non-appearance of certain phenomena in one of the two languages, more convincing evidence for the early differentiation between languages consists in the application of grammatical devices specific for French or German. This is the case with the verb-second position required by the German system. Objects and adverbials may be fronted in both languages in order to topicalize these constituents. In French, this results in sequences with the verb in third position: AdvSV(O) or OSV(Adv). Fronting of objects is not used by the children during the period under consideration. Fronted adverbs, however, appear in P's speech. In these cases, the order of elements correctly follows the adult norm. Fronting of these constituents in German, on the other hand, necessarily triggers subject-verb inversion, leading to AdvVS or OVS sequences; compare example (2) above. As can be seen from the figures, both children use such structures in German but never in French. In fact, they never deviate from the adult norm. In other words, whenever they do front a constituent in German, the verb appears in second position whereas in French the verb remains in third position. This is especially remarkable since monolingual German children, as has been mentioned above, tend to leave the verb in third position for some time, thus violating the target norm. Note that verb-second position is only motivated by the grammatical system; it does not serve stylistic purposes, nor does it express specific semantic or pragmatic functions. In the light of this observation, it is even more revealing to observe that both children use constructions of this type from the very beginning of the multi-word phase onwards, beginning within Brown's stage II, approximately at MLU 2.0. I therefore want to claim that this is strong evidence in support of the hypothesis that bilingual children are, in fact, able to differentiate between two languages as soon as they use what may be interpreted as *syntactic* means of expression.

A similar argument can be used to explain the observation already mentioned that non-finite verbs in German are placed in final position. In the French utterances of the children, such constructions do not exist.

Let me add one remark concerning word order in subordinate clauses. It has been mentioned above that verb placement in German which requires clause final position, in this case does not cause acquisitional difficulties. Rather, monolinguals always use these constructions as prescribed by the adult norm. The bilingual data available are not unambiguous. First of all, subordinates are rather rare during this period. Secondly, C uses a few utterances which might be interpreted as – incorrect – SVO orders. And similar examples can be found in the literature for bilingual children acquiring German as one of their languages, e.g. Park (1981), Taeschner (1983). P, on the other hand, behaves quite like monolinguals and uses correct SOV sequences in embedded sentences. This seems to indicate that subordinate constructions might also be used as evidence in favor of the differentiation hypothesis since both children always use SVO order in French.

In sum then, I believe I have adequately shown that bilingual children use different word order sequences in both languages as soon as they begin to produce multi-word utterances. The two target systems are distinct in these cases; and monolingual children also use different orders in the respective languages. In addition, there are very good reasons to assume that these phenomena may rightly be called syntactic ones. If semantic and/or pragmatic functions were determining these uses, one would have to expect that similar or identical functions should be expressed similarly in both languages. This is definitely not the case in these instances. Instead, the children follow the requirements of the grammatical systems of both target languages quite closely, even when these merely express grammatical necessities without any apparent semantic–pragmatic motivation. In other cases, certain constructions may well be motivated pragmatically, such as the topicalization of complements, yet their formal properties are merely determined by the respective grammatical system, e.g. verb in second or third position after fronting of complements.

Subject-verb agreement

Another promising area to find evidence in support of the differentiation hypothesis is the use of subject pronouns and of subject-verb agreement. It is generally agreed that these phenomena are grammatical ones. Even Bates (1976), who otherwise argues against syntactic explanations, states that rigid adherence to SVO order (in Italian) and the use of such devices should be "explained by the possibility that the child has just discovered the concept of syntactic subject" (p. 209). The function of person and number markings on the verb is thus primarily a syntactic one, namely to encode the grammatical function of *subject*. And the respective coding devices are sufficiently distinct in German and in French.

A very brief look at the two adult target systems reveals that German uses a fairly rich system of suffixes to encode person and number, whereas French has lost most of its suffixes serving similar purposes. We may restrict this discussion to present-tense forms, since other tenses appear later in child language and are used much less frequently. The German paradigm for main verbs and modals is as follows:

	sagen (to say)		*können* (to be able)	
(4)	ich sage ich sag'	I say	ich kann	I am able to
	du sagst	you say	du kannst	you are able to
	er sagt	he says	er kann	he is able to
	sie sagt	she says	sie kann	she is able to
	wir sagen	we say	wir können	we are able to
	ihr sagt	you say	ihr könnt	you are able to
	sie sagen	they say	sie können	they are able to

Consequently there is a difference between main verbs and modals. The zero suffix for the first person singular is the one commonly used in colloquial speech. The suffixes, in other words, carry the following functions:

		main verbs	modals
(5)	—ø	1st sg. (coll)	1st/3rd sg.
	—e	1st sg.	—
	—st	2nd sg.	2nd sg.
	—t	3rd sg. 2nd pl.	2nd pl.
	—en	1st/3rd pl. infinitive	1st/3rd pl. infinitive

In French, the corresponding suffixes have mainly survived in the writing system. In spoken language, only some plural forms are left:

	parler (to speak)	
(6)	je parle	I speak
	tu parles	you speak
	il parle	he speaks
	elle parle	she speaks
	nous parlons/on parle	we speak
	vous parlez	you speak
	ils parlent	they speak
	elles parlent	they speak

In colloquial speech where the 1st person plural is regularly realized as "on", we are therefore normally left with only two forms, zero and -*ez* (2nd person plural). Certain additional variants may be ignored here, for they are unlikely to appear in early child speech, for example the 3rd person plural form of certain "irregular" verbs. Merely with the auxiliary and the copula do we find a pattern of verbal markings for person and number which is used in early phases of language development. But this cannot be generalized as a productive system of verb inflection.

Given this situation, the study of subject pronouns in French turns out to be of prime importance. In fact, it could be argued that the clitic subject pronoun in French forms part of the verb rather than being a syntactic subject. Similar proposals have been put forward repeatedly in studies on French syntax: for example see the discussion in Joly (1973). Recent generative analyses conclude that the subject clitic should be regarded as a constituent of the auxiliary in the INFL node but not of the subject NP (see Jaeggli, 1982). A number of phonological, morphological, and syntactic facts lend support to analyses of this kind. Its status as a clitic already points in this direction. The frequency of patterns like (7)(i) in colloquial speech also supports this hypothesis. Note that in cases like (7)(ii) where a non-clitic subject pronoun is used, the clitic cannot be omitted:

(7) (i) Lui il mange tout   He, he eats everything
    (ii) *Lui mange tout
    (iii) Pierre il mange tout   Pierre, he eats everything

For reasons of space, this problem will not be discussed in any detail. It is enough to notice that the clitic pronoun in subject position cannot simply be treated as a variant of the usual subject NP. Rather, it is possible to argue that it is part of the subject–verb agreement system in French. Syntactically, it can be regarded as a constituent of INFL or of V'; a slightly more radical version of this hypothesis would claim that it functions as a prefix of the verb.

Monolingual German children's acquisition of verb inflection has been studied recently by Clahsen (1986); in addition, results from a few other studies are summarized by Mills (1985). They all seem to agree that -ø, -(e)n, and -t are the first suffixes used. Leaving aside phonological variants (e.g. -ø replacing -e, -e replacing -en) and non-finite forms (infinitives and past participles), -t is clearly the first form which may be interpreted as a suffix of a finite verb. In a second step, most or all other forms come into play within a relatively brief period of time. There is some disagreement as to whether the early uses of -t can be regarded as syntactic markings of agreement. Clahsen (1986:95ff.), for example, argues that they encode a semantic function, namely non-transitivity. Although I do not find this suggestion very plausible, I will not pursue the problem any further for the time being (see Meisel, forthcoming). What matters for the present discussion is that all authors apparently agree that subject–verb agreement as a syntactic phenomenon emerges quite early (probably no later than at stages III–IV, as defined by

Table 2.2. *Order of acquisition of German verb forms*

C 1;11–2;1		P 2;6–2;9	
is	3rd sg. "to be"	*is*	3rd sg. "to be"
-t	3rd sg.	*-t*	3rd sg.
C 2;4–2;6		**P 2;9–2;11**	
		-e	1st sg.
ø	1st sg.	*ø*	1st sg.
ø	3rd sg. (modals)	*ø*	3rd sg. (modals)
-st	2nd sg.	*-st*	2nd sg.
-en	3rd pl.	*-en*	3rd pl.
sind	3rd pl. "to be"		
C 2;8–2;10		**P 3;3–3;11**	
-en	1st pl.	*-en*	1st pl.
bin	1st sg. "to be"	*bin*	1st sg. "to be"
sind	1st pl. "to be"	*sind*	1st pl.
		sind	3rd pl. "to be"
-e	1st sg.		

Brown). And this development parallels another one, namely the acquisition of finite verb placement in second position. Mills (1985) as well as Clahsen (1986:91) suggest that these two phenomena are logically connected. This is in accordance with the claims made by Bates (1976), alluded to above.

As for monolingual acquisition of French, we actually know very little about the phenomena discussed in this section of the chapter (see Clark, 1985). It has been mentioned above that the crucial issue here concerns clitic pronouns in "subject" position. A short glance at the relevant literature indicates that subject pronouns appear quite early in the speech of French children, approximately at age 2;0. *Il* is usually the first pronoun attested, but the others follow within a brief time span of a few months. Apart from the fact that plural forms emerge later than the singular forms, a clear developmental pattern apparently does not exist. To my knowledge, the use of these forms in French child language has never been studied in connection with the problem of subject–verb agreement. In fact, even the general question of when and how syntactic functions such as "subject" are acquired by French-speaking children is still wide open.

Analyzing the speech of the bilingual children reveals that they acquire *each* of the two languages very much like monolingual children. In German, they begin using verbs at age 1;9 (C) and 2;6 (P), respectively. The first forms which are modeled on adult finite verb inflection appear at age 1;11 (C) and at 2;7 (P). Most of these emerge within a relatively short period of time, as is evidenced by table 2.2 (for more details, see Meisel, forthcoming).

It is easy to see that for each child there are two phases during which most of the suffixes are acquired. The late appearance of some forms of *sein* "to be" is not pertinent to the present discussion. And the fact that C begins to use the *-e* suffix only after everything else has been acquired, can probably be accounted for by means of phonological arguments. This form competes with the colloquially preferred zero marking; it is in fact not used frequently. On the other hand, P occasionally overgeneralizes the *-e* suffix to modals.

This brings us to the crucial point of this discussion: apart from overgeneralizations in P's speech such as *man kanne* "one can", both children make almost *no errors* in person marking on verbs. There are a few errors in number marking, where singular is used instead of plural (3 in C's speech and 2 in P's), but this happens fairly late, for C at 2;8 and for P at 3;10–3;11. Indeed, I find only three errors where P uses an inappropriate form to encode person, but this, too, happens long after verb inflection has already been firmly established in the child's grammatical competence, at 3;5 and at 3;11:

(8) (i) nein du nimmt nicht   no you take – 3rd sg. – not
   (ii) der hab aufgegessen   this one have – 1st sg. – eaten all up
  (iii) der hab ja gesagt   this one have – 1st sg. – said yes

It seems to be safe to assume that these examples may be interpreted as performance errors. At any rate, there can be no doubt that verb inflection is acquired early, within a brief time span, and virtually without errors. As with monolingual children, *-t* is the first marking to appear, together with the colloquial *is*, replacing the standard variant *ist*. Note, however, that P acquires 3rd sg. *-t* and 1st sg. *-e* almost simultaneously. The former is attested only once at age 2;7 and then again at 2;9; from then on, it is used productively. As a conclusion, I would like to suggest that inflectional markings for finite verbs develop at about age 1;11 (C) and 2;9 (P), respectively. This corresponds to an MLU value of approximately 2.0, thus to stage II, as defined by Brown. It remains to be seen whether these forms do in fact serve a *syntactic* function at this point, i.e. whether they are used to encode subject–verb agreement.

It is important to realize that the same children have been found to use the first *grammatical* tense markings at exactly the same point of development (see Meisel, 1985). Also, we have seen above that language-specific word order patterns – and particularly verb-second placement in German – begin to appear during this phase.

Concerning verb inflection in French, as mentioned before, one has to rely on rather scanty evidence. By examining the contrast between finite and non-finite forms, and by evaluating the amount of variability in form across the whole range of verbs used by one child at a given time, we do, nevertheless, have two criteria which enable us to decide whether and when the children are using a form class *verb*.

Candidates for this syntactic label appear much earlier in French than in German. The first examples are attested at about age 1;3–1;4. But these are probably the result of rote learning; they never vary in form and they all belong to a small set of items reflecting certain routine patterns in adult–child interaction, e.g. *tiens, donne, attends* "hold/take," "give," "wait." The first type which appears in different forms is documented for C at age 1;10. Using the two criteria just mentioned (finite *versus* non-finite contrast; variability in form), leads us to the conclusion that C is in fact using the syntactic category of verbs and verb inflection no later than at age 2;0. At this point, some twenty different verbs are used, and they are marked for *present tense, past participle, imperative*, and *infinitive*. Applying the same criteria in the analysis of P's speech, shows that he uses verbs and verb inflection at about age 2;9. In other words, this syntactic category develops during the same period of time, in French as well as in German.

It should not be overlooked, however, that we used defining criteria for what might be syntactic entities, which makes it impossible *per definitionem* to find evidence for *syntactic* operations before a child reaches stage II (MLU 1.75–2.25). It remains to be seen whether a less restrictive definition would not allow us to identify instances of grammatical categories and processes much earlier than has been possible here. For the time being, we will assume that both children have access to the syntactic mode of processing no later than at stage II.

At this point, it is necessary to look at the emergence of subjects and to examine the question whether early verb morphology is indeed used to encode agreement with the subject. I will be very brief here, referring again to Meisel (forthcoming) for a more detailed discussion. The following remarks apply to multi-word utterances; infinitives and imperatives will not be included in this discussion for the obvious reason that they do not require subject–verb agreement.

At about age 1;11 (C) and 2;8 (P), subjects are normally supplied by both children in contexts where the adult norm requires them in German. C omits them only occasionally. These instances can be interpreted as elliptic utterances, most of which are perfectly normal in adult casual speech, e.g. *geht nicht* "doesn't work". Most of these omissions occur with the verbs *is/ist* "is" and *will* "want". P omits subjects more frequently, but he tends to leave out other obligatory elements as well. I would like to suggest that once an element is used productively, such omissions should be interpreted as resulting from a performance strategy. This claim is supported by the fact that, as in C's omissions, this is restricted to a small set of verbs: *ist, gehen*, and *will*. In fact, all but one of the omissions in P's speech at age 2;10 occur with *geht kaputt* "goes broken = is breaking" (see figure 2.4). Similarly, all but one of the

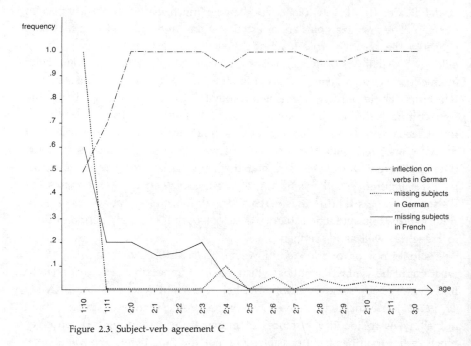

Figure 2.3. Subject-verb agreement C

missing subjects at 3;5 (P) occur with the construction *will* + verb. In other words, omissions are highly predictable and usually happen in very specific contexts. In conclusion, subjects are used productively in German by C and P from age 1;11 and 2;8 respectively. It should be noted that up to age 2;9 (C) and 3;3 (P), these are almost exclusively pronominal subjects.

Analyzing the use of subjects in French leads to very similar conclusions. The subject position is frequently not filled until age 1;10 (C) and 2;9 (P). Missing subjects after this point of development can be interpreted as in the German data, i.e. as resulting from performance strategies. And again, this only happens in connection with a small set of verbs, i.e. almost exclusively with *veux/veut* "will/wants". The observed preference for pronominal subjects is even more marked in French than in German. The children either use only a clitic pronoun in subject position, or they dislocate the subject (preferably to the left) and leave a clitic copy in subject position. Non-pronominal subjects in a position adjacent to the verb *never* occur in C's speech and only very rarely in P's. Note that this reflects to a large degree the use of such constructions in colloquial adult French. But this observation, too, indicates that the children adhere to the respective target systems. This again leads to a differentiation between the two languages.

Some of the most crucial facts discussed above are shown in Figures 2.3 and 2.4. They indicate that verb inflection in German develops very rapidly. Once

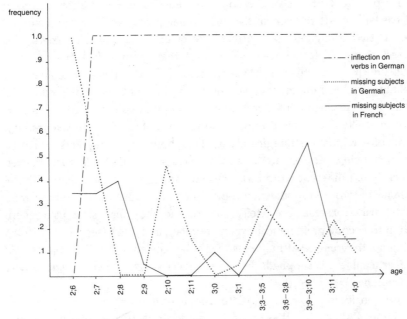

Figure 2.4. Subject-verb agreement P

it is attested, it is almost without exception used in all contexts where it is required in the adult language. At the same time, the frequency of omitted subjects drops in both languages – except for some instances in P's speech which have been explained above as a phenomenon peculiar to his language use. Most importantly, the two figures show quite clearly that constructions where the subject position is not filled, fade out as inflected verbs come in. If one bears in mind that markings for the grammatical person on the verb always agree correctly with the subject, these facts represent strong evidence in favor of the claim that the children's use of language can be described adequately as being organized according to *syntactic* categories and processes. The function of early verb inflection is thus to encode subject–verb agreement. The correct use of these devices in each of the bilingual's two languages implies that they are differentiated from early on.

Conclusions

In the introduction to this chapter, the question was raised whether it might be possible, in principle, that an individual exposed to two languages from early on should be capable of separating the two grammatical systems without going through a phase of temporary confusion. I believe that our findings lend strong support to the claim that this is indeed possible. The evidence provided here is of the sort required above. In addition, a strong effort has been made to back up the further claim that early differences in the use of the two languages may correctly be qualified as *syntactic* in nature, as discussed above. In fact, I want to suggest that grammatical processing is possible much earlier than is usually assumed on the basis of analyses of monolingual child language. I would guess that this might be explained by the fact that the task of acquiring two grammatical systems simultaneously will be easier if the child focuses his attention on problems of form, rather than relying on semantic-pragmatic strategies alone. This, however, is rather speculative for the time being. At any rate, I believe I have shown that bilingual children consistently use different word order in both languages no later than with the appearance of two – or more – word utterances. At about the same time, they begin to mark for case (see Meisel, 1986) and they also start using verb inflection to encode grammatical person, number, and tense (see Meisel, 1985). In doing so, they use what may reasonably be labeled syntactic subjects, and whenever a subject is supplied, the verb agrees with it in person and usually also in number.

Before concluding, I would like to add a terminological remark. In the introduction, I suggested that some of the contradictory claims concerning language "mixing" are due to the fact that "mixing" is not clearly distinguished from "code-switching". Rather superficial definitions, as suggested by Redlinger and Park (1980), cannot but result in a terminologically motivated confusion. In fact, the few researchers who do distinguish the two phenomena and who then explicitly ask which of the two occurs in specific contexts, seem to agree that in most cases even lexical "mixing" has to be interpreted as code-switching which frequently helps to improve communication, for example Oksaar (1976, 1978) and Saunders (1982).

As I have used the two terms, *mixing* was defined as the fusion of two grammatical systems, i.e. a possible characteristic of a bilingual's *grammatical competence*. *Code-switching*, on the other hand, was defined as a specific skill in the bilingual's *pragmatic competence*. These two definitions, however, do not cover a third phenomenon which should be distinguished from the two others.[7] Namely, the child may well use two different grammatical systems, as evidenced by distinct word order patterns, etc., and yet may still choose the "wrong" language occasionally. (Which language is the "right" or "wrong" one is usually determined by the same sociolinguistic factors as in code-switching, e.g. interlocutor, topic, etc.) This may correspond to an error in what Grosjean (1982:127) calls "language choice", or it may be a case of "code-mixing" (Grosjean, 1982:204), i.e. the child switches "to express a word or an expression that is not immediately accessible in the other language" (Grosjean, 1982:206). In any case, it is a phenomenon which would have to be explained by the bilingual's *pragmatic competence*. From this it follows that language differentiation is a necessary but not a sufficient prerequisite for successful code-switching. Even though two grammatical systems have been internalized, the child might still violate the rules which govern choice or switching, e.g. in the case of the children discussed here, speaking German to the French-speaking mother. If we want to call *this* "mixing", we should find a different term to refer to the phenomenon treated in this paper, i.e. the alleged inability to separate two grammatical systems. I would suggest calling this *fusion* (of grammatical systems).

Terminological quarrels are certainly boring. And I will not necessarily insist on the terminology proposed above. But I would urge keeping the three phenomena apart, whatever labels one may finally use to refer to them. If, however, one adopts these terms, the results of this chapter can be phrased in the following way: bilinguals are capable of differentiating grammatical systems; fusion is not necessarily a characteristic of bilingual language development, but mixing may occur until code-switching is firmly established as a strategy of bilingual pragmatic competence.

Notes

1 This summary draws on the studies which are also included in the overviews given by Taeschner (1983) and McLaughlin (1984). A number of other studies have been included in this survey, for example Fantini (1982), Hoffmann (1985), Kadar-Hoffmann (1983), Kielhöfer and Jonekeit (1983), Porché (1983), Pupier, Connors and Lappin (1982).

2 In fact, one finds a second but contradictory statement on this issue; see Volterra and Taeschner (1978:320): "It is at the end of this stage [stage II], that bilingual children amaze observers because of their extraordinary skill in passing from one language to another during the same verbal interaction" – followed by an example to illustrate this point, taken from Lisa, age 3;3!

3 In fact, "mixing", as used by Redlinger and Park (1980), is a rather ill-defined term. The vast majority of the "mixes" are "single lexical substitutions" (pp. 345 ff.). It is quite unlikely that these may adequately be treated as syntactic phenomena. I would suspect that most instances of "mixing" in their data could easily be explained as lexical transfer from the dominant language, probably even as code-switching (compare "code-mixing", as defined by Grosjean, 1982:204). Redlinger and Park (1980:342) themselves observe that at least in some cases, the children were consciously aware of the fact that they were switching.

4 I find it somewhat strange to argue (see Volterra and Taeschner, 1978:324) that the child uses a common syntax for adjective constructions, based on the observation that during this phase (i.e. up to age 2;9) one does not find a single example of this construction in Italian; and the German examples stick perfectly to the target norm.

5 Traute Taeschner (personal communication) confirmed, in fact, that this is the intended interpretation. I should also point out that she apparently does not defend the single-system hypothesis any more. It is only lexical development which is described in Taeschner (1983) in the same fashion as in Volterra and Taeschner (1978). As for morphology and syntax, Taeschner (1983) also mentions three stages, but those are not defined in terms of one single grammatical system. Rather, she suggests that, by and large, development is very similar in bilingual and in monolingual children. (See chapters 3 and 4, and table 7.1 in chapter 7 of Taeschner, 1983.) She concludes that the simultaneous acquisition of two

languages is "the formation of two linguistic systems under conditions of complex interaction which are both based or depend upon the same process of cognitive, linguistic, social, and emotional maturation" (Taeschner, 1983:113). Nevertheless, I find her statements to this effect somewhat confusing. To mention one example, in section 4.13 (Taeschner, 1983:166f.) she claims that the child "believes that both languages have the same rules." And "During the second period, the child very gradually realizes that the rules involved in linguistic processing must be separated." It would have been helpful if she had stated explicitly which claims contained in the Volterra and Taeschner (1978) model have now been abandoned. Unfortunately, this previous model is not discussed in any detail.

6 This study forms part of a research project which was started in 1980 as an enterprise of the research group DUFDE (Deutsch und Französisch – Doppelter Erstspracherwerb). During the period when this chapter was written, the researchers in this team were Swantje Klinge, Teresa Parodi, and Suzanne Schlyter. Students collaborating as research assistants were Marianne Dieck, Pascale Guénard, Martina Jürgens, Caroline Koehn, Marie-France Lavielle, Natascha Müller, and Anke Sigerist. Elvira Behrend was kind enough to lend me her intuitions as a native speaker. I want to thank all of them for their most valuable help. Furthermore, I want to thank those friends and colleagues who commented on an earlier version of this chapter, Harald Clahsen, Kathleen Connors, Charlotte Hoffmann, Annick de Houwer, Kenneth Hyltenstam, and Loraine Obler. I also acknowledge gratefully that the Deutsche Forschungsgemeinschaft has given a research grant (1986–88) to the author of this study to support this research project.

7 This was pointed out to me by Suzanne Schlyter. I want to thank her for her persistence and her patience, for it took me quite a while, I must confess, to accept this.

References

Bates, Elizabeth (1976), *Language and Context: The Acquisition of Pragmatics*. New York: Academic Press.

Bates, E. and MacWhinney, B. (1982), Functionalist approaches to grammar. In Wanner, E. and Gleitman, L. R. (eds.), *Language Acquisition: The State of the Art*. Cambridge University Press. 173–218.

Bergman, Coral R. (1976), Interference vs. independent development in infant bilingualism. In Keller, G. D., Teschner, R. V. and Viera, S. (eds.), *Bilingualism in the Bicentennial and Beyond*. New York: Bilingual Press (York College/CUNY), 86–96.

Bloom, L. and Lahey, M. (1978), *Language Development and Language Disorders*. New York: Wiley.

Brown, Roger (1973), *A First Language. The Early Stages*. Cambridge, MA: Harvard University Press.

Clahsen, Harald (1982), *Spracherwerb in der Kindheit*. Tübingen: Narr.

    (1984), Der Erwerb der Kasusmarkierung in der deutschen Kindersprache. *Linguistische Berichte* **89**. 1–31.

    (1986), Verb inflections in German child language: acquisition of agreement markings and the functions they encode. *Linguistics* **24** (1). 79–121.

Clark, Eve (1985), Acquisition of Romance: with special reference to French. In: Slobin, D. (ed.), *Crosslinguistic Study of Language Acquisition*. Hillsdale, N.J.: Erlbaum. 687–782.

Fantini, Alvino E. (1982), *La adquisición del lenguaje en un niño bilingüe*. Barcelona: Editorial Herder.

Fletcher, P. and Garman, M. (eds.) (1979), *Language Acquisition: Studies in First Language Development*. Cambridge University Press.

Garman, Michael (1979), Early grammatical development. In Fletcher, P. and Garman, M. (eds.), *Language Acquisition: Studies in First Language Development*. Cambridge University Press, 177–208.

Givón, Talmy (1979), *On Understanding Grammar*. New York: Academic Press.

(1985), Function, structure and language acquisition. In: Slobin, D. I. (ed.), *The Crosslinguistic Study of Language Acquisition*. Hillsdale, N. J.: Erlbaum, 1005–1027.

Grosjean, François (1982), *Life with Two Languages*. Cambridge, MA.: Harvard University Press.

Hoffmann, Charlotte (1985), Language acquisition in two trilingual children. *Journal of Multilingual and Multicultural Development* 6(6). 479–495.

Jaeggli, Osvaldo (1982), *Topics in Romance Syntax*. Dordrecht: Foris.

Jekat, Susanne (1985), *Die Entwicklung des Wortschatzes bei bilingualen Kindern (Frz.-Dt.) in den ersten vier Lebensjahren*. Master's Thesis, University of Hamburg, Dep. of Romance Languages.

Joly, André (1973), Sur le système de la personne. *Revue des Langues Romanes* 80. 3–56.

Kadar-Hoffmann, Gisela (1983), *Trilingualer Spracherwerb: Der gleichzeitige Erwerb des Deutschen, Französischen und Ungarischen*. Universität Kiel: Dissertation.

Kielhöfer, B. and Jonekeit, S. (1983), *Zweisprachige Kindererziehung*. Tübingen: Stauffenberg Verlag.

Leopold, Werner F. (1939), *Speech Development of a Bilingual Child*. Evanston, Ill.: Northwestern University Press.

Lindholm, K. and Padilla, A. M. (1978), Language mixing in bilingual children. *Journal of Child Language* 5. 327–335.

McLaughlin, Barry (1984), *Second Language Acquisition in Childhood. Vol. 1: Preschool Children*. Hillsdale, N.J.: Erlbaum.

Maratsos, Michael (1982), The child's construction of grammatical categories. In: Wanner, E. & Gleitman, L. (eds.), *Language Acquisition: The State of the Art*. Cambridge University Press. 240–266.

Meisel, Jürgen M. (1983), Transfer as a second-language strategy. *Language & Communication* 3(1). 11–46.

(1985), Les phases initiales du développement de notions temporelles, aspectuelles et de modes d'action. *Lingua* 66. 321–374.

(1986), Word order and case marking in early child language. Evidence from simultaneous acquisition of two languages. *Linguistics* 24(1). 123–183.

(forthcoming) Subjekt-Verb Kongruenz. Hamburg: *Arbeitspapier DUFDE*.

Meisel, J. M., Clahsen, H. and Pienemann, M. (1981), On determining developmental stages in natural second language acquisition. *Studies in Second Language Acquisition* 3(2). 109–135.

Mikès, Melanija (1967), Acquisition des catégories grammaticales dans le langage de l'enfant. *Enfance* 20. 289–298.

Mills, Anne E. (1985), The acquisition of German. In: Slobin, D. I. (ed.), *The Cross-Linguistic Study of Language Acquisition*. Hillsdale, N.J.: Erlbaum, 141–254.

Oksaar, Els (1976), Code switching as an interactional strategy for developing bilingual competence. *Child Language* (= Word 27). 377–385.

(1978), Preschool trilingualism: A case study. In: Peng, F. C. and v. Raffler-Engel, W. (eds.), *Language Acquisition and Developmental Kinesics*. Tokyo, 129–137.

Park, Tschang-Zin (1981), *The Development of Syntax in the Child. With Special Reference to German*. Innsbruck: Innsbrucker Beiträge zur Kulturwissenschaft 45.

Pavlovitch, M. (1920), *Le langage enfantin. Acquisition du serbe et du français par un enfant serbe*. Paris: Champion.

Pfaff, Carol (1979), Constraints on language mixing: Intrasentential code-switching and borrowing in Spanish/English. *Language* 55. 291–318.

Poplack, Shana (1980), Sometimes I'll start a sentence in Spanish y termino en español: Toward a typology of code-switching. *Linguistics* 18. 581–618.

Porsché, Donald C. (1983), *Die Zweisprachigkeit während des primären Spracherwerbs*. Tübingen: Narr (TBL 218).

Pupier, P., Connors, K. and Lappin, K. et al. (1982), *L'acquisition simultanée du français et de l'anglais chez des petits enfants de Montréal*. Gouvernement du Québec, Office de la Langue Française.

Redlinger, W. and Park, T. (1980), Language mixing in young bilinguals. *Journal of Child Language* 7. 337–352.

Ronjat, Jules (1913), *Le développement du langage observé chez un enfant bilingue.* Paris: Champion.

Saunders, George (1982), Der Erwerb einer "zweiten" Muttersprache in der Familie. In: Swift, J. (ed.), *Bilinguale und multikulturelle Erziehung.* Königshausen: Neumann, 26–33.

Slobin, Dan I. (ed.) (1985), *The Crosslinguistic Study of Language Acquisition.* Hillsdale, N.J.: Erlbaum.

Taeschner, Traute (1983), *The Sun is Feminine. A Study of Language Acquisition in Bilingual Children.* Berlin: Springer.

Valian, Virginia (1986), Syntactic categories in the speech of young children. *Developmental Psychology* 22. 562–579.

Vihman, Marilyn M. (1982), The acquisition of morphology by a bilingual child: A whole-word approach. *Applied Psycholinguistics* 3. 141–160.

(1985), Language differentiation by the bilingual infant. *Journal of Child Language* 12. 297–324.

(forthcoming), A developmental perspective on code-switching: Conversations between a pair of bilingual siblings.

Volterra, V. and Taeschner, T. (1978), The acquisition and development of language by bilingual children. *Journal of Child Language* 5. 311–326.

Wanner, E. and Gleitman, L. (eds.) (1982), *Language Acquisition: The State of the Art.* Cambridge University Press.

Wode, Henning (1977), Four early stages in the development of L1 negation. *Journal of Child Language* 4. 87–102.

(1981), *Learning a Second Language. An Integrated View of Language Acquisition.* Tübingen: Narr.

3. Variation in children's ability to learn second languages

MARGARET HUMES-BARTLO

Introduction

The question of individual differences in cognition is one which draws the interest of many disciplines. What causes the vast variation in individual skills and aptitudes? The most obvious response is that a combination of genetic and environmental factors shape our cognitive personalities much as they shape our emotional personalities. As a neuropsychologist, my focus is on the different areas of the brain in which linguistic and other cognitive functions are processed.

Neuropsychology, a comparatively young science, has over the last century identified the areas of the brain which are responsible for the processing of specific cognitive skills such as language, visuo-spatial abilities, and reading. In order to identify and associate brain areas and cognitive skills, neuro-psychological research has traditionally focused upon the similarities between the abilities of human subjects. A large amount of information on brain function was gathered from stroke and head trauma victims in whom disabilities caused by damage to certain areas were studied. Currently, interest in research is being directed toward individual differences, within the structure of species similarity. For instance, interest in the brain organization of left handers and women has been increasing. Evidence is mounting that individual differences in brain organization are important. Given the infinite permutations of human genetic, hormonal, prenatal and postnatal environments, I find it easy to agree with Gray (1948) that each person's "brain is as individual to its possessor as his face."

The aim of this study was to suggest some patterns of neuropsychological development of the brain which would shed some light on these questions:

(1) Why do some people find it easy to learn or acquire a foreign language, while others in comparable situations find it to be a nearly impossible task?

(2) Is there a cluster of cognitive and linguistic skills which can be identified as being advantageous or disadvantageous to an individual in attempting to learn a second language?

The present paper reports on the results of a study in which the differences between good and poor second language learners were investigated. The current evidence of variation in the ability to learn a second language, and reasons for this variability will be reviewed first. Differences between cognitive profiles of good and poor language learners will then be discussed, and a model for the brain structures underlying the cognitive differences will be presented.

Variation in L2 acquisition – previous studies

Variation in the ability to learn second languages has been studied frequently in adults, notably by such researchers as Carroll (Carroll and Sapon, 1959; Carroll, 1962, 1979), Pimsleur (Pimsleur, Stockwell and Comrey, 1962, Pimsleur, Sundaland and McIntyre, 1964; Pimsleur, 1966), and Gardner (Gardner, 1960, Gardner and Lambert, 1972). Research by Nelson (1973), Vihman (1982), and Wong-Fillmore (1979), among others, has shown that children differ in their styles of both first and second language acquisition. It is clear that children vary widely, as do adults, in the ease of acquisition of other skills, such as reading, mathematics, and motor skills. Children also vary widely in the degree to which they master their first language, as adults vary widely in their linguistic talents. Individual differences in style of second language acquisition in children have been studied (Wong-Fillmore, 1979), but variation in children's ability to learn a second language has not been closely investigated, despite the important ramifications for bilingual education.

The relative ease or difficulty which a particular child may have in learning a second language may be predictable on the basis of his or her profile of cognitive strengths and weaknesses. Hartnett (1976) identified two groups of adult language learners with distinct styles and preferred teaching methods. It may be possible to identify groups of child language learners with similar acquisition styles. Children with similar cognitive profiles may learn a second language more easily using a particular style of language instruction.

There are many possible reasons for difficulty in learning or acquiring a second language. Students who are poor students in general, or who have low general intelligence may have difficulty acquiring a second language, and students who have attitudinal or motivational problems may also be slower than average, as Gardner and Lambert's research has shown (1972). A third group of children may have serious L1 problems. For example, some learning disabled children may have serious processing difficulties in L1, which cause them difficulty in learning a second language. A fourth group of children, who are of at least average intelligence and who are good students otherwise, just cannot seem to learn another language. The last group of students is the one this study will focus on, since there is no apparent reason for their failure.

Some of these children are capable of learning a second language at the level of Cummins' "basic interpersonal communications skills" (1979) when they must, such as in the case of immigrant children who must learn the host country's language in order to survive. English-speaking children born in the United States have a choice. Among the native English-speaking children who drop out of high school language courses, eschew the elective language courses in college, and avoid the language requirement in graduate school in favor of computer languages, are a percentage for whom attitude and motivation are not a factor in their failure to learn until after they have tried and failed.

A study by the Canadian Public Service (Wells, 1976) estimates the percentage of adults who have a "negative prognosis" for foreign language learning to be 11 percent, with 21 percent borderline cases. This study advances the proposition that this group of poor language learners possesses a cognitive profile which happens to be disadvantageous to language learning, and that it applies to children as well as to adults.

Cognitive differences between good and poor learners

The observed differences between groups of good and poor learners may provide information about the origin of these differences, as well as ways to narrow the gap between the groups.

A study by Diaz (1985) compared bilingual kindergarten and first grade children who were high or low English proficient during two test periods on a variety of cognitive tasks. He found that the high English proficiency group had significantly better test scores on a verbal analogies task at both the first and second test periods. In addition, scores on the verbal analogies task predicted Time 2 proficiency for the low English group. Diaz concluded that there is a strong relationship between the degree of bilingualism and cognitive variability in early stages of proficiency, but this relationship is weak in children of high proficiency. ·

Diaz's groups were not controlled for the number of years they were exposed to English. The range of home language situations for bilingual children is large, and there could easily be a wide variation in years of exposure to English within each proficiency group. For instance, a child with two years of exposure to English may have passed Diaz's proficiency test, while another child with the same amount of exposure to English remained

Spanish dominant. Since Diaz did not control for years of exposure to English, information about cognitive variability among his high and low proficiency groups may be obscured.

Other researchers have targeted poor second language learners for investigation. Trites and Price (1976) studied thirty-two 7 and 8-year old children who were experiencing difficulties in French immersion programs in the Ottawa area. The researchers were interested in discovering whether the immersion failures could be identified as a group distinct from immersion successes and from learning disabled children. The children were compared on a number of cognitive and linguistic tasks. The immersion failures performed generally at a level between the immersion successes and the learning disabled children, supporting the theory that they constitute a distinct group.

The two immersion groups were not distinguishable on the basis of overall intelligence, although the failure group tended to have an above average Performance IQ coupled with an average Verbal IQ. The success group showed no discrepancy between the Verbal and Performance IQs. Other group differences included higher performance by the immersion successes on academic achievement tests, auditory and visual memory tests, fine motor skills, and behavior adjustment ratings. Trites and Price concluded that "some children of above average potential and normal ability for school progress in native language experience difficulty or fail in immersion programs, due to a mild specific maturational lag."

Trites and Price's theory of a developmental lag causing failure for some children in immersion programs is an intriguing one which deserves further attention. The causes of variation in the ease with which children learn languages may lie in individual differences in brain structure. These differences may be caused by anomalies or lags in the development process.

Earlier I mentioned that I believe that our brains are as different as our faces. What I meant by that statement was that the actual structure of each human brain is unique, within the limitations of species. Studies of stroke and trauma victims have allowed us to identify general areas of the brain responsible for speech formulation, auditory discrimination, and other subunits of language processing. The size of these brain regions differs significantly among individuals (Geschwind and Levitsky, 1968), and so does the arrangement and type of neurons found in different areas of the brain (Galaburda, Sanides, and Geschwind, 1979). This is true for the entire cortex of the brain but especially for those brain regions devoted to language.

Variation in the size and structure of brain regions subserving language does not necessarily correlate with variation in language skills, nor is the degree of variation necessarily comparable. For example, a particularly large total language area does not always indicate that language skills will be exceptional. However, in some cases, variation in organization of the brain has been shown to be associated with differences in function, such as the case reported by Galaburda and Kemper (1979) in which the brain of a dyslexic was found to have a disordered pattern of brain lateralization, in addition to abnormalities of neuronal growth, especially in the areas of the brain involved with language. This study and others more recently reported provide evidence that variation in cognitive performance may be associated with variation in the structure of the brain. The next step would be to observe specific cognitive profiles which would be predicted by expected types of variation in brain structure. The following model proposes such a relationship.

The model draws heavily upon Geschwind and Galaburda's (1985) theory of the association between individual differences in cognitive skills, such as language, and individual variation in neuroanatomical structure. Geschwind and Galaburda hypothesize that "slowed growth within certain zones of the left hemisphere is likely to result in enlargement of other cortical regions, in particular, the homologous contralateral area, but also adjacent unaffected regions." This pattern of anomalous dominance is thought to be due to abnormal hormone levels during fetal development, or to unusual fetal sensitivity to normal hormone levels.

The resulting variation may be associated with left-handedness and with superior talents and/or learning disorders, as well as with certain immune disorders, such as allergies and asthma. Specifically, an individual with language deficits due to unusual neuroanatomic development may have exceptional skills in other areas, especially areas which are subserved by adjacent areas or by the right cerebral hemisphere (Geschwind and Galaburda, 1985). My study expands this model to investigate a subset of language skills, that of ability in second language learning.

In their book *The Exceptional Brain*, Obler and Fein (1988) discussed the Geschwind and Galaburda theory in connection with several types of special talents, including special talent in second language learning. Case studies of talented language learners by Novoa, Obler and Fein (1988) and by Desmarais (1986) lend credence to the theory that special talent in second language learning may be associated with deficits in another area.

Present study

The study presented in this chapter investigates the opposite end of the ability continuum, that of poor ability for second language learning. The premise of the study is that difficulty in second language learning may be associated with ability in other skills subserved by brain areas which are adjacent or homologous to language regions. Conversely, those individuals with notable

Table 3.1. *Types of tasks*

Language
Peabody Picture Vocabulary
Test de Vocabulario en Imagenes Peabody
Woodcock Analogies
Auditory Discrimination

Memory
Digit Span (WISC-R)
Associative Pairs (WMS)
Memory for Designs (WMS)

Handedness
Harris Test of Lateral Dominance-subtests

Intellectual Screening
Raven Colored Progressive Matrices

Tasks expected to dissociate from language learning skill
Arithmetic (WISC-R)
Block Design (WISC-R)

---

ability in acquiring or learning a second language may perform significantly worse in another cognitive area.

The central hypothesis is that those with low ability in second language learning, as compared with peers of comparable age and level of general intelligence, would exhibit subtle language deficits in L1, coupled with above average abilities in mathematical reasoning and visuo-spatial construction. Both mathematical reasoning and visuo-spatial manipulation skills are subserved by a brain region adjacent to the language region, and by the right hemisphere. Conversely, students with high ability for language learning would exhibit overall better L1 language skills than the low ability group, as well as less ability in the visuo-spatial skills.

Materials

The names and types of tests used are outlined in Table 3.1. These are: language, memory, handedness, intelligence, and tasks which were expected to dissociate from language learning skill.

A screening battery consisting of Ravens Coloured Progressive Matrices and the Peabody Vocabulary tests in Spanish and in English were administered first, in order to control for the effects that low intelligence or language impairment may have on second language learning. The Ravens is a test of the child's ability to make visual analogies by choosing the correct design segment to complete a pattern. The Ravens has been used as a culture-fair intelligence

Table 3.2. *Auditory discrimination*
(Humes-Bartlo, 1986)

Examples: lo-la
　　　　　dar-par
1. *macho-nacho*
2. *carta-tarta*
3. *nos-nos*
4. *beber-deber*
5. *si-se*
6. *lave-llave*
7. *caro-paro*
8. *lago-lago*
9. *falta-salta*
10. *como-coma*
11. *claro-claro*
12. *dia-guia*

---

test, and was used in this study as a gross measure of overall intellectual ability.

Next, the English version of the Peabody Picture Vocabulary Test-Revised was administered. The child must choose the correct picture which corresponds to the word the experimenter has just named. The Spanish version of the test, *Test de Vocabulario en Imagenes Peabody* (*TVIP*), is similar but not identical, and the scores cannot be directly compared. The vocabulary tests were used as a separate measure of English and Spanish proficiency, and to screen out children with obvious language impairments. The English vocabulary test was always given first to minimize transfer effects to the second vocabulary test.

For both the Ravens and the Spanish vocabulary test, children who scored more than one standard deviation below the mean were disqualified from the study. After completing the initial screening battery, children received further language testing in Spanish. A test of verbal analogical reasoning from the Woodcock-Johnson Psychoeducational Battery was chosen because analogical reasoning has been found by other researchers to be important in second language learning, and because of its availability in Spanish. In this test, the child must complete verbal analogies such as: "Mother is to father as sister is to——."

For a test of the ability to discriminate minimal phoneme pairs in Spanish, a list was constructed of ten word pairs which represent most of the major phonetic contrasts in Spanish (see Table 3.2). Good L1 phonemic discrimination skills may help a child to learn to discriminate phonemic contrasts in a new language. In the Rapid Automatized Naming Test (Denckla and Rudel, 1976), the child named as quickly as possible the colors or objects which are printed

Table 3.3. *Paired Associates (Wechsler Memory Scale)*
(trans. Humes-Bartlo, 1986)

---

 1. *metal-hierro*
 2. *nene-llora*
 3. *moler-oscuro*
 4. *norte-sur*
 5. *escuela-bodega*
 6. *rosa-flor*
 7. *arriba-abajo*
 8. *correr-onza*
 9. *fruta-manzana*
10. *repollo-pluma*

---

in random series across a board. The test measures the child's automaticity of language, and is used clinically to detect latent difficulties in naming.

A Spanish translation of the paired associates test from the Wechsler Memory Scale (Wechsler and Stone, 1945) was used as a measure of associative memory (see Table 3.3). Rote verbal memory was measured by means of the Digit Span subtest from the Wechsler Intelligence Scale for Children (WISC-R) (Wechsler, 1981). The task requires a child to repeat after the experimenter increasingly longer strings of digits. Children with a good verbal associative memory were expected to find language learning easier, while a good rote memory may or may not be helpful. A good visual memory was not expected to be related to success in language learning.

The Arithmetic subtest from the WISC-R and the Block Design subtest from the WISC-R were measures which were chosen as likely to dissociate from skill in language learning. Block Design requires the child to copy a geometric design with blocks. Another test which was chosen as likely to dissociate from skill in second language learning was the memory for designs subtest of the Wechsler Memory Scale. The child was required to reproduce a geometric design from memory.

Handedness and lateralization tasks were administered to determine whether the fast language learners had left language lateralization, as Geschwind and Galaburda's theory predicts.

In the course of the study, children also carried home a questionnaire for their parents to fill out concerning birth and development information, as well as family information about hand preference, school and language history, cognitive talents, and asthma and allergy sufferers, in order to provide information regarding the Geschwind and Galaburda hypothesis.

Procedure

Students were tested individually in three half-hour sessions, including screening sessions. All tests were in Spanish except the English vocabulary test.

Subjects

A total of 71 third to fifth grade children attending bilingual classes in New York city schools received intelligence and language screening after obtaining parental permission to participate in the study. Only children who had not yet passed the school's standardized proficiency test, the Language Assessment Battery (LAB) (New York City Board of Education, 1982), by the Fall of 1986 were eligible to participate in the study. The LAB test is administered by the school system each fall and spring to determine whether Limited English Proficient children are ready to move to an English classroom. (Validity and reliability data on the LAB may be found in the appendix.) Although the LAB was not a part of the current test battery, the final LAB scores were utilized in assigning children to fast and slow language learning groups.

Twenty five children who scored more than 1 standard deviation below the mean on the Ravens or on the Spanish Peabody test were excluded from the study. Thus children who remained in bilingual classrooms for reasons other than lack of English proficiency were excluded from the study.

At the end of the school year, the school re-administered the standardized English proficiency test to all students attending bilingual classes. When these scores were made available, children were grouped into fast, slow, and unclassified groups. The groups were determined on the basis of number of years attending U.S. schools and final passing or failing in the Spring of 1987 on the LAB. Children who passed the English proficiency test in 3 years or less of attendance in a U.S. school constituted the fast learning group. Children who had had 3 or more years of exposure to English while attending school in the U.S., and who failed so far to reach criterion on the LAB were placed in the slow English learning group. The scores of children who had been in the school system for less than three years and who had not yet passed the proficiency test have been analyzed separately for use in the prediction of their future scores, to test the model presented here. The accuracy of predictions for group membership will be reported when final scores are available from the schools.

Table 3.4. *Significance levels of contributory variables in discriminant analysis*

Step	Variables	Significance
1	Verbal analogies	0.0279
2	Arithmetic	0.0266
3	Auditory discrimination	0.0338
4	Block Design	0.0380
5	Associative memory	0.0380
6	English vocabulary	0.0480

Results

Discriminant analysis was used to distinguish statistically between the fast and slow English learners. The discriminant procedure weights and combines the scores of the variables on which the researcher believes the two groups are likely to differ; in this case, on the cognitive variables mentioned earlier. The method may be used both for the identification of the most highly discriminating variables in a battery and for classification of unknown groups.

Six variables were identified as being contributory to the discrimination of the fast and slow groups (see Table 3.4). The variables so identified were verbal analogies, arithmetic, auditory discrimination, block design, verbal associative memory, and English vocabulary. Using the children's scores for these six variables, the discriminant procedure was able to assign correctly 83 percent of the cases, including 90 percent of the slow English learners.

Interestingly, high scores for block design and arithmetic scores more strongly identified the slow English group, while high scores for verbal analogies, auditory discrimination, verbal associative memory and English vocabulary identified the fast English learners.

These results are in agreement with the original hypothesis, which stated that fast English learners would be identified by their overall better language skills, while the slow English learners would be characterized by their relative skill in visuo-spatial skills.

T-test differences between the fast and slow English learners were significant only on verbal analogies, on which the fast learners outperformed the slow learners. In comparison with the standardized population norms, neither group is significantly above or below the mean, thus the difference is a subtle, yet statistically significant one. Fast learners also had a slightly but not significantly higher score on the Spanish vocabulary test ($p = .091$). The results on these language tests indicate that the fast English learners have more highly developed first language skills than the slow English learners, as was hypothesized. The slow English learners' low, but not pathologically low scores on L1 tasks suggest a language processing system which is adequate for L1 but is overloaded by L2.

No differences between the fast and slow learners were found on the lateralization task, although interesting within-group patterns were observed, suggesting that the fast learners are *more* highly lateralized for language than the slow learners, contradicting the hypothesis based upon Geschwind and Galaburda's work. It has been suggested (Obler, personal communication, 1987) that the fast learner group may be too large (10 percent of the total) to represent the proportion of superior learners with anomalous cerebral dominance which is proposed by Geschwind and Galaburda.

The slow English learners had higher scores than the fast learners on Block Design, Arithmetic, and on Digit Span (the rote verbal memory task), but these differences were not significant. The slow group did not have a higher score on the memory for visual designs task. A larger subject sample might have produced more robust findings regarding the skills of the slow English learners.

Differences between the groups were not manifested for any of the factors associated with Geschwind's theory of unusual lateralization patterns. This may have been due to the rate of return of the questionnaires (77 percent) which reduced the possibility for robust differences.

Conclusions

This chapter has reported a study on the cognitive differences between children who are fast and slow learners of English. Differentiation between the two groups of children was accomplished using a discriminant analysis procedure. High scores for verbal analogical reasoning, auditory discrimination, verbal associative memory, and English vocabulary tended to identify the fast learning group, while high scores for arithmetic and copying block designs more strongly identified the slow learning group. Correct group assignments were received by 83 percent of the subjects according to this method.

Only verbal analogical reasoning stood out as exhibiting a significant difference between the groups on separate T-tests. The analogies test was also the most significant predictive variable throughout the discriminant procedure, suggesting that a mild difficulty in making verbal analogies is a necessary but not sufficient condition for the identification of a slow second language learner. Factors of auditory discrimination, ability to remember associated word pairs, and ability to retain foreign vocabulary stand out as skills which are advantageous to second language learning in children.

In contrast, children for whom second language learning is difficult may have skills in arithmetic or in constructing visuo-spatial designs. Strengthening the first language skills and verbal memory of children at risk of being slow second language learners may be helpful in preparing them for the task.

The results of this study provide a neuropsychological framework for the study of second language learning aptitude, and underline the existence of individual differences in human cognitive skills among average subjects. More specifically for the field of second language learning, this study indicates that differences in ability may be based on factors which have not previously been widely considered.

Appendix

Language Assessment Battery (LAB) – 1982

New York City Board of Education: Internal Memo

The Office of Testing in the Division of Curriculum and Instruction of the New York City Board of Education has developed a completely new edition of the Language Assessment Battery, LAB-1982. This was undertaken as a result of needs expressed by professional staff in the field who reported that the earlier edition, LAB-1976, not only had been overused but, also, was an inappropriate measuring instrument for required purposes. Both LAB-1982 and LAB-1976 were designed to comply with the Aspira Consent Decree which mandated the creation of an instrument to identify non-native speakers of English who lack sufficient proficiency in English to participate effectively in an English-speaking instructional environment and who are, therefore, eligible and entitled to a specific bilingual or English-as-a-Second-Language education program. The new edition, LAB-1982, however, is designed also to comply with other legal mandates, including the Lau guidelines. LAB-1982 continues to measure four content areas (speaking, listening, reading and writing) in both English and Spanish. The Spanish version, which is not a translation, was developed concurrently with the English and closely parallels it. It was designed to identify language dominance of Hispanic students whose English proficiency is limited. In each language, LAB-1982 provides for four levels (K-2, 3-5, 6-8, 9-12) and two parallel forms at each level. Results are reported as raw scores and grade percentiles. All subtests except speaking are group administered and items are in multiple-choice format.

It should be noted that while the content areas measured in LAB-1982 (listening, reading, writing, speaking) remain the same as in LAB-1976, there have been major changes in how the areas are measured as well as changes in test administration procedures. This resulted largely from the use of an integrative rather than a discrete point approach to the measurement of language proficiency. The latter takes language apart and measures its discrete individual segments whereas the former combines language segments into large units and measures the ability to make use of these larger language elements in the context of normal communication. As a result, all the items are new, none having been carried over from LAB-1976.

Content changes in the Listening Test at Levels I and II consisted of replacing picture vocabulary with pictorial items dependent upon sentence comprehension and at Levels II, III and IV of replacing minimal pairs with dictated questions and a listening cloze procedure. In the Reading Test, the traditional paragraph and question format was replaced by a reading cloze procedure. The Writing Test which continues to resemble a language usage test now contains constructions that follow curriculum.

Administrative changes are most extensive at Level I. In LAB-1982, kindergarten students now take only the combined Listening/Speaking test while grade 1 and 2 students take both the combined Listening/Speaking and combined Reading/Writing tests. Also at Level I the listening, reading and writing items are presented in a format that permits small group administration in order to reduce teacher administration time. In the individually administered

Speaking Test, at all levels, a response is now scored separately for relevance and for grammar.

Pilot testing was conducted in the fall of 1981. The English version of the pilot test was administered to an English-proficient sample of students and to a limited-English-proficient sample of students who were non-native speakers of English and whose home languages included languages in addition to Spanish. The Spanish version was administered to a Spanish-proficient sample of students. Samples were selected to be representative of the populations of interest. In order to provide sufficient "floor" so that reliable measurement of the limited-proficient students would result, the test was designed to be very easy for English-proficient students and of average difficulty for the limited-English-proficient students.

Final Forms A and B of LAB-1982 were based upon data from the pilot testing and have been administered to all pupils of limited-English-proficiency in the New York City Public Schools: Form A in Spring 1982 and 1984 and Form B in Spring 1983. For both Forms A and B, spring and fall grade norms have been developed for subtests and total test. At present, however, total test norms for grades 3–12 exclude Speaking. It is planned that norms will be developed for Speaking and Total Test including Speaking. The grade norms were generated for each of the groups mentioned above: English-proficient students on the English version, limited-English-proficient students on the English version, and Spanish-proficient students on the Spanish version. Scores for LAB-1982 are reported as raw scores and percentiles. Scale scores are in process of being developed.

In the New York City Public Schools System, LAB-1982 is used both for entry into and exit from bilingual and ESL programs. New entrants to the NYC school system whose home language is other than English are tested with the English version at the time of entry – usually fall. Any such student who scores at or below the court-mandated criterion score on the English-proficient norms is entitled to bilingual or ESL services. All students in ESL or bilingual programs are tested every spring. Any such student who, in the spring testing, scores above the court-mandated criterion score on the English test is no longer entitled to services and may move into general education classes.

Because Hispanics constitute about three-quarters of the non-native speakers of English in the New York schools, a parallel test was developed in Spanish. The results are used primarily for instructional purposes. There are very different instructional implications for a student who is a proficient reader in his or her own native language, but is a deficient reader in English compared with a student who cannot read well in either language. It is hoped that LAB-1982 versions in other languages may eventually be developed.

Note

This chapter was presented in an earlier form at the XIth University of Michigan Conference on Applied Linguistics, October 9, 1987.

References

Carroll, J. B. (1962), The prediction of success in intensive foreign language training. In Glaser, R. (ed.) *Training Research and Education*. University of Pittsburgh Press.

(1979), Psychometric approaches to the study of language abilities. In Fillmore, C., Kempler, D. and Wang, W. (eds.) *Individual Differences in Language Ability and Language Behavior*. New York: Academic Press.

Carroll, J. B. and Sapon, S. (1959), *Modern Language Aptitude Test*. New York: The Psychological Corporation.

Cummins, J. (1979), Cognitive/academic language proficiency, linguistic interdependence, the optimal age question and some other matters. *Working Papers in Bilingualism* **19**.

Denckla, M. and Rudel, R. (1976), Rapid Automatized Naming Test (R.A.N.), *Neuropsychologia* **14**. 471–479.

Desmarais, C. (1986), Talent en acquisition des langues secondes: perspectives neuro-psychologiques. Unpublished Master's Thesis, University of Ottawa, Ontario.

Diaz, R. (1985), Bilingual cognitive development: Addressing three gaps in current research. *Child Development* **56**. 1376–1388.

Galaburda, A., Sanides, F. and Geschwind, N. (1979), Human brain: Cytoarchitectonic left-right asymmetries in the temporal speech region. *Archives of Neurology* **35**. 812–817.

Galaburda, A. and Kemper, T. L. (1979), Cytoarchitectonic abnormalities in developmental dyslexia: A case study. *Annals of Neurology* **6**. 94–100.

Gardner, R. C. (1960), Motivational variables in second-language acquisition. Unpublished doctoral dissertation, McGill University.

Gardner, R. C. and Lambert, W. E. (1972), *Attitudes and Motivation in Second Language Learning*. Rowley, MA: Newbury House.

Geschwind, N. and Levitsky, W. (1968), Human brain: Left-right asymmetries in temporal speech region. *Science* **161**. 186–187.

Geschwind, N. and Galaburda, A. (1985), Cerebral lateralization. Biological mechanisms, associations, and pathology. Parts I, II, & III. *Archives of Neurology* **42**. 428–459, 521–552, 634–654.

Gray, G. W. (1948), The great ravelled knot. *Scientific American* **179** (4). 26–39.

Hartnett, D. (1976), The relationship of cognitive style and hemispheric preference to deductive and inductive second language learning. Presented at the Conference on Human Brain Function, UCLA, Los Angeles, CA.

Nelson, K. (1973), Structures and strategy in learning to talk. *Monographs of the Society for Research in Child Development* **38**. 149.

New York City Board of Education (1982), *Language Assessment Battery*. New York: Riverside.

Novoa, L., Obler, L. K. and Fein, D. (1988), A neuropsychological approach to talented second language acquisition: A case study. In: Obler, L. K. and Fein, D. A. (eds.) *The Exceptional Brain*. New York: Guilford.

Obler, L. K. and Fein, D. A. (eds.) (1988), *The Exceptional Brain*. New York: Guilford.

Pimsleur, P. (1966), *The Pimsleur Language Aptitude Battery*. New York: Harcourt Brace Jovanovich.

Pimsleur, P., Stockwell, R. P. and Comrey, A. L. (1962), Foreign language learning ability. *Journal of Educational Psychology* **53**. 15–26.

Pimsleur, P., Sundaland, R. and McIntyre, R. (1964), Underachievement in foreign language learning. *International Review of Applied Linguistics* **2**. 113–150.

Rudel, R., Denckla, M. and Broman, M. Rapid silent response to repeated target symbols by dyslexic and non-dyslexic children. *Brain and Language* **10**. 111–119.

Trites, R. L. and Price, M. A. (1976), Learning disabilities found in association with French immersion programming. The Ministry of Education, Ontario. Queen's Park, Toronto, Canada.

Vihman, M. (1982), The acquisition of morphology by a bilingual child: A whole-word approach. *Applied Psycholinguistics* **3**. 144–160.

Wechsler, D. (1981), *Manual for the Wechsler Intelligence Scale for Children – Revised*. New York: Psychological Corporation.

Wechsler, D. and Stone, C. P. (1945), *Wechsler Memory Scale*. New York: Psychological Corporation.

Wells, W. (1976), Validité du processus d'orientation. Internal Report. Orientation Service, Staff Development Branch, Public Service Commission of Canada, Ottawa, Canada. Reported in Wesche, M. Language aptitude measures in streaming, matching students with methods, and diagnosis of learning problems. In Diller, K. C. (Ed.) *Individual differences & universals in language learning aptitude*. Rowley, MA: Newbury House, 1981.

Wong-Fillmore, L. (1979), Individual differences in second language acquisition. In Fillmore, C. J. *et al.* (eds.) *Individual differences in language ability and language behavior*. New York: Academic Press, 1979.

4. Idiomaticity as an indicator of second language proficiency

CARLOS A. YORIO

Introduction

The issue of conventionalized language (idioms, formulas, prefabricated patterns, etc.) has long been a problem in linguistic theory, albeit a relatively marginal one. Despite the high frequency and pervasiveness of these forms and the efforts of a few interested linguists, conventionalized language has never really found a clear place in theories of language (Jespersen, 1922; Katz and Postal, 1963; Austin, 1965; Chafe, 1968; Weinreich, 1969, 1972; Searle, 1969; Newmeyer, 1972; Fraser, 1970, 1971, 1976; Mitchell, 1971; Makkai, 1972, 1978; Ferguson, 1976; Bolinger, 1977; Fillmore, 1979, 1983; Wood, 1986; Wierzbicka, 1987). This literature will not be reviewed here; the theoretical background it provides, however, has greatly influenced the research reported here and the work of the other applied linguists that will be mentioned.

Probably because of their interest in language use, various kinds of applied linguists have also dealt with conventionalized language. Their individual interests and foci have been so disparate, however, that their work cannot be said to constitute a coherent background (Whitaker, 1971; Brown, 1973; Clark, 1973; Hakuta, 1974; Wong-Fillmore, 1976; Peters, 1977; Fraser, 1978; Scarcella, 1979; Coulmas, 1979; Yorio, 1980; Ellis, 1984; and others). Neither has recent work in the area of speech act acquisition in a second language, by researchers like L. Beebe, S. Blum-Kulka, C. Candlin, A. Cohen, M. Eisenstein, G. Kasper, E. Olshtain, N. Wolfson, and others, yet crystallized into an integrated theory (Schmidt and Richards, 1980).

This lack of a coherent theoretical and empirical background creates serious definitional problems. For this reason, the very general term "conventionalized language" has been chosen here as the operational cover term. Definitions will be given when dealing with more specific types of conventionalized language (idioms, formulas, collocations, etc.).

Since language is conventionalized by its very nature, the term conventionalized language in this paper is used to mean "language forms that are *more* conventionalized than other language forms." These forms appear to have special characteristics:

(1) They are thought to be learned as wholes, largely unanalyzed.
(2) They cannot always be analyzed like other lexical items or syntactic strings. They are often exceptional or constrained syntactically, semantically or situationally.
(3) They make language performance appear "native-like", hence the notion of "idiomaticity".

In this paper I will deal with two issues: (1) the role of conventionalized language in adult second language acquisition and (2) the notion of idiomaticity in adult second language performance.

The idea that children learning L1 utilize "whole chunks" in early communication and that these chunks, which are usually expressions of high frequency, are later broken down and incorporated into the child's grammar is not new (Brown, 1973; Clark, 1973; Peters, 1977). These "prefabricated" strings have been said to perform the same psycholinguistic learning function in child second language learners (Hakuta, 1974). L. Wong-Fillmore (1976) and E. Hatch (1978) have also shown that children use social interactions and formulaic discourse-level expressions as the basis for syntactic and lexical development. S. Krashen and R. Scarcella (1978) and M. Vihman (1982) provide excellent reviews of much of this literature.

Whether adult learners also use conventionalized language in the same way or to what extent, and how their knowledge of conventionalized language might be related to other kinds of linguistic development has not been as extensively studied or even documented, and the studies that do exist do not present a clear picture of the issues involved (Huebner, 1983).

The background issues

Brown (1973) described the use of "prefabricated routines" by his L1 learning subjects. These routines were defined as unanalyzed utterances of varying length which were memorized and used as wholes. These "routines" were also observed by second language researchers (Huang and Hatch, 1978; Hakuta, 1976). Hatuka (1974) makes a distinction between "prefabricated routines" and "prefabricated patterns"; the latter he defines as "segments of sentences which operate in conjunction with a movable component." He then advances the notion that these chunks are simply memorized and used as wholes and implies that they become input to the rule formation process. Along similar lines, Wong-Fillmore (1976) claims that the five children she was studying made extensive use of very functional "prefabricated utterances" which they later broke down into constituents, a step seen as necessary for the learning of the underlying rules.

Although there are differences among these researchers, their views of these prefabricated utterances (routines, patterns or formulas) have several elements in common:

(1) Prefabricated utterances consist of words or strings of high frequency.
(2) They are used as both communicative and learning strategies.

The question still remains of how important conventionalized, prefabricated or routinized language is in second language acquisition, what precisely its role is and whether or not adults use and/or learn this kind of language the same way as children appear to do.

Four of the most detailed longitudinal studies in the adult L2 literature (Hanania and Gradman, 1977; Shapira, 1978; Schumann, 1978; and Huebner, 1983) do not appear to find extensive use of prefabricated language in untutored adult learners. Schmidt (1983), on the other hand, documented extensive use of conventionalized language by his subject Wes. In all five studies, however, researchers found that whatever prefabricated patterns, formulas or routines these adults used had a purely functional, communicative role and did not lead to further grammatical development.

Hanania and Gradman (1977) studied Fatmah's language development for eighteen months. Only in the very early stages did the subject appear to use "memorized utterances" (p. 78) which she used appropriately in particular situations. These included *thank you, I'm sorry, see you, you're welcome, come in, sit down, what's your name?*, etc. These expressions appear to be mostly "routine formulas" which have been defined as "highly conventionalized pre-patterned expressions whose occurrence is tied to a more or less standardized communication situation" (Yorio, 1980: 434). These routine formulas are very different from the prefabricated routines or prefabricated patterns that Brown and Hakuta described; they are "more sociolinguistic" in nature. Wong-Fillmore's subjects' "formulas" also appear to have had a clear sociolinguistic function but unlike them, Fatmah's memorized utterances do not seem to have furthered her grammatical development.

Shapira (1978) followed Zoila's English language development, also for eighteen months, and unambiguously characterised her subject's accomplishments as "non learning of English." Although Shapira concentrated primarily on the acquisition of grammatical morphemes, she categorically affirms that "Zoila used the same basic structure in April, 1975, as she did eighteen months earlier in November, 1973" (p. 254). Shapira also notes, however, that, "there is evidence that she is adding a number of alternative structures – in a few cases – which she uses in highly controlled environments.

These added structures are unanalyzed phrases, or formulae, learned as a unit, through constant exposure" (p. 225). Although Shapira gives no further detail, she does conclude that Zoila uses these formulas "in their restricted environments without even using analogy to expand their application" (p. 225).

As part of a ten-month project, Schumann (1978) studied the linguistic development of Alberto, a thirty-three year old Costa Rican, and concluded that during the course of the project the subject had "evidenced very little linguistic development" (p. VII). Although Schumann does not specifically discuss the use of conventionalized language by Alberto, his Appendix A (p. 117) shows a few clearly memorized phrases: *you're welcome, I'm sorry, I don't understand, I don't care*. The data clearly show the paucity and lack of consistency in the use of these formulas; they also show that no grammatical development resulted from their sporadic use.

Huebner (1983) studied the English language development of Ge, a bilingual Hmong/Lao speaker, for one year, and provides us with one of the most detailed and interesting studies of untutored early L2 acquisition by an adult. Although Huebner does not focus on the acquisition of conventionalized language by his subject, he acknowledges that "the learner has access to both individual words and patterns as input for his/her analysis of the language being acquired" (p. 45). Huebner further appears to support the view that adults, even more than L1 or L2 children, should be able to utilize their previous knowledge of L1 as a rich source for hypotheses for L2 development.

Because of Ge's lack of development of tense and aspect during the year of the study, Huebner limited his analysis to "the form *is(a)*, ... the article *da*, and the anaphoric devices of pronouns and zero" (p. 53). Of these, only *is(a)* and the discovery of the right contexts for its use might be called an example of a "prefabricated pattern". However, because of Huebner's extensive discussion of the role of prefabricated patterns and routines in L1 and L2 acquisition in the introductory chapter to his book (pp. 38–45), we must assume that his lack of further discussion of this topic is an indication that no evidence was found in his data that warranted a return to it and that, in consequence, this kind of conventionalized language did not play a significant role in Ge's early English language development.

Schmidt's (1983) longitudinal study of his Japanese subject Wes presents a very different picture from those described above. Wes can be characterized as an outgoing "communicator". According to Schmidt, "Wes has a rather rich repertoire of formulaic utterances, memorized sentences and phrases which increase the appearance of fluency in English. It is not always clear which of Wes's utterances are memorized wholes, except for those which clearly exceed the limits of his acquired grammatical system, but it is clear that he has chosen this as a major language strategy" (p. 150). Schmidt's fascinating paper clearly shows that Wes has become a very able, fluent communicator and that he uses routine formulas (situation formulas and gambits, Yorio, 1980) extensively and usually successfully. It also shows that Wes's "accomplishments appear on the whole better in the area of sociolinguistic than grammatical competence" (p. 155). Wes's use of grammatical morphemes presents a "dismal picture" (p. 149) and the same appears to be true of other aspects of grammar (question formation, dummy subjects, relative clauses, passives, etc.). Wes's case is different from those of Fatmah, Zoila, Alberto, and Ge in that he makes extensive use of conventionalized language and can be considered a "good learner and communicator"; like them, however, his grammatical development has not been impressive.

Three other studies deserve mention here: R. Scarcella's (1979) cross-sectional study of the acquisition of "verbal routines", R. Ellis's (1984) study of formulaic speech in the classroom, and S. Irujo's (1986) cross-sectional study on the acquisition of idioms. These three studies differ from the ones described earlier, not only in the fact that they are cross-sectional rather than longitudinal, but also because they focus on the performance of *instructed* second language *adults* on specific kinds of conventionalized language: *routine formulas* (already defined above), *idioms* ("expressions whose meaning is more or less unpredictable from the sum of the meanings of its morphemes" (Yorio, 1980)) and *scripts* (entire conversational sequences which are more or less fixed and predictable (Ellis, 1984)).

Scarcella found, as she had hypothesized, that adults have "difficulty acquiring very common routines" (p. 84). Ellis found that his subjects learned and used various types of memorized formulas and scripts and that some were later used for syntactic development. He appeared to have found, however, considerable variation from learner to learner not only in what formulas they learned but also in the extent to which these formulas were used for further development. Irujo found that even her advanced learners (over 500 on TOEFL) showed heavy reliance on their native language in both recognition and production of idioms, and performed well only when positive transfer was possible and when idioms were most transparent in meaning. Kellerman (1977) and Jordens (1977) had also found similar results.

What all these studies appear to indicate is that:

(1) Adults have considerable difficulty in the L2 acquisition and/or use of conventionalized language.
(2) Adults do not appear to use conventionalized language to the same extent as children do, or in the same way as children do; namely, as a psycholinguistic *learning* strategy.

(3) Tutored adult learners appear to perform better than naturalistic adult learners or at least appear to be able to use conventionalized language to further their linguistic development.

The present studies

Although I have been interested in conventionalized language for many years, the data for this paper came to me almost by accident. While involved in some preliminary studies in the area of fossilization, some obvious facts jumped out at me – facts easy to observe but certainly not easy to describe, let alone explain. I must also add that my data comes from written language and is, in consequence, different from the oral data used in all the studies mentioned previously. I will present three sets of data, ask many questions and venture very few answers in the hope that the questions will prompt other researchers to enter this largely unexplored field.

The first set of data comes from the case study of the written production of K., a native speaker of Korean and a freshman in one of the colleges of the City University of New York. At the time of the study, K. was 18 years old, had been living in New York City for five years and had attended grades 8 through 12 in Queens. He had taken *one* ESL class during his first semester in grade 8 and had later completed the rest of his schooling using English as the medium of instruction. My data consisted of 14 compositions written by K. at home on topics related to his life (activities, plans for the future, his past, his family, etc.) as part of his work in a writing class. I must also add that K. had been working in the Bronx as an assistant manager in a wine and liquor store for a period of 2 years. I was interested in K.'s linguistic development, particularly his morphology and syntax. Appendix I is K.'s seventh composition, the one written in the middle of the series. Because traditional linguistic units of analysis, like sentences, are too restrictive when a large number of errors are present, T-units were used for the general quantitative analysis in this study. A T-unit "is exactly one main clause plus whatever subordinate clauses are attached to that main clause" (Hunt 1970:197). T-units have been used successfully in first and second language acquisition studies (Hunt, 1965; Larsen-Freeman and Strom, 1977; Gaies, 1980; and others) and proved to be very useful and revealing here. The T-unit analysis of the entire corpus revealed that although only 32 percent of the T-units were error-free, 98 percent of them were perfectly comprehensible. In order to explain at least partially this great degree of comprehensibility, and because of K.'s background and acquisitional history, I hypothesized that his writing would reveal good command of idioms, set phrases and patterns, and lexical collocations. I was both right and wrong.

Table 4.1 shows a few examples taken from K.'s compositions. Although K.

Table 4.1. *Correct and incorrect forms (used by K.)*

1	She's O.K.
2	I know what's going on
3	No matter what happens
4	in a row
5	right now
6	at this point
7	Most of the time
8	*Sunday was lousiest day
9	*just two of us
10	*for short time
11	*I have lots money
12	*at the morning

used a number of conventionalized expressions, he did not have *formal* command over them; he made the same types of errors when using "regular" language, as when using conventionalized language. But how could this be? The language acquisition literature had led me to believe that this kind of language was different, memorized and impermeable to the formal rules that govern regular, propositional language! Besides, if K., who had just spent 5 years in a New York City school being educated in English, and 2 years in the Bronx, working in English, had not mastered this kind of language, who could? And finally, isn't it supposed to go the *other* way: from wholes to rules? Why are these faulty grammatical rules creeping into these wholesome, memorized chunks?

My second source of data is a cross-sectional study in which I compared the written production of 25 ESL students, with a minimum of 5, and a maximum of 7 years of residence in the United States, with the written production of 15 English speaking students of the same college. Both natives and non-natives had scored 6 (out of a possible 12) in the Writing Assessment Test, which is a global measure of writing proficiency required in all of the colleges of the City University of New York. A score of 6, which is considered a failing score, means that two different readers had, independently, given each one of these writers a mark of 3. The minimum passing score requires two marks of 4. Appendix II is a randomly chosen example from these data. From these compositions, I will extract two pieces for our puzzle. The first is a fairly careful study of the conventionalized language (idioms, formulas and collocations) used by the L2 learners which reveals that everything that could go wrong with them, did!

Table 4.2 shows a few stylistic formulas (Yorio, 1980) which these learners have probably learned in their composition classes. Tables 4.3 through 4.8

Table 4.2. Correct forms (learned)

In conclusion
According to
By way of illustration
In summary
For example

Table 4.3. Lack of grammatical control

*take advantages of
*he had chance
*are to blamed for
*at the present
*those mention above
*being taking care of
*a friend of her

show the results of an error analysis done on the data. It is clear from these examples that these advanced learners are making extensive use of conventionalized language, but it is also clear that, as was the case with K. (the subject of my earlier study), they have no formal control over them. Once again we see examples of grammatical errors creeping in (as shown in Table 4.3). On the positive side, we must say that these learners are using a lot more of these forms than K. was and, in doing so, are taking more risks and making more errors. What I find interesting is that, in written discourse, it is the *advanced* L2 learners rather than the beginning L2 learners who appear to make more extensive use of conventionalized language. This appears to agree with the findings for adults described in the studies mentioned earlier using *oral* data. The large number of errors found also suggests that these expressions are not simply memorized or taken in as wholes but that, in fact, they are subject to whatever interlanguage rules the learner is operating under. There is also evidence from other studies that only the more advanced L2 learners use, for example, communication strategies with an idiomatic or cultural base, and when they do, they show clear evidence of both native and target language influence (Paribakht 1982, 1984). I have already mentioned an experimental study, also with advanced learners, in which Irujo (1986) found that in all the categories of idioms that she studied, the idioms that proved easiest were those that were semantically more transparent and lexically and syntactically simpler. It appears to be the case, then, that in adult bilinguals

Table 4.4. *Wrong lexical choice*

---

*today date (today)
*made a great job (did a great job)
*make a great influence (have a great influence)
*to have their own lives (lead/live)
*on the meantime (in)
*in return (in turn)
*in the way (in the sense)
*with my own experience (in ...)
*by my own experience (in ...)
*put more attention to (pay ...)

Table 4.5. *Mixed idioms*

---

*give up their freedom of mobility
    — their freedom of movement
    — their mobility
*it always strikes the mind of the employer
    — strikes their employers
    — crosses the mind of the employers

Table 4.6. *Wrong meaning*

---

on the other hand (however)
in this way (for this reason)
in the way (in the sense)
their early days (in their youth)
men under arms (armed men)
in addition to (in order to)

Table 4.7. *Attempted idioms*

---

*they don't do with them (they have nothing to do with them)
*cultivate herself (go back to school)
*at the end of the road (ultimately)
*to work to my best (to do my best)
*turn on his mind as a blank (their minds go blank)
*they feel suspended upon their heads, the Damocles' sword (they feel the sword of
  Damocles suspended over their heads) (they feel as if —)
*where my performance would fall on the scale (— on a scale from — to —)

Table 4.8. *Mixed registers*

---

*a good head and education
*a better society without crime and headaches
*no wonder!

Table 4.9. L_1 *and* L_2 *use of two-word verbs*

	L_1 tokens	L_2 tokens
Conjugated verbs	742	955
Two-word verbs	145 (19.5%)	138 (14%) (59% correct)
Idiomatic	52 (36%)	9 (6.5%) (4%)

there is a non-trivial connection between the development of rule-governed language or propositional language, and the development and use of conventionalized language. This relationship appears to be different from that which has been described for L1 and L2 children.

The second piece of the puzzle that I extracted from this second cross-sectional study was a quantitative analysis of what are known in ESL as "two-word verbs". I was looking for indicators of *idiomaticity*, that native-like quality which seems so easy to detect and so difficult for L2 learners to achieve. Idiomaticity is a non-phonological "accent", not always attributable to surface language errors, but to a certain undefined quality which many frustrated L2 composition teachers define as "I don't know what's wrong with this, but we just don't say that in English." Many of the examples in Tables 4.3, 4.4, 4.5, 4.6 and 4.7 are examples of this lack of idiomaticity. I also thought that there might be constructions that were differentially used by native and non-native speakers; that is, that certain constructions were under- or overused by L2 learners. I had two candidates for scrutiny: sentences using the copula BE as their main verb and the ubiquitous two-word verbs.

Based on my observations, I hypothesized that L2 learners made much more extensive use of BE sentences than native speakers. This did not turn out to be true. The range of BE-sentence use was almost identical for both groups.

Table 4.9 shows that although the *proportion* of two-word verbs used by these advanced L2 learners was similar to that of native speakers, the *kind* of two-word verbs used was not the same. Notice that 36 percent of those used by L1 writers were idiomatic in nature (like "bring up") whereas only 6 percent of those used by L2 writers were. Furthermore, one learner (in a group of 25) was responsible for 3 of the 9 tokens. The percentage then would be even smaller if this anomalous subject were eliminated from the pool. In addition, only 59 percent of the tokens used by the L2 learners were correct. In another study (McPartland, 1983) similar findings were obtained for oral data. She compared the spoken production of six native speakers of Russian with that of one native speaker of English performing the same task. McPartland's results are identical to mine; not only did she find that bilinguals use significantly fewer two-word verbs; she also found that they use verbs with a low degree of idiomaticity. These data appear to agree with the findings on idioms cited earlier, and further support the hypothesis that there may be items or constructions that are avoided or are under-used by even fairly proficient, fluent bilinguals which may affect the degree of idiomaticity of their oral and written performance.

In a very recent study, Reid (1987) showed evidence that there *is* a quantitative difference in the writing of ESL learners as compared with native writers. One of her findings, for example, is that non-native writers use more personal pronouns than native writers do in contexts where the latter would use noun phrases.

My third and last set of data comes from another cross-sectional study involving two groups of ESL learners performing the same task under identical conditions. Group I is made up of immigrant students, native speakers of Spanish, who have lived in the United States for 5 or 6 years and who are currently enrolled in an advanced ESL class at Lehman College. Group II is made up of English majors at the Universidad de Cordoba in Argentina (a free public university). They have been studying English for 3, 4 or 5 years and have never been in an English-speaking community. Appendices III and IV show randomly chosen samples of Groups I and II respectively. My hypothesis was that the Argentine subjects would show greater grammatical accuracy but that the Lehman subjects, having lived in the United States for a longer period than the Argentinians had studied the language, would be better at conventionalized language and that their compositions would appear more idiomatic. I was partially right. Subjects in Group II *are* grammatically more accurate; however, they also appear to use more idioms and their written English, despite errors, is more authentic than that of the subjects in the immigrant group. This impression of greater idiomaticity was apparent to me and to other colleagues whose native-speaker impressions I sought. If correct, this finding agrees with my previous findings: the higher the level of linguistic proficiency, the higher the level of idiomaticity. The problem, however, remained: what exactly constitutes idiomaticity? So far, I had identified two components: one related to linguistic or formal error; and one unrelated to formal error. Table 4.10 shows what I call the "cumulative effect" of formal

Table 4.10. *The cumulative effect*

---

a   "I agree that from every old person that their families do not care, there is a lifetime of knowledge and experience that is going into a waste."

b   "High School students are more interested in — dance the night out, or go to watch the game or spend the time walking on the streets with their peers, wasting most part of the time. Time that should be spended in the library doing their homework or doing research on some papers of the kind."

---

errors; both examples *a* and *b* are semantically clear and idiomatically rich but they are so plagued with errors that they are unlikely to be considered native. The second component of idiomaticity is given by the frequency of occurrence of certain forms or constructions. This might be the case with two-word verbs in English, which appear to be *less* frequently used by bilinguals than by natives, or by the presence of personal pronouns which appear to be used *more* frequently by bilinguals than by natives.

What else constitutes idiomaticity? It was clear to me that it was not necessarily the number of actual "idioms" employed, since these are not very frequent in native speech and writing.

Pawley and Syder (1983) make a distinction between *native-like selection* and *native-like fluency*. Native-like selection is defined as "the ability of the native speaker routinely to convey his meaning by an expression that is not only grammatical but also native-like; what is puzzling about this is how he selects a sentence that is natural and idiomatic from among the range of grammatically correct paraphrases, many of which are non-native-like or highly marked usages" (p. 191). Native-like fluency is "the native speaker's ability to produce fluent stretches of spontaneous connected discourse" (p. 191). It is clear that second language learners or users are quite capable of developing native-like fluency. Schmidt's subject Wes and my own subject K. can easily produce fluent oral and written discourse respectively. In addition, there is abundant anecdotal and experimental evidence of fluency in bilinguals. Native-like selection, however, is another matter. Of its two components, grammaticality and idiomaticity, only the former is well-understood, or at least easily identified through the absence of formal error. Idiomaticity, particularly in non-native production, appears much more elusive and difficult to describe.

After reading the two sets of compositions (the Lehman and the Argentinian data) many times, it became clear to me that, in addition to having fewer formal errors, the compositions that appeared more native-like contained many more "English phrases", or word combinations that a native speaker would use without thinking much, without an active search for the right

Table 4.11 *Collocational phrases*

```
 1  most of the time
 2  late in the evening
 3  summer holidays
 4  special flavor
 5  in my heart
 6  a quiet life
 7  good friends
 8  childhood memories
 9  It gives me great pleasure
10  special moments
11  up to now
12  the typical problems
13  a happy childhood
14  a big family
15  a good Catholic education
16  improved greatly
17  two close friends
18  one of the happiest periods
19  behavior patterns
20  a human being
21  a spoilt child
22  free from troubles
23  a very big place
24  outdoor activities
25  dress up
26  ride our bicycles
27  favorite pastime
28  without taking into account
29  *with no doubt (without any doubt)
30  *the latest fashion (the latest fashions)
31  *changing presents (exchanging presents)
32  *two very closed friends (two very close friends)
```

word – every-day word combinations. These syntagmatic–lexical relations have been called *collocations* by British linguists, particularly Firthian linguists. Collocation is defined as the habitual co-occurrence of individual lexical items. They are formal rather than semantic statements of co-occurrence and are governed by restrictions similar to the selectional restrictions of generative grammar. (For an English dictionary of collocations, see Benson, Benson and Ilson, 1986.) Table 4.11 shows a few examples (both correct and incorrect) found in the Argentine data. Pawley and Syder argue that, in oral data, they found not only large numbers of collocations but also what they call "sentence stems". These are "units of clause length or longer whose grammatical form and lexical content is wholly or largely fixed; its fixed elements form a standard label for a culturally recognized concept, a term in the language" (pp. 191–192). Although I did not find any examples of these units in my written data, they appear to be what Ellis (1984) called "scripts" in his oral data.

Idiomaticity, or native-like quality in written language, appears to be a property characterized primarily by the presence of collocations and/or sentence stems rather than by actual idioms. In second language performance, idiomaticity is further characterized by the absence of grammatical errors and by the use of quantitatively appropriate amounts of certain language-specific features, such as phrasal verbs or personal pronouns, as yet largely unidentified.

Conclusion

The acquisition of conventionalized language forms by adults learning a second language appears to be a long and arduous task. Unlike children, they do not appear to make extensive early use of prefabricated, formulaic language, and when they do, they do not appear to be able to use it to further their grammatical development. It is not surprising that conventionalized language should be difficult to acquire and use if we believe that markedness contributes to difficulty. All kinds of conventionalized language are highly marked (Kellerman, 1983). It is not clear, however, why children appear to be immune to markedness-based difficulties in this case.

The data that we have collected or reviewed here appear to show a correlation between grammatical proficiency and the successful use of conventionalized language. Indeed, it seems that although fluency is possible without grammatical accuracy, idiomaticity is not. Idiomaticity then becomes an excellent indicator of bilingual system proficiency and, as such, it deserves to be further studied and understood.

Appendix I

(Korean speaker, 18 year old, 6 years' residence in New York City, English medium of instruction in high school)

I haven't much thoughts about plans for weekend. On Saturday I'd work. Have a part-time job at the Bronx doing salesman and manager at a Wine and Liquor store. I can't make any plans on the Saturday, except working.

On Sunday I always go to a church and I spend time all day at the church. But not this weekend because I have a very important exam is coming up next week. So I'd stay home do my study. No matter what happens tomorrow, I'd not miss the baseball game. This Sunday there is the National League Championships finals. Also I'm big fan of the footballs. Anyway good luck to both teams. I'm very excited about it. I hope if I could do well on the exam.

Appendix II

(Spanish speaker, 6 years' residence in the United States, Writing Assessment Test Score 6)

I agree with the idea that women are working more today for the good of them and for the economy, but it is not good for the children of working mothers.

From my experience it is clear that mothers with children can't work, because children will suffer and they will feel isolated and abandoned. A mother should provide to her children love, care, protection and time, but if she is a working mother, she won't have time to provide her kids all those mention above. For example, my mother placed my little brother in a Day Care Center to go to work. My brother was being taking care fine for the two first week, but a month later he got sick. He had some kind of disease on his stamach. the doctor said that he was not getting the right amount of food per day. Either he was eating too much or not enough. After he was released from the hospital, my mother took care of him, he started to do fine.

From my observation of others, I believe that mothers should stay home. They should not go out to work for the good of their own children.

For example, my cousin has 3 beautiful daughters. They are in a school few blocks away from their house. They ages are six, seven and eight. One day she was tired of being indoor all of the time. She decided to get a job. She found a job. The three little girls were taking care of themselves. The oldest one used to supervise the younger. But one day when they were open their apartment door, a man who was coming upstairs saw those three little girls. He got into the apartment with them. He raped them, and he robbed all of what he could from the apartment. When my cousin came from work, she saw what haf happen she almost died.

In conclusion, mothers should be more aware of their children. If they decided to go to work they should get a good babysitter; otherwise, they should stay home taking care of their children. Children are the future men, so they need care, time, love and security. If you are mother please don't go out to work. Stay with your children. They need you more than anything else.

Appendix III

(Spanish speaker, 5 years' residence in the United States, advanced ESL student/developmental course)

I was born in ——————, on Septemberr 7, 1959. My parents got separated before I was born. My mother stayed alone and growup us by herself. My childhood was very pleasant.

I have three brothers and one sister. We always have arguments between one another since we were children but we loved each other very much. Specially with my sister because we were only two girls and exited jealous between us. If my mother bougth a doll for myself she had to buy another one for my sister. Amoung my brothers the relationship were very good. Because I was younger they always cared and watched for me.

I remember some of my teachers and classmates. Some of my classmates became my friends and today we still seen one another. Sometimes we sat down and remembered some memories that we had from our childhood. In my second grade I had a teacher that even today asked my aunt about me. I remember the yard of the school, the games we used to play.

I had very good friends on my neighbourhood. We had a lot of fun playing about doctors, about mothers or artists. We ran around the houses and claimbs the tress. Althougt I loved to go to the river to swim or fishing.

I had very nices memories about my childhood with my family, with my teachers and classmates and with my friends in my neiborhood.

Appendix IV

(Spanish speaker, native and resident of Argentina, English language college major, 3 years of study)

In spite of the fact that I've lived a normal childhood (that is to say a childhood without nothing particularly interesting or extra-ordinary) and that I have beautiful memories of that period of my life, I must say honestly that period is not precisely the one I like best. Why? I have many reasons for that assert but I can refer here mainly to three of them: The continuious dependancy a child have to endure, the limited scope of reactions, emotions and feelings a child possess, and (very related) the child's narrow scope of knowledge and wisdom needed to develop his potential and comply with his role in society as a fully fullfiled person.

That the child is a completely dependant creature is out of question. He depends on his parents for almost every aspect of his life; to be fed, dressed and protected. And much time after the first years of his life have placed he may be still dependant psichollogically on his parents, a situation that many times leads to problems of mental adjustment. Of course, this dependancy is obvious and can't be skipped, but all the same, I don't consider a person completely developed or self-accomplished of he depends continually on others, and to be an uncompletely developed person is not the goal at which a human being must tend to.

Besides this, a fully matured person finds his highest happiness when he gives to his most inner feelings in a controlled way and be incapable of discover new emotions and reactions every day out of experience, and the experience a child posses is very limited and doesn't allow him to have great, really deep emotions.

Finally, what a person longs for more than any other thing on earth is to feel "fullfilled" himself, when he feels that he has found his place in the world and that he is useful to society, and can a child to proclaim that he is such a person? No, he can't. Therefore, I prefer to be an adult person and not a unrippen child with such a long way to go.

I conclude, then, saying that childhood is a very important period of our lives and a very necessary one, obviously, but where it is compared with all the advantages that adult life provides, in spite of their risks, undoubtely the later offers a life that is fuller, richer and that rewards with unsuspected sources of joy.

References

Austin, J. L. (1965), *How To Do Things with Words*. New York: Oxford University Press.

Benson, M., E. Benson and R. Ilson (1986), *The BBI Combinatory Dictionary of English. A Guide to Word Combinations*. Amsterdam: John Benjamin Publishing Company.

Bolinger, D. (1977), Idioms have relations. *Forum Linguisticum*, vol. 2, pp. 157–169.

Brown, R. (1973), *A first language: The early stages*. Cambridge, MA: Harvard University Press.

Chafe, N. (1986), Idiomaticity as an anomaly in the Chomskian paradigm. *Foundations of Language*, vol. 4, pp. 109–125.

Clark, R. (1973), Performing without competence. *Journal of Child Language*, vol. 1, pp. 1–10.

Coulmas, R. (1979), On the sociolinguistic relevance of routine formulas. *Journal of Pragmatics*, vol. 3, pp. 239–266.

Ellis, R. (1984), Formulaic speech in early classroom second language development. In Handscombe, J., R. Orem and B. Taylor (eds.), *ON TESOL '83: The Question of Control*. Washington, D.C.: TESOL.

Ferguson, C. (1976), The structure and use of politeness formulas. *Language and Society*, vol. 5, pp. 137–151.

Fillmore, C. (1979), On fluency. In Fillmore, C., D. Kempler, and W. S. Wang (eds.), *Individual Differences in Language Ability and Language Behavior*. New York: Academic Press.

(1983), Syntactic constraints and idiomatic language. Lecture delivered at the Department of Linguistics, University of Toronto, TESOL Summer Institute.

Fraser, B. (1970), Idioms within transformational grammar. *Foundations of Language*, vol. 5, pp. 137–151.

(1971), The applicability of transformations to idioms. *Papers from the Seventh Regional Meeting, Chicago Linguistic Society*, pp. 198–205.

(1976), *The Verb-Particle Combination in English*. New York: Academic Press.

(1978), Acquiring social competence in a second language. *RELC Journal*, vol. 9, (2), pp. 1–26.

Gaies, S. (1980), T-unit analysis in second language acquisition research: applications, problems and limitations. *TESOL Quarterly*, vol. 14, pp. 53–60.

Hakuta, K. (1974), Prefabricated patterns and the emergence of structure in second language acquisition. *Language Learning*, vol. 24, pp. 287–297.

(1976), A case study of a Japanese child learning English, *Language Learning*, vol. 26, pp. 321–351.

Hanania, E. and H. Gradman (1977), Acquisition of English structures: A case study of an adult native speaker of Arabic in an English speaking environment. *Language Learning*, vol. 27, (1), pp. 75–91.

Hatch, E. (1978), Discourse analysis and second language acquisition. In Hatch, E. (ed.), *Second Language Acquisition: A Book of Readings*. Rowley, MA: Newbury House.

Huang, J. and E. Hatch (1978), A Chinese child's acquisition of English. In Hatch, E. (ed.), *Second Language Acquisition: A Book of Readings*. Rowley, MA: Newbury House.

Huebner, T. (1983), *A Longitudinal Analysis of the Acquisition of English*. Ann Arbor: Karoma Publishers.

Hunt, K. W. (1965), *Grammatical structures written at three grade levels*. Research Report No. 3. National Council of Teachers of English, Urbana, Illinois.

(1970), Recent measures in syntactic development. In Lester, M. (ed.), *Readings in Applied Transformational Grammar*. New York: Holt, Rinehart and Winston.

Irujo, S. (1986), Don't put your leg in your mouth: Transfer in the acquisition of idioms in a second language. *TESOL Quarterly*, vol. 20, (2), pp. 287–304.

Jespersen, J. O. (1922), Formulas and free expressions. *The Philosophy of Grammar*, Norton Library Edition, pp. 18–24.

Jordens, P. (1977), Rules, grammatical intuitions, and strategies in foreign language learning. *Interlanguage Studies Bulletin-Utrecht*, vol. 2, (2), pp. 5–76.

Katz, J. and P. Postal (1963), Semantic interpretation of idioms and sentences containing them. *Quarterly Progress Report*, vol. 70, MIT Research Laboratory of Electronics, pp. 275–282.

Kellerman, E. (1977), Towards a characterization of the strategy of transfer in second language learning. *Interlanguage Studies Bulletin-Utrecht*, vol. 2, (1), pp. 58–145.

(1983), Now you see it, now you don't. In Gass, S. and L. Selinker (eds.), *Language Transfer in Language Learning*. Rowley, MA: Newbury House.

Krashen, S. and R. Scarcella, (1978), On routines and patterns in language acquisition and performance. *Language Learning*, vol. 28, 283–300.

Larsen-Freeman, D. and V. Strom (1977), The construction of a second language acquisition index of development. *Language Learning*, vol. 27, pp. 123–134.

McPartland, P. (1983), What the non-native speaker of English leaves out. Unpublished manuscript; Department of Linguistics, Graduate School, CUNY.

Makkai, A. (1972), *Idiom structure in English*. The Hague: Mouton.

Makkai, A. (1978) Idiomaticity as a language universal. In Greenberg, J. H. (ed.), *Universals of Human Language*, vol. IV. Stanford University Press. pp. 402–448.

Mitchell, T. (1971), Linguistic "goings-on": Collocations and other lexical matters arising on the syntactic record. *Archivum Linguisticum*, vol. 2 (new series), pp. 35–69.

Newmeyer, F. (1972), The insertion of idioms. In *Papers from the Eighth Regional Meeting, Chicago Linguistic Society*, pp. 294–302.

Paribakht, T. (1982), The relationship between the use of communication strategies and aspects of target language proficiency: A study of Persian ESL students. Ph.D. Thesis, University of Toronto.

(1984), *The Relationship between the Use of Communication Strategies and Aspects of Target Language Proficiencies – A Study of ESL Students*. International Centre for Research on Bilingualism, Quebec.

Pawley, A. and F. Hodgetts Syder (1983), Two puzzles for linguistic theory: Native-like selection and native-like fluency. In Richards, J. and R. Schmidt (eds.), *Language and Communication*. New York: Longman.

Peters, A. (1977), Language learning strategies. *Language*, vol. 53, (3), pp. 560–573.

Reid, J. (1987), Does ESL writing differ quantitatively? Paper presented at the 21st Annual Convention of TESOL, Miami, Florida.

Scarcella, R. (1979), Watch up: A study of verbal routines in adult second language performance. *Working Papers on Bilingualism*, vol. 19, pp. 79–88.

    (1983), Discourse accent in second language performance. In: Gass, S. and L. Selinker (eds.), *Language Transfer in Language Learning*. Rowley, MA: Newbury House.

Schmidt, R. W. (1983), Interaction, acculturation, and the acquisition of communicative competence: A case study of an adult. In: Wolfson, N. and E. Judd (eds.), *Sociolinguistics and Language Acquisition*. Rowley, MA: Newbury House.

Schmidt, R. and J. Richards (1980), Speech acts and second language learning. *Applied Linguistics*, vol. 1, (2), pp. 129–157.

Schumann, J. H. (1978), *The Pidginization Process*. Rowley, MA: Newbury House.

Searle, J. R. (1969), *Speech Acts: An Essay in the Philosophy of Language*, Cambridge University Press.

Shapira, R. (1978), The non-learning of English: A case study of an adult. In Hatch, E. (ed.), *Second Language Acquisition: A Book of Readings*. Rowley, MA: Newbury House.

Vihman, M. M. (1982) Formulas in first and second language acquisition. In Obler, L. K and L. Menn (eds.), *Exceptional Language and Linguistics*. New York: Academic Press.

Weinreich, U. (1969) Problems in the analysis of idioms. In Puhvel, J. (ed.), *Substance and Structure of Language*. Berkeley, CA: University of California Press.

    (1972), *Explorations in Semantic Theory*. The Hague: Mouton.

Wierzbicka, A. (1987), Boys will be boys: "radical semantics" vs. "radical pragmatics". *Language*, vol. 63, (1), pp. 95–114.

Whitaker, H. A. (1971), *On the representation of language in the human brain*. Edmonton: Linguistic Research Inc.

    (1979), Automatization – A neurolinguistic model. Forum Lecture delivered at the 1979 Summer Institute of the Linguistic Society of America in Salzburg, Austria.

Wong-Fillmore, L. (1976), *The Second Time Around: Cognitive and Social Strategies in Language Acquisition*. Ph.D. dissertation, Stanford University.

Wood, M. (1986), *A Definition of Idiom*. Bloomington, IN: Indiana University Linguistics Club.

Yorio, C. (1980), Conventionalized language forms and the development of communicative competence. *TESOL Quarterly*, vol. 14, (4), pp. 433–442.

    (1985), (Many) questions and (very few) answers about fossilization in second language acquisition. Plenary Address presented at the New York TESOL Applied Linguistics Conference.

5 Prefabs, patterns and rules in interaction? Formulaic speech in adult learners' L2 Swedish

MARIA BOLANDER

Studies on learner language have shown formulaic speech to be a common phenomenon, especially in early phases of development. In this paper the occurrence of formulaic speech will be further evidenced by the results from studies on tutored adult learners' acquisition of word order rules in Swedish as a second language. The investigation of favorable/unfavorable contexts for the application of these rules in spontaneous speech showed that the rule application is often related to the actual words involved. The results thus indicate not only that memorization of strings and formulaic speech are important in language learning as a means of facilitating conversation in early learner language, but also that they affect the application of syntactic rules in several respects.

The term "formulaic speech" is used here in a broad sense and includes complete expressions like *jag vet inte* "I don't know", and different types of frequent combinations of words constituting various parts of sentences, that appear to be used as ready-made units in processing. The criterion for regarding a sequence as a chunk/prefab is the learners' manifestation of them as such in their speech, as shown either by a more frequent than average correct production of a certain structure, or by errors in structures that are otherwise correct.

Analyses of the application of word order rules indicate that learners select certain frequent and needed combinations of words out of longer sequences, store them as units, and use them as "prefabs" in production, e.g. *kan inte* "can not", *har gått* "has gone", and *inte så mycket* "not very much". Moreover, one sees "patterns", i.e. formulae with open slots, constituting frames for production of whole clauses, e.g. *det kan man göra* "it/so can one do". As Bolinger writes:

> Our language does not expect us to build everything starting with lumber, nails, and blueprint, but provides us with an incredibly large

> number of prefabs, which have the magical property of persisting
> even when we knock some of them apart and put them together in
> unpredictable ways. (Bolinger 1976:1)

Many studies of second language acquisition have aimed at uncovering the
transitional grammatical rules assumed to govern the learners' language
production and intuitional judgments of target language sentences. The focus
on grammatical rules in many studies has often meant that little attention has
been paid to which specific words co-occur in the investigated structures.
However, several analyses of spontaneous speech show that formulaic speech
is common in both L1 acquisition and children's L2 acquisition (e.g. Brown,
1973; Hatch, 1973; Hakuta, 1974; Huang and Hatch, 1978; Fillmore, 1979;
and Peters, 1983). In some studies formulaic speech has also been reported for
adult L2 learners (Hanania and Gradman, 1977; Hellwig, 1983; and Ellis,
1984).

Although most authors in this research area distinguish formulae from
propositional "creative speech", there is a debate as to whether routines and
rules develop independently, or whether routines develop into creative rules.
Other terms used to denote the phenomenon are "ready-made utterances"
and "schemata" (Lyons, 1968), "prefabricated routines" (e.g. Brown, 1973),
"prefabricated patterns" (e.g. Hakuta, 1974), "units" (Peters, 1983), and
"formulaic speech" (e.g. Ellis, 1986).

Factors often pointed out as bringing about reliance on formulaic speech are
the learners' communicative needs, the frequency of input and output, and
perceptual salience (e.g. in Brown, 1973 and Dulay and Burt, 1978). In this
context the term "communicative needs" is used in the broader psychological
sense, i.e. it implies different personal needs to communicate as they are
linguistically manifested.

The role of patterns or prefabs in language processing has also been
discussed with reference to the role of memory processes and brain function
in language processing. Seliger (1982) discusses the different functions of the
two hemispheres of the brain, emphasizing the co-operation between the
right and the left hemispheres. The right hemisphere appears to be involved
in holistic processing, whereas the left hemisphere appears to be responsible
for segmental analytic processing associated with traditional linguistic levels
(phonemic, morphemic, etc.). As Grosjean (1982) suggests, it is conceivable
that the left hemisphere as well as the right takes part in the processing of
formulae.

This paper presents two studies on the acquisition of syntactic rules
demonstrating the existence of different types of formulaic speech. In the

discussion, several explanations for formulaic use are evaluated in the light of the data. In particular, general communicative necessity and frequency of input and output are considered, as well as perceptual saliency, lexical needs, and lexical frequency.

Evidence for formulaic speech among adult learners of Swedish

The studies on formulaic speech investigate the acquisition of (1) the rule for subject-verb-inversion after sentence-initial elements other than subject in declarative main clauses (X-V-S), and (2) the rules for placement of the negative particle *inte* "not" and some adverbs with the same placement. Full command of these grammatical rules is acquired at a late stage in second language learners' acquisition of Swedish.

Data come from 60 adult learners: 20 Finnish, 20 Polish, and 20 Spanish native speakers. Half of the learners in each native language group are high proficiency learners, the other half are low proficiency. The allocation of the subjects to the high level and low level, respectively, was done at a labor training center, where the subjects took a four month intensive course in Swedish.

The results presented and discussed are based on data of two types: (1) free speech from a 15 minute interview conducted at the beginning and at the end of the course, and (2) speech from a picture description task elicited on the same occasion as the interviews. All the data were transcribed in a modified standard orthography. Then all instances of negation in both main (n = 1729) and subordinate clauses (n = 313) and main clauses with sentence-initial non-subjects (n = 3288) were compiled and judged as correct or erroneous. (Further details about the data and the methods used are given in Bolander, 1987b; 1988.)

The inversion study

In Swedish statements, as in German, the inversion of subject–verb after a sentence-initial non-subject is an obligatory rule that is most often motivated solely by grammatical considerations, but that may sometimes be selected for pragmatic reasons, i.e. when the rule results in the placement of new information towards the end of the sentence.

In the inversion study reviewed here, the effects of different types of subjects, verbs and sentence-initial elements in the inversion clauses were investigated. In the learners' correct applications of the inversion rule, the most frequent type of subject is a first person pronoun, either in the singular

Table 5.1. *Learners' frequencies for different types of sentence-initial elements*
(upper values − total numbers; lower values − relative frequencies of correctness)

Adverbs	PP	Objects	Sub-clauses	Pred	Total
1932	561	403	373	19	3,288
0.36	0.35	0.82	0.19	0.35	0.40

Abbreviations: PP − prepositional phrases, Sub-clauses − subordinate clauses, Pred − predicatives

or the plural. The most frequent verb is the copula, and then the main verb *komma* "come". The reason for the high frequency of *komma* is a large number of presentatives, e.g. *sen kommer ambulans* "then comes ambulance", in which the word order is governed by pragmatic principles. In these occurrences the learners' application of the inversion rule is more correct than in narrative clauses, e.g. *sen går han* "then goes he" (Bolander, 1987a).

A comparison between the combination *kommer det* and combinations with the most frequent verb in the data, the copula *vara* "be", provides some support for the suggestion that perceptual salience gives rise to chunk learning. Despite its high frequency, the copula is not the verb in the most frequent, correctly inverted combinations. One explanation for this may be low perceptual salience in the combinations with *det* "it/there". The semantically empty combination *är det* "is it/there" is often pronounced fast and unstressed, in contrast to the combination *kommer det* "comes it/there" which is mostly pronounced /*komme re*/. The relative frequency of correctness for *är det* is 0.26 and for *kommer det* 0.45. The importance of pronunciation for the perception and acquisition of these combinations is also evidenced by the fact that some of the subjects use the form /*re*/ instead of *det* in initial positions too, e.g. /*re tycke ja*/ "it/so think I".

The categories of sentence-initial elements studied were adverbs, prepositional phrases, objects, predicatives, and subordinate clauses (see table 5.1).

As expected, the most frequent sentence-initial non-subjects are adverbs. However, clauses with the highest values for correctness are those containing sentence-initial objects, a somewhat surprising result, since sentence-initial objects are often said to have a low frequency in Swedish. Moreover, in pedagogical grammars for Swedish as a second language, it is sometimes recommended not to introduce this type of clause in the early stages of teaching. However, Dahlbäck (1981) also finds that sentence-initial objects seem to be a favorable context for the application of the inversion rule.

A more detailed analysis of the object clauses in our data, however, provides some explanation for the results. Most of these clauses are of the following type:

(1) det har jag läst
   "it have I read"
(2) det kunde man göra
   "it/so could one do"
(3) det tror jag
   "it/so think I"
(4) det utnyttjade jag
   "it made I use of"

Although all elements but *det* are varied in (1)–(4), the clauses give a stereotyped reading. Inversion in the kind of clauses presented above also appears when the object is omitted:

(5) Ø [det] kan man säga
   "Ø [it/so] can one say"
(6) Ø [det] tycker jag
   "Ø [it/so] think I"
(7) Ø [det] måste jag säga
   "Ø [it/so] must I say"

Thus, this pattern seems to be rather well integrated in the interlanguage of most of these learners. The results for the other inversion-clauses with sentence-initial objects indicate that the formula-like clauses promote application of the inversion rule in these cases as well. The relative frequency of correctness for the rest of the object clauses is 0.6, which is a higher value than average for the inversion clauses. Furthermore, the elicitation tasks in Dahlbäck's study (1981) mainly consisted of object clauses other than the formula-like ones presented above. Thus, the results for the object clauses lend support to the hypothesis that creative language may develop out of familiar formulae.

Besides the formulaic clauses with sentence-initial *det* "it/so", we find formulaic-like speech in the following constructions after main clauses:

(8) han pratar bra spanska *tycker jag*
   "he speaks good Spanish think I"
(9) de håller värme bättre *menar jag*
   "they keep warm better mean I"

116 of 122 of these clauses have the first person pronoun *jag* "I" as subject, and all of them contain one of a small number of verbs expressing opinions and attitudes.

In table 5.2, the two types of object clauses presented are compared to the inversion clauses with the most frequent sentence-initial adverbs. The most correct inversion clauses are the *det*-clauses and the *då*-clauses among adverb clauses. The most frequent adverb clauses are clearly those with sentence-initial *sen*.

Table 5.2. *Learners' frequencies for inversion clauses with different sentence-initial elements*

(upper values – total numbers; lower values – relative frequencies of correctness)

det "it/so"	"main clause"	då "then"	så "then"	här "here"	nu "now"	sen "then"
249	122	134	94	96	164	1,011
0.9	0.61	0.75	0.56	0.52	0.42	0.27

The hypothesis on chunk learning of frequent invariant strings is also supported in this study by some learners' overgeneralizations of the inversion rule to subordinate clause contexts:

(10) han ser att *kommer det* en flicka med
"he sees that comes there a girl with"
(11) om kursen som *kan man* låna på bibliotek
"about the course that can one borrow at the library"
(12) *måste jag* ta ledigt i juli
"must I take holiday in July"

The combinations italicized in (10)–(12) are frequent and often correctly inverted combinations. One concludes that both usage data and error data from Swedish L2 learners indicate their use of formulaic speech.

The negation study

The use of formulaic speech has also been found in the learners' acquisition of negation. Our data are from a study of favorable/unfavorable contexts for the correct application of the rules for placement of the negative particle.

In Swedish, the negative particle *inte* takes different positions in main and subordinate clauses. In main clauses *inte* has the marked position after the finite verb, whereas in subordinate clauses, its position is the unmarked placement before the finite verb. (For a discussion of markedness conditions see Hyltenstam, 1984.) In learner language, a common placement of *inte* in main clauses is before the finite verb, i.e. the unmarked position. When the learner subsequently produces subordinate clauses, the placement of *inte* is the main clause position after the finite verb (cf. Hyltenstam, 1977; 1978 and Bolander, 1987b; 1988).

Most of the learners in this study are beyond the earliest stage in the learning process: thirty of the subjects have acquired the rule for the placement of negation in main clauses before the onset of the investigation, and the majority of the other learners make only a few errors. The number of correctly negated main clauses is 1,663 out of the total number of 1,729.

However, the frequency of negation in subordinate clauses is much lower than in main clauses, and errors are more common (55 correct ones out of 313).

With regard to different contexts favorable to negation placement, the results of the present study corroborate those of Hyltenstam's study (1978). The most favorable context for the application of the rule for placement of negation in main clauses, is the copula and the modul verbs, simple as well as in combination with main verbs. The values for relative frequency of correctness for simple modals are even higher than for the combinations. This suggests that the placement of the particle between the modal and the main verb in complex verb phrases is a placement after the modal as in Hyltenstam's analysis (1977 and 1978), rather than before the main verb, as suggested in discussions of Hyltenstam's data (cf. Hammarberg, 1979; Jordens, 1980; Rutherford, 1982).

Furthermore, the spontaneous data yield some interesting results with regard to the application of these word order rules in clauses containing AUX + V. In 3 out of 17 error clauses, the negative particle *inte* is placed before the finite verb. However, two of these clauses have the negation placed sentence-initially, and the third contains the verb group *brukar använda* "often uses" – a finite verb somewhat different from the "ordinary" auxiliaries. In all the other error clauses, the negation is placed after the non-finite verb, a position not discussed in earlier studies.

The negative element in some of these latter types of clauses may be seen as a negation of constituents (cf. Clahsen, Meisel and Pienemann, 1983), e.g.

(13) jag ska prata inte svenska
    "I will speak not Swedish"
(14) hon vill ha inte någonting
    "she wants to have not anything"

Another possible explanation could be that these tutored learners operate the verb group (AUX + V) as a prefab, and consequently keep the verbs together and therefore place the negative particle after the non-finite verb. A third possibility might be that the negative particle is always placed after the main verb, V + *inte*.

Support for a hypothesis on chunk learning and use of prefabs in processing may be found in the following utterances:

(15) men vi har fått inte
    "but we have become not"
(16) jag har läst inte jag har inte läst
    "I have read not I have not read"
(17) men min barn kan inte ut lek/kan gå inte ut leka
    "but my child can not out pla–/can go not out play"

In (15) and (16) the two verbs of the present perfect tense are kept together, and it may be tentatively suggested that the affirmative present perfect tense, due to high frequency and drill in formal instruction, emerges as a prefab during speech production. The negation is then postposed. In (16) the adjustment reveals that the learner knows the placement rule on a more conscious level, but the application is too distant in the speech production chain.

Also interesting is (17) in which the speaker first says *kan inte*, but in the context of modal + V, she places the negation after the verb phrase. This might be seen as an example of (a) a readiness to produce *kan inte* with postposed negation, (b) a preference for keeping the later uttered verb phrase together with the negative particle placed after, or (c) a preference for placing the negation immediately before the intended negated element. (a) and (b) support a hypothesis that frequent combinations are stored and used as prefabs.

In addition, none of the error clauses containing present perfect or past perfect tense and the negative particle, except (16) presented above, have the subject *jag* "I", a result indicating early acquisition of the placement of negation in these contexts.

However, a second and more frequent error type is this:

(18) vi har läst inte så mycket
      "we have read not very much"
(19) dom hade haft inte så många kompisar innan
      "they had had not so many friends before"
(20) man kan studera inte så mycket
      "one can study not very much"
(21) som vill bli fotograferad och in-
      har inte så snyggt va
      "who want is to have herself photoed and no-
      has not very good"

In (18)–(21) the negation seems to be linked to the following sequence of words instead of to the verb. Particularly interesting is (21), in which the speaker, a learner with high fluency, alters his intended correct placement in the subordinate clause. Perhaps this is done because of two conflicting prefabs, *inte har* and *inte så*, and a judgment of *inte så snyggt* as a unit not amenable to splitting. In addition, the speech by one learner who has notably more negated subordinate clauses than the others, supports the chunk hypothesis. Out of 13 negated subordinate clauses 10 have the correct placement of the negation before the finite verb, but two of the three error clauses contain *inte så* "not very".

Problematic effects of some kind of chunk learning may also be the reason for the errors in the following clauses:

(19) jag inte förstår
"I not understand"
(20) nu jag förstår mera
"now I understand more"
(21) de inte prata finska
"they not speak Finnish"
(22) efter skolan jag pratar bara polska
"after school I speak only Polish"

The two verbs *förstå* "understand" and *prata* "speak" should be frequent in early L2 learner communication, when the learners have still not acquired the rules for the placement of negation and the inversion rule for main clauses (see Bolander, 1988). Some errors of this kind are the only errors in the application of the rule in question for these learners. Subsequently, they might be idiosyncratic prefabs that are fossilized from the earliest stages of acquisition, later resisting rule application (cf. Peters, 1983:111 and Hyltenstam, 1985:131).

In summary, the negation data also suggest that memorization of chunks may play a part in the learners' L2 acquisition.

Chunks and prefabs – economy in language learning and language use?

In the previous sections results are presented from studies on 60 tutored adult learners' acquisition of some word order rules in Swedish. As in earlier studies of learner language, the results indicate that memorizing frequent sequences of various types is a common phenomenon, not only as "routines" like *jag vet inte* "I don't know" or "patterns" like *det kan man göra* "it/so can one do", but also as ready-made smaller parts of utterances, here called chunks or prefabs. These memorized chunks are not always the constituents considered in linguistic theory, i.e. phrases like, for example, NPs, but frequent and "needed" words that often occur together in input and output, e.g. *kan inte* "can not" and *inte så mycket* "not very much" and *har fått* "has got". This does indicate that language learning and processing employ chunks/prefabs of frequent and useful words to a greater extent than normally assumed (cf. Bolinger, 1976). Let us consider the various factors that seem to motivate use of prefab utterances and structures.

For language learning, as well as for other human activities, a decisive factor for perception is motivation. The learner's communicative need predisposes her/him to focus on selected concrete utterances in input. However, to make learning possible, the learner needs frequently occurring, perceptually salient words and constructions. A conceivable strategy then, would be to extract chunks that can be slotted into communicative needs and that subsequently become some kind of "prefabs" that can be used in processing.

With regard to the type of structures studied, *communicative needs* and *frequency in input and output* seem to be interdependent and both are likely to explain chunk learning of the types shown in our data. Prefabs or patterns that are more often used correctly by the learners, i.e. more often than in other occurrences of the corresponding structure, are the following:

> structures containing combinations of the first person pronouns and some verbs expressing personal attitudes and opinions, respectively
>
> the negative particle in combination with the relatively few, but needed and frequent modal verbs and the copula, compared to combinations with the many different main verbs (cf. Hatch, 1978)
>
> correct inversion clauses with sentence-initial *det* "it/so", e.g. *det kan man göra* "it/so can one do", which are frequent in spoken Swedish (Jörgensen, 1976) and used to display confirmation of prior utterances.

Thus, these suggested prefabs are of different types, and only the last examples are of a type similar to the ones discussed in earlier studies reporting formulaic speech.

The influence of *perceptual salience* may be a further explanation of some of the studies' results. Thus, similarity in prosody may explain the type *det kan man göra* "it/so can one do", and these adult learners might use a strategy similar to that common for children who "seem to pick up and produce intonational patterns before they control other aspects of speech" (Peters, 1977:568). Clauses with *det* share a similar intonational contour: *det* is unstressed in most of these clauses where the stress is often on the main verb. This is also mostly the case for clauses with sentence-initial *då* "then/at that moment", in which the inversion rule is more correctly applied than, for instance, in clauses with sentence-initial *sen* "then/after that" (see table 5.2 above). *Sen* often carries a heavier stress, which distinguishes the intonation of *sen*-clauses from *det*-clauses.

These results suggest that a prosodic frame has been "tuned in" for the *det*- and *då*-clauses which is not the case for the *sen*-clauses. The difference in prosody between clauses preposed by *det* and *sen* is a consequence of their different textual function and meaning. The function of *sen* seems very often to be to facilitate enumerations of events in narrative contexts, i.e. a function similar to that of *och* "and", *dessutom* "besides", or *vidare* "further". This leads to a considerable variation with regard to subjects and verbs in these clauses, and rule operating seems to be the only reasonable way to produce correct inversion clauses. Perhaps this is the reason why the clauses preceded by *sen* are less correct with regard to the inversion rule, and why several of these learners "correct" themselves, as in *sen går* "then goes" immediately corrected to *sen hon går* "then she goes". The interpretation of this may be that the learner, when hearing her/his utterance, becomes conscious of the rule for obligatory pronominal subject, restarts and adds the subject with the dominant order S-V. Despite the high frequency of the grammatical structure ADV + V + S and *sen*-clauses, this does not seem to promote the acquisition of the rule, but the "tune-in" factor seems to do so (contra Krashen and Scarcella (1978:297) who maintain that "adults may use routines and patterns but not tunes").

A dependence on *spoken input* for these learners is further supported by the fact that the learners use constructions that are very unlikely topics for formal instruction, but probably occur frequently in the teachers' own talk (Håkansson, 1987). One example of this is the placement of negation with main clause word order in some asserted subordinate clauses e.g. beginning with *att* "that", which are common in everyday Swedish. Furthermore, the importance of input is shown by the learners' use of *då/så* immediately after sentence-initial subordinate clauses, *om du vill så kommer jag* "if you want then I come", and pronominal copies after sentence-initial subjects or objects, *Peter han är snäll* "Peter he is kind".

In all these cases, the input from native speakers' speech and perhaps certain types of written texts is presumably the main source for the acquisition of idiomatic Swedish, since all these constructions are often looked upon as "inappropriate language" in written texts, and are not topics for class-room instruction.

The importance of input is also indicated by the acquisition of the rule for the placement of some adverbs, compared to the acquisition of the rule for the placement of the negative particle. These many different adverbs have three different positions in main clauses, one of which – the most frequent – is common to that of negation. The similarities between the placement of negation and these adverbs are focused on in formal instruction, but the acquisition of the rule for placement of adverbs is later than the placement of negation. In addition to L1 influence, this is conceivably due to both the larger number of different adverb items and the variation of placement in input for these adverbs compared to the single word *inte* and the relative lack of variation in the placement of the negation (see also Bolander, 1988).

Note that many of the syntactic errors occur when the learners lack adequate words. A common assumption supported by many studies is that language use – including most learners' language use – is more correct in more formal situations. If this is the case, the learners' speech in the present study ought to be more correct in the picture description task, when more focusing on the linguistic form is possible, than in the more informal interviews studied. However, in all but a few cases, there are more errors in the description task, and the errors occur mostly when the learners lack adequate words to describe the pictures. This indicates that the syntactic rules under acquisition are neglected when problems in expressing intended meaning arise (cf. Hene, 1988).

Tarone (1984:39) raised a pertinent question on the relationship between the degree of formality in the speech situation and the variability in learner language. She reviews the results from a study on style-shifting and shows that not all structures are produced most correctly when using a careful style (the articles and the direct object pronouns were not). Tarone then asks "what sort of capability underlies an IL [interlanguage] system made up of sets of structures which shift in opposite directions along the style continuum?" (Tarone, 1984:39–40).

One answer to Tarone's question would be that the learners have two kinds of capacity: (1) one consisting of frequent invariant strings of words that have been extracted and memorized and are used as prefabs in production, and (2) one consisting of processing by means of syntactic rules operating on more or less isolated strings of words. This might then explain the different style-shifting for different structures. What looks like rule application might in fact be prefabs and the degree of correctness is then due to the actual words constituting the utterance (cf. Hyltenstam, 1985).

The influence of lexicon on the application of grammatical rules is also discussed by Hyltenstam (1984:52) in a study on pronominal copies in relative clauses in Swedish. Hyltenstam proposes that one explanation for the unexpected findings of a high frequency of correct omissions of pronominal copies in the context of "the very common verb *titta på*" "look at", may be "that a pronominal copy would more often be deleted in familiar lexical environments."

If the discussed interrelation between vocabulary and syntax (i.e. that the actual words of an utterance are important also for the application of syntactic rules) holds true, this has implications for the construction of elicitation instruments and tests for studies on the acquisition of grammatical rules. Items comprising similar constructions, but different words, may yield different outcomes and be one reason for variation in rule application.

Thus, formulaic speech in learner language sometimes leads to error clauses and sometimes the prefabs generate target language structures before the rule is actually acquired. It appears then that at least some syntactic rules – the marked ones? – are loosely integrated in the learner language. As Peters (1983:90) states:

> Syntax and lexicon are thus seen to be complementary in a dynamic and redundant way. The same information may be present in both, in different forms: It may be present implicitly in the lexicon fused into an expression or formulaic frame, and at the same time it may be explicitly represented in the syntax.

A subsequent hypothesis based on the evidence for formulaic speech in learner language might be that chunk processing is an effective and economic means for language processing in general, comparable with, for example, memorizing a long telephone number. There are even similarities to how we learn and organize movements. As Ladefoged (1972:282) notes:

> There is a great deal of evidence that muscular movements are organized in terms of complex, unalterable chunks of at least a quarter of a second in duration (and often much longer) and nothing to indicate organization in terms of short simultaneous segments which require processing with context-restricted rules.

Thus, from the perspective of human neurofunctional processing, a hypothesis on language learning might be that when the number of prefabs stored in memory is large enough, syntactic rules are derived as help for the memory to economize and rationalize processing (cf. Wadell and Johansson, 1984). As Bolinger (1976:2) put it succinctly "speakers do at least as much remembering as they do putting together."

References

Bolander, M. (1987a), On the acquisition of word order rules in Swedish as a second language. Paper presented at the 8th World Congress of Applied Linguistics, 16–21 August, 1987, Sydney.
   (1987b), Man kan studera inte så mycke. Om placering av negation och adverb i vuxna invandrares svenska. *SUM-rapport 5*. Department of Linguistics, University of Stockholm.
   (1988), Is there any order? On Word Order in Swedish Learner Language. *Journal of Multilingual and Multicultural Development*, **9**, 97–113.
Bolinger, D. (1976), Meaning and memory. *Forum Linguisticum* 1: 1–14.
Brown, R. (1973), *A First Language: The Early Stages*. Cambridge MA: Harvard University Press.
Clahsen, H., Meisel, J. M. and Pienemann, M. (1983), *Deutsch als Zweitsprache. Der Spracherwerb ausländischer Arbeiter*. Tübingen: Gunter Narr.
Dahlbäck, H. (1981), Datatyp och interimspråkskompetens 1. En variationsanalys av olika slags testdata på inversion och rak ordföljd i invandrares svenska. Department of Linguistics, University of Lund.
Dulay, H. and Burt, M. (1978), Some remarks on creativity in language acquisition. In Ritchie, W. C. (ed.), *Second Language Acquisition Research: Issues and Implications*. New York: Academic Press, Inc.
Ellis, R. (1984), Formulaic speech in early classroom second language development. In Handscombe, R., Orem, R. and Taylor, B. (eds.), *On TESOL '83: The Question of Control*. Washington, D. C.: TESOL.
   (1986), *Understanding Second Language Acquisition*. Oxford University Press.
Fillmore, W. (1979), Individual differences in second language acquisition. In Fillmore, C., Kempler, D. and Wang, W. (eds.), *Individual Differences in Language Ability and Language Behavior*. New York: Academic Press.
Grosjean, F. (1982), *Life with Two Languages. An Introduction to Bilingualism*. Cambridge, MA: Harvard University Press.
Håkansson, G. (1987), *Teacher Talk. How teachers modify their speech when addressing learners of Swedish as a second language*. Lund: University Press.

Hakuta, K. (1974), Prefabricated patterns and the emergence of structure in second language acquisition. *Language Learning*, **24**. 287–97.

Hammarberg, B. (1979), On intralingual, interlingual and developmental solutions in interlanguage. In Hyltenstam, K. and M. Linnarud, (eds.), *Interlanguage*. Workshop at the Fifth Scandinavian Conference of Linguistics, Frostavallen, April 27–29, 1979.

Hanania, E. A. B. and Gradman, H. L. (1977), Acquisition of English structures: A case study of an adult native speaker of Arabic in an English-speaking environment. *Language Learning* **27**:75–92.

Hatch, E. (1973), Second language learning – universals? *Working Papers on Bilingualism*, **3**, 1–18.

(1978), Discourse analysis. In Hatch, E. (ed.), *Second Language Acquisition. A Book of Readings*. Rowley, MA: Newbury House.

Hellwig, L. (1983), A Prefabricated Pattern as a Communication Strategy. Paper given at BAAL Annual Conference, Leicester.

Hene, B. (1988), Language Development of Inter-Country Adoptees. Presentation of a Swedish research project. *SPRINS* Report No 39. Department of Linguistics, University of Göteborg.

Huang, J. and Hatch, E. (1978), A Chinese child's acquisition of English. In Hatch, E. (ed.), *Second Language Acquisition: A Book of Readings*. Rowley, MA: Newbury House.

Hyltenstam, K. (1977), Implicational patterns in interlanguage syntax variation. *Language Learning*, **27**, 383–411.

(1978), Variation in interlanguage syntax. *Working Papers* **18**. Lund: Department of General Linguistics.

(1984), The use of typological markedness conditions as predictors in second language acquisition: the case of pronominal copies in relative clauses. In Andersen, R. W. (ed.), *Second Languages*. Rowley, MA: Newbury House.

(1985), L2 learners' variable output and language teaching. In Hyltenstam, K. and Pienemann, M. (eds.), *Modelling and Assessing Second Language Acquisition*. Avon: Multilingual Matters.

Jordens, P. (1980), Interlanguage research: interpretation or explanation. *Language Learning* **30**, 195–207.

Jörgensen, N. (1976), *Meningsbyggnaden i talad svenska*. Lund: Studentlitteratur.

Krashen, S. D. and Scarcella, R. (1978), On routines and patterns in language acquisition and performance. *Language Learning* **28**, 283–300.

Ladefoged, P. (1972), Phonetic Prerequisites for a Distinctive Feature Theory. In Valdman, A. (ed.), *Papers in Linguistics and Phonetics in Memory of Pierre Delatre*. The Hague: Mouton.

Lyons, J. (1968), *Introduction to Theoretical Linguistics*. Cambridge University Press.

Peters, A. M. (1977), Language learning strategies: does the whole equal the sum of the parts? *Language* **53**, 560–73.

(1983), *The Units of Language Acquisition*. Cambridge University Press.

Rutherford, W. (1982), Markedness in second language acquisition. *Language Learning* **32**, 85–106.

Seliger, H. (1982), On the possible role of the right hemisphere in second language teaching. *TESOL Quarterly* **16**, 307–14.

Tarone, E. T. (1984), The interlanguage continuum. In Wheatley, B. *et al.* (eds.), *Current Approaches to Second Language Acquisition: Proceedings of the 1984 University of Wisconsin-Milwaukee linguistics symposium*.

Wadell, I. and Johansson, H. (1984), Betydelsen av sensorisk feedback vid motorisk inlärning. *Finlands Fysioterapeutförbunds terapeutdagar*, 11–12 oktober 1984. Abstract of papers. Helsingfors.

6. The imperfect conditional

ERIC KELLERMAN

Introduction

The Dutch have a reputation for being good at speaking English. Their prowess in this regard cannot simply be attributed to the presence of English in the school curriculum. For one thing, Dutch and English are typologically close; for another, there is also considerable exposure to English through the media. English and American productions feature regularly on Dutch TV and in the cinema and are never dubbed, and English-medium radio and television are becoming widely available. English-language books sell so well that the British publishing trade apparently sees the Netherlands as simply another part of the home market. The Dutch success in learning English also reflects an attitude fully commensurate with the commercial importance of the nation and the insignificance of Dutch as a world language. Furthermore, the Dutch language, unlike French, does not have its official band of zealous guardians; it is a language that borrows happily, particularly from English.

Despite the high level of linguistic achievement, it is obvious to any experienced observer that the majority of Dutch speakers remain unmistakably Dutch in their command of English. This is not merely a matter of pronunciation, but also of "accent" in other linguistic domains (see Scarcella, 1983). These particular "accents" take the form of characteristic features which are said to have *fossilized* (Selinker, 1974). Fossilization occurs when learners stop learning, having arrived at a point where their language consistently deviates from native speaker norms, or when they regress to stages of development they had supposedly left behind. It is a phenomenon whose existence carries considerable theoretical import, since its absence in child language development constitutes one of the cornerstones of the argument that the processes of first and second language acquisition are distinct.

Although fossilization has been frequently discussed in the literature, very little is known about its workings. Biological explanations relating to changes in the brain ("the critical period hypothesis") have been put forward to account for the failure of learners to achieve native-like proficiency, and so have psychosocial ones (see, for example, Klein, 1986:151 for a discussion of this). However, such explanations are concerned with understanding the causes of fossilization; they do not lead to predictions about what linguistic features of the interlanguage are candidates for fossilization (for this point, with slightly different emphasis, see Selinker, 1974:42f.). There has been virtually no discussion as to why certain "accents" may come to typify a whole community of language learners irrespective of differing proficiency levels within that community. An understanding of fossilization may only come from a detailed analysis of such "accents".

The existence of fossilization presents a further challenge in environments in which formal language training takes place. At university level in the Netherlands, a great deal of attention is paid to the appropriate morphology of English *if–then* conditionals, and it is well described in various grammars. Yet explicit teaching does not seem to chalk up much success. Dutch learners go on using *would + infinitive* (instead of a past tense) in the *if*-clause, producing such sentences as *If I would be able to live all over again, I would be a gardener.*[1] Why then are Dutch learners even at this advanced level still immune to pedagogical blandishments? The causes of errors that persist at this level of general achievement deserve serious investigation.

One might want to argue that the source of the learner's difficulty with conditionals is the native language, since Dutch in fact permits a *would*-equivalent in the conditional subclause. However, this in itself is not an explanation for fossilization. Nor does it explain why Dutch should continue to influence the learner's language in this area of the grammar when its influence is more easily overcome in so many other areas where Dutch and English contrast. All one could reasonably say about the L1 is that it could be the formal source of the learner's difficulties. Clearly an explanation will have to be sought elsewhere.

This chapter is an elaboration of the possible causes of the difficulty that even advanced learners have with the morphology of English conditionals. Instead of putting forward a straightforward structural explanation for the problem, I propose that the errors come about as a result of Dutch learners of English[2] (a) reacting against ambiguity in the verb forms of conditional sentences, and (b) creating morphological symmetry in verb forms of the two clauses that make up these sentences. However, I shall also suggest that in the case of Dutch learners of English, these tendencies are inextricably linked to crosslinguistic influence.

The structure of the chapter is as follows: Section 1 provides brief descriptions of hypothetical conditionals in English and Dutch. Section 2 describes the errors made by Dutch learners and reports briefly on experimental data from L1 Dutch and L2 English. I will then show that these same forms are also produced by learners with different language backgrounds, appear as variants in languages where they are sometimes stigmatized in standard descriptions, and are the accepted forms in others. I will also present evidence that disambiguation can play a role in determining the structure of Dutch conditionals. I will conclude that the avoidance of ambiguity and the promotion of morphological symmetry are primarily what cause the error and contribute to its fossilization.

Hypothetical conditionals in English and Dutch

This section presents a brief sketch of English and Dutch hypothetical conditionals. The former are well described in the literature (see e.g. Quirk, Greenbaum, Leech and Svartvik, 1985 and references therein), but Dutch conditionals have received only the most cursory attention (for a notable exception, see Nieuwint, 1984). It is not the aim of this section to remedy the current lack of an adequate description of Dutch conditionals, conditionals being complex structures on a number of levels. Rather, I shall offer a characterization of their structural properties, followed by some speculation about the meaning differences entailed by different structure types.

I shall assume that a conditional sentence[3] consists of two clauses: the first, introduced typically by *if*, will, following traditional practice, be called the *protasis*. The protasis states the condition on which the second clause is contingent. This second clause, again according to tradition, will be called the *apodosis*. It may contain the correlative conjunction *then*.[4] I will not in this section be considering other devices for indicating the contingency between clauses such as inversion of subject and tensed verb in the protasis, the use of other subordinating conjunctions such as *unless*, or co-ordination and juxtaposition of clauses.

English conditionals

Comrie (1986:88–89) claims that languages organize conditionals along a hypotheticality continuum, and that different languages cut up that continuum in different ways, allowing speakers to express different degrees of hypotheticality by purely grammatical means. Hypotheticality is defined by Comrie as follows: "...the degree of probability of realization of the situations referred to in the conditional, and more especially in the protasis...a factual sentence would represent the lowest degree of hypotheticality, while a counterfactual clause would represent the highest degree."

Conditionals, Comrie argues, say nothing about whether the propositions in either clause are factual or not, although it may be possible to infer their truth from other knowledge sources. This means that what are traditionally called *open* or *real* conditionals (see Leech, 1971:110) have, strictly speaking, very low hypotheticality since the speaker intimates that the probability of their fulfilment is relatively high. Thus if someone says *It's nice out*, he presents this statement as a fact, and it has zero hypotheticality. On the other hand, *If it's nice out, we'll go to the park* does not state that either proposition is factual, even if the speaker believes that it actually is nice out, e.g.

> (1) A: Is it nice out at the moment?
>   B: Yes
>   A: Well, if it's nice out, we'll go to the park

Note that A's second remark can only be appropriate if A's knowledge of local weather conditions derives entirely from hearsay, i.e. B's reply (Akatsuka, 1986:340). If A is normally sighted and co-operative, he could not say *If it's nice out, we'll go to the park* while looking out of the window at the sunlit street below. Clearly, these conditionals do bear a degree of hypotheticality. However, backshifted tenses (i.e. a past tense to refer to non-past time and the pluperfect to refer to past time) in protasis and apodosis would indicate a lower probability of realization, i.e. higher hypotheticality:

> (2) If it was nice out, we would go to the park

Consequently, since we are dealing in known facts ("it's nice out") such a sentence would be decidedly odd if placed in the preceding interchange, because of its counterfactual reading:

> (3) A: Is it nice out?
>   B: Yes
>   A: !Well, if it was nice out, we would go to the park

However, as Comrie (1986:89) amongst others points out, it would be wrong to assume that conditionals with backshifted tenses are necessarily to be interpreted as counterfactual, as the next example shows:

> (4) A: Will you buy me a beer?
>   B: If you gave me a kiss, I'd buy you a beer

It is true that B might have said "If you give me a kiss, I'll buy you a beer" (Comrie 1986:90), but the point is that both backshifted and non-backshifted verb forms are possible, unlike in the preceding dialogue about the weather. The difference in the two sentences resides in the greater tentativeness of *If you gave me a kiss, I'd buy you a beer* (cf. James, 1982:391). The difference in interpretation as to the degree of hypotheticality between *If it was nice out* and *If you gave me a kiss* can only come about as a result of pragmatic considerations and not grammatical ones. The clearest cases of non-counterfactual readings for conditional sentences with backshifted tenses is when they occur in conjunction with a future time adjunct, e.g.

(5) If it rained tomorrow, we'd just stay home

Comrie's next example concerns what might seem an even stronger candidate for counterfactual status, a conditional sentence with a pluperfect in the protasis and *would + perfect infinitive* in the apodosis. *If it had been nice out, we would have gone to the park* implies that the weather was unpleasant and we did not go to the park. However, Comrie again shows that counterfactuality is really an inference and not part of the grammatical *meaning* of the conditional:

(6) If the butler had done it, we would have found just the clues that we did in fact find

This sentence leaves open the possibility that the butler really did do it (see also Davies, 1979). That past time conditionals of this kind are usually interpreted as counterfactual is presumably because we generally have more certainty about situations that may or may not have happened than we have about those yet to occur. Like other languages such as French and German, then, English conditionals distinguish grammatically only two degrees of hypotheticality – low and high. There is no specifically morphological means of expressing counterfactuality in such sentences (cf. James, 1982:377–78).

We have seen that conditionals displaying high hypotheticality employ backshifted tenses. The rules for forming such conditionals in English are these:

> the protasis requires a finite verb with backshifted tense (preterite in non-past conditionals, pluperfect in past conditionals) or *could, might* and *should + (perfect) infinitive, but not *would*;[5]

> the apodosis requires a periphrastic conditional (*would + (perfect) infinitive). Other auxiliaries are possible, but since *would* is the most common modal verb in the apodosis (Quirk *et al.*, 1985:1010), they will not be referred to further.

Comrie's claim that conditional structures can be placed along a continuum of hypotheticality obviates the need to make "the contorted and often empty formulations attempting to distinguish between real and hypothetical conditionals" (Comrie, 1986:88). Accordingly, I shall from now on be dealing only with those conditionals whose backshifted tenses explicitly mark their high hypotheticality. Such conditionals will be known by the abbreviation HC (for "highly hypothetical conditionals").

Dutch conditionals

As suggested above, the organisation of the Dutch conditional system is more problematic than its English counterpart. Dutch conditionals of low hypotheticality are similar to English ones in using non-backshifted tenses. The difficulties start with the high hypothetical conditionals (HCs), where, on the face of it, there seems to be a number of choices in the morphological structure of the verb phrases of the two clauses.

In Dutch HCs with present or indefinite time reference (equivalent to *if it was nice out now/more often*) the protasis and the apodosis may be respectively marked either by a preterite or a periphrastic conditional (with what is formally a past tense modal equivalent of English *would, zou(den)*). That is to say, there are theoretically four possible structure types in Dutch HCs, all grammatical, as the following examples show:

(7) (a) Als je dat zou doen, zou ik je zo de trap afschoppen
(b) Als je dat deed, zou ik je zo de trap afschoppen
(c) Als je dat deed, schopte ik je zo de trap af
(d) Als je dat zou doen, schopte ik je zo de trap af
(If you did that, I would kick you downstairs)

Similarly, with past time reference, either the pluperfect or the perfect conditional may be used in either clause:

(8) (a) Als je dat gedaan zou hebben, zou ik je zo de trap hebben afgeschopt
(b) Als je dat gedaan had, zou ik je zo de trap hebben afgeschopt
(c) Als je dat gedaan had, had ik je zo de trap afgeschopt
(d) Als je dat gedaan zou hebben, had ik je zo de trap afgeschopt
(If you had done that, I would have kicked you downstairs)

In conditional sentences with explicit future reference (*If it rained tomorrow, the match would be cancelled*), the preterite in either clause is usually considered unacceptable:

(9) (a) Als het morgen zou regenen, zou de wedstrijd afgelast worden
(b) *Als het morgen regende, zou de wedstrijd afgelast worden

This difference between conditionals with future and non-future reference in Dutch seems consistent with the observation by James (1982:378), who notes that past tenses are more common in non-future HCs than in future ones crosslinguistically. In this respect, English, and for that matter, French, are exceptional for requiring past indicative tenses with HCs with future reference.

For convenience, I shall code the grammatical structures of the clauses of a HC as follows:

+signifies that the auxiliary verb *would*, or its equivalent in Dutch, *zou(den)*, is present in the protasis and/or apodosis, followed by the infinitive of a lexical verb, e.g. *If it would rain/*If it would have rained: als het zou regenen/als het zou hebben geregend* (periphrastic conditional tense).

—signifies that *would* or its Dutch equivalent is absent, the finite verb being in a past tense form, such as preterite or pluperfect, e.g. *if it rained/if it had rained: als het regende/als het had geregend* (past tense).

HC sentence structure will always be given as if the order were (1) protasis, (2) apodosis, the clauses being separated by a slash, e.g. $+/+$, $-/+$ etc. even where the order of clauses is reversed. Therefore both *If you gave me a kiss, I'd buy you a beer* and *I'd buy you a beer if you gave me a kiss* are coded as $-/+$.

Thus in (7) and (8) above (a) will be coded $+/+$, (b) $-/+$, (c) $-/-$, and (d) $+/-$. Only (b) is generally correct in English. Dutch grammars have had very little to say about the distribution and meaning of these structures, apart from noting that all four occur (Van Es and Van Caspel, 1975:191–94). Geerts, Haeserijn, de Rooij and v.d. Toorn (1984:468) maintain that the choice among the various structures in (7) and (8) is essentially stylistic. The Nijmegen corpus of HCs being collected by Herman Wekker and myself shows that notion to be quite incorrect, as will become clear later in the chapter. The one writer who has studied the significance of the formal diversity of Dutch HC morphology is Nieuwint (1984). His arguments are subtle and difficult to test, since they depend critically on the reader's acceptance of Nieuwint's intuitions about Dutch. Accordingly, the description of Nieuwint's ideas is coupled here with our own observations on the Nijmegen corpus.

It will be assumed that the principal difference between Dutch and English HCs is that Dutch does have the capacity to mark counterfactuality grammatically. Specifically, in Dutch, speaker evaluation of the degree of hypotheticality may be expressed by a binary tense choice. The use of a past tense $-/$ (preterite or pluperfect, according to time frame), in the protasis signifies the assertion on the part of the speaker that the preposition in the protasis is counterfactual (which is why the preterite cannot co-occur with a future time adjunct). This assertion may be even further underlined by the use of a past tense in the apodosis as well, which is then not only counterfactual by implication, but by grammatical marking (which is why past tenses are most common in past time HCs, where one can be most certain about what did or did not happen).

The use of the periphrastic conditional, on the other hand, only asserts hypotheticality, just as it does in English; counterfactuality is not part of the meaning of periphrastic conditional tenses, though it may be interpreted by the listener as such in the appropriate context. The examples in (7) and (8) above are arranged in this putative order of hypotheticality (though we must exclude $+/-$ structures for the moment), from the hypothetical $+/+$ (a) to counterfactual $-/+$ and doubly counterfactual $-/-$ (b and c).

Periphrastic conditional HCs may be termed the unmarked or "default" HC structures in Dutch. That they can be used to refer to the same segment of the hypotheticality continuum in their meanings as the putative counterfactuals, may be seen from the observation that there is probably no Dutch HC with a past tense in either clause where that past tense cannot be rewritten by a periphrastic conditional (with one very minor exception). That is to say that any HC of the structure $-/+$, $-/-$ or $+/-$ may be reformulated as $+/+$ without loss of acceptability. It is certainly not the case that any $+/+$ can be written as $-/+$, $-/-$ or $+/-$. The one exception to this "rewrite rule" is *als ik jou was* ("if I were you"), where **Als ik jou zou zijn* is unacceptable. Although this expression really has idiomatic status, it can be assumed that the preterite is required here because of the physical difficulty involved in being someone else.

As an example of this directionality in the substitutability of a structure by another, there seems, as noted above, to be general agreement that in non-past time frames it is unacceptable to have a preterite in the protasis with a future time adjunct, viz.

> (10) *Als het morgen regende, zou de wedstrijd afgelast worden
> (If it rained tomorrow, the match would be cancelled)

presumably because no one can be so omniscient that they can rule out the prospect of rain. Instead it would be necessary to have the periphrastic conditional in the protasis:

> (11) Als het morgen zou regenen, zou de wedstrijd afgelast worden

When the time frame is indefinite, however, the speaker has a choice. Thus, with an indefinite time adjunct like *vaker* ("more often"), all combinations of + and − are possible:

> (12) Als het vaker zou regenen/regende, werd het gras groener/zou het gras groener worden
> (If it rained more often, the grass would get greener)

If past tenses seem to be less than acceptable in what are clearly *potentialis* contexts, the converse is not true. The conditional is perfectly acceptable in contexts which are *irrealis*, though presumably in the following example, the speaker is more concerned with fantasizing than asserting the inability of houses to speak:

> (13) Als dit huis zou kunnen spreken, wat voor verhalen zou het niet kunnen vertellen!
> (If this house could speak, what stories it could tell!)

The same is true in past time frames (although the result is a little inelegant with its piled-up auxiliaries):

(14) Als dit huis zou hebben kunnen spreken, wat voor verhalen zou het niet hebben kunnen vertellen!
(If this house could have spoken, what stories it could have told!)

An example quoted by Dierikx (1985 : 50) may help to illustrate the intimate link between past tenses and counterfactual meaning, even in non-past contexts:

(15) "Dat wil niet zeggen dat ik een beest zou wezen. Er zijn genoeg mensen die me willen helpen, die me mogen. *Als ik zo'n rotvent was (-PRET), hielpen (-PRET) ze me niet."* Nou het is niet zo dat Bruessing een jongen is die op hulp zit te wachten. ("That does not mean that I am a brute. There are enough people who want to help me, who like me. *If I was such a bastard, they wouldn't help me."* Now it's not the case that Bruessing is the sort of bloke who sits around waiting to be helped.)

Here "Bruessing" has said quite explicitly that he is not a bastard, and that people are actually willing to help him. Thus both protasis and apodosis are counterfactual. $-/+$ and $+/+$ structures would have been equally acceptable, but the speaker's explicit commitment to the falsity of the propositions would have become progressively weaker, if still recoverable from the surrounding context.

This leaves us with the $+/-$ structures. It must be said that they are problematic, since in the present framework the protasis is hypothetical and the apodosis counterfactual. Nieuwint (1984) claims that such structures mean that the speaker makes a categorical statement about what would happen at some point in time other than the present (apodosis) in a given situation which may or may not occur (protasis). It seems to be the case that these structures are often interpreted as overt promises or threats:

(16) Als je dat zou doen, schopte ik je zo de trap af

or

(17) Als je beter zou zingen, verlengde ik je contract

The English equivalents would be sentences like

(18) Do that and I'll kick you downstairs

and

(19) Sing better and I'll prolong your contract

That the $+/-$ structure seems to be restricted to such cases is supported by the awkwardness of such sentences as

(20) ?Als je dat zou doen, speet me dat erg/vond ik je een naarling

English equivalents also sound strange:

(21) Do that and I'll be sorry/and I'll consider you a fool

Table 6.1. *Distribution of structure types, Nijmegen Hypothetical Conditional Corpus*

	Structure								
Time frame	+/+	−/+	−/−	+/−	+/x	−/x	x/+	x/−	Total
Non-past	155	88	13	15	70	23	36	1	401
Past	22	66	110	9	1	0	3	0	211
Mixed	7	9	5	4	1	2	0	1	29
									641

NB. x: absent clause *or* verb form not realized by either past tense of lexical verb or conditional. In non-past HCs, many of these are present tenses. Mixed: Both non-past and past time frames used, e.g. *If I had seen her, I wouldn't be sitting here now.*

However, there are so few examples of +/− sentences in our corpus that it is difficult to check this characterization against data. The reader is referred to Nieuwint (1984) for discussion.

This description of Dutch HCs leads to a number of testable predictions about their distribution. The first is that −/ protases should be commoner in past time frames than +/ ones. The converse should also hold: +/ protases should be commoner in non-past time frames than −/ ones. The third prediction is that in non-past time frames, −/ protases referring to the present or indefinite time should be more frequent than those referring to the future.

Stable linguistic judgements on the acceptability of HCs are very difficult to elicit from native speakers. Clear intuitions about what is or is not acceptable seem the exception rather than the rule. Consequently the appropriate methodology for testing these predictions is to study HCs as they are actually used in non-experimental contexts, i.e. in ordinary language use (cf. Lavandera, 1975). This is what Wekker and I are doing at the University of Nijmegen. To date, the Nijmegen corpus contains about 700 Dutch HC sentences collected principally from written sources accompanied by the contexts in which they appear. Table 6.1 gives the distribution of structure type by time frame in this corpus.

If we exclude +/− structures from consideration (their frequency is small in any case), we see that in non-past time frames, there are 225 +/ protases (56 percent) and 126 −/ protases (30.8 percent). In past time frames, there are 23 +/ protases (10.9 per cent) and 176 −/ protases (83.3 percent). Thus the first two predictions are confirmed. The third prediction has yet to be tested. However, a quick perusal of the 64 −/ HCs in Dierikx (1985) suggests that this prediction may well be correct.

Furthermore, Table 6.1 makes it quite clear that although all four HC structures are supposed to be grammatical, there are considerable differences in their distribution which cannot be attributed to stylistic choice. $+/+$ is almost exclusively non-past, and $-/-$ almost exclusively past. $+/-$ is rare. Only the $-/+$ structure appears frequently in both time frames.[6]

In summary, the principal differences between English and Dutch HCs are that Dutch seems able to distinguish grammatically the counterfactual in addition to the hypothetical. English cannot do this. A prediction about learner behavior in English based solely on structural differences between the two languages would anticipate that Dutch learners would overuse incorrect $+/$ protases in non-past HCs with future reference, and incidentally produce correct $-/$ protases in past and non-past HCs whenever they wished to mark counterfactuality grammatically as they would in Dutch. As far as the English apodosis is concerned, $/-$ would predominate in past HCs and $/+$ in non-past HCs. Whether these predictions have any substance is the topic of the next section.

A comparison of performance in L1 and L2

Errors made by Dutch learners of English

Now that we have briefly described HCs in both English and Dutch, we must consider the errors that Dutch learners of English make. As has already been pointed out in the introduction, advanced Dutch learners of English frequently use *would* in the protasis of HCs, as in (22):

(22) (a) *If it would rain, they would cancel the concert in Damrosch Park $(+/+)$
(b) *If it would have rained, they would have cancelled the concert in Damrosch Park $(+/+)$

Such use constitutes an error in that English HCs do not normally allow the modal auxiliary *would* to occur in the protasis. Less frequently, one finds errors like (23) (a) and (b):

(23) (a) *If it rained, they cancelled the concert in Damrosch Park $(-/-)$
(b) *If it had rained, they had cancelled the concert in Damrosch Park $(-/-)$

The rule violated here is that English HCs do require a construction with *would* (or some other past tense modal auxiliary) in the apodosis (matrix clause). Double mistakes also occur, though they seem rare:

(24) (a) *If it would rain, they cancelled the concert in Damrosch Park $(+/-)$
(b) *If it would have rained, they had cancelled the concert in Damrosch Park $(+/-)$

The correct versions of (22)–(24) would thus be (25) (a) and (b):

(25) (a) If it rained, they would cancel the concert in Damrosch Park $(-/+)$
(b) If it had rained, they would have cancelled the concert in Damrosch Park $(-/+)$

Two experiments

Wekker, Kellerman and Hermans (1982) investigated performance on non-past and past hypothetical conditional sentences in Dutch and English under experimental conditions, using Dutch learners of English as their own controls. That is to say, subjects performed the same task in both languages, thus permitting comparison both within and across individuals. Wekker *et al.* also collected data using two slightly different elicitation instruments. The first required the subjects to complete paragraphs with a contextually appropriate conditional sentence. The second elicitation format also required subjects to complete a paragraph, this time by choosing from four alternative contextually appropriate HCs, each with the same content and representing one of the permissible Dutch structures in (7) and (8) above. The first instrument (Experiment 1) was thus more "natural", while the second (Experiment 2) invited subjects to consider the structure of the response quite explicitly. Subjects were drawn from 1st, 2nd and 3rd year students at the University of Nijmegen, generally considered to be advanced after between 7 and 9 years of English instruction.

The distribution of L2 HC structures obtained in the two experiments is shown in Tables 6.2 and 6.3. These figures show that where the focus is not explicitly on form (Experiment 1), even 3rd year students have not mastered non-past HC syntax, although all three groups score highly in past HCs. All in all, performance in Experiment 2 is better for non-past HCs, while 1st year subjects are somewhat worse for past HCs than they were in Experiment 1.

At first sight, Tables 6.2 and 6.3 might be seen to support the idea that Dutch is the source of the distribution of structures in English, since these frequencies bear some resemblance to the distribution of Dutch structures in Table 6.1 in the previous section, at least as far as the choice of verb-form in the protasis is concerned. Thus, it might be argued, the reason why Dutch learners put *woulds* into their protases is that they transfer the periphrastic conditional distribution from Dutch. However, such an explanation still does not account for the tendency for this error to fossilize. It says merely that Dutch and L2 English are structurally similar. Nor does it account for the clear differences in distribution revealed in Tables 6.1, 6.2 and 6.3 for the − / − structure in Dutch and L2 English past HCs.

As noted above, having subjects as their own controls permits us to compare Dutch and English responses on an individual and group basis. In fact, the application of a simple procedure we called *shift analysis* (Wekker *et al.*, 1982) enabled us to point out that the similarities between Dutch and English performance were less apparent once one began to examine behavior

Table 6.2. *Experiment 1 — Relationships between "non-past" and "past" HCs, and the preference for English HC structures per proficiency group*

English structure	Non-past		
	1st year	2nd year	3rd year
+/+	56 (75%)	59 (81%)	22 (47%)
−/+	19 (25%)	14 (19%)	25 (53%)
+/−	0	0	0
−/−	0	0	0
	Past		
	1st year	2nd year	3rd year
+/+	20 (24%)	8 (10%)	7 (12%)
−/+	60 (73%)	73 (88%)	50 (85%)
+/−	1 (1%)	0	0
−/−	2 (2%)	2 (2%)	2 (3%)

Table 6.3. *Experiment 2 — Relationships between "non-past" and "past" HCs, and the preference for English HC structures per proficiency group*

English structure	Non-past		
	1st year	2nd year	3rd year
+/+	77 (56%)	55 (45%)	22 (25%)
−/+	44 (32%)	56 (46%)	61 (70%)
+/−	17 (12%)	8 (7%)	3 (3%)
−/−	2 (1%)	3 (2%)	2 (2%)
	Past		
	1st year	2nd year	3rd year
+/+	57 (41%)	22 (18%)	11 (13%)
−/+	68 (49%)	97 (79%)	75 (85%)
+/−	6 (4%)	1 (1%)	1 (1%)
−/−	9 (6%)	2 (2%)	1 (1%)

beyond the level of the group. Shift analysis compares performance in the two languages for each subject on the same stimulus and notes (a) whether the same or different structures are chosen in both languages, and (b) if different structures are chosen, what the direction of the change is (i.e. towards the target English structure, or towards another Dutch-like structure).

The analysis reveals that 50 percent of the English responses were shifts and that shifting was overwhelmingly in the direction of either the correct −/+ structure or +/+ structure in both experiments. The percentage of shifts to

Table 6.4. *Proportion of total shifts to* +/+ *contributed by each proficiency group*

(*Not calculated as frequencies too small)

	Non-past		Past	
	Expt. 1*	Expt. 2	Expt. 1	Expt. 2
1st year	—	.56	.61	.58
2nd year	—	.31	.18	.27
3rd year	—	.13	.22	.15

Table 6.5. *Factors by which frequency of shifts to* −/+ *exceeds shifts to* +/+

(*These figures are based on very small +/+ frequencies, see Table 6.3)

	Non-past		Past	
	Expt. 1*	Expt. 2	Expt. 1	Expt. 2
1st year	8	1.55	2.35	1.14
2nd year	0	4.50	11.10	3.08
3rd year	23	12.25	5.67	5.57

+/+ contributed by each group is proficiency-related, with first year students providing the most (Table 6.4). The ratio of shifts to −/+ against shifts to +/+ shows another clear proficiency-related progression (Table 6.5). Taken together, Tables 6.4 and 6.5 show that increasing nominal proficiency goes hand-in-hand with more native-like performance on HC structure. However, Table 6.2 reveals that even third year students do not behave like native speakers. To sum up, shift analysis revealed that subjects did not merely use the same structure in English as they did in Dutch. All groups showed at least some tendency to select +/+ as the English target, irrespective of their choice in Dutch. As a result, alternative explanations for the occurrence of this structure will have to be sought.

An alternative explanation

Structural disambiguation

In this section I shall propose that the influence of the L1 in the acquisition of English hypothetical conditionals is a great deal more subtle than a simple structural comparison of Dutch and English conditionals might suggest. I shall argue that the difficulty experienced by Dutch learners with these structures is related to their attempts to deal with polysemous verb morphology in English and Dutch HCs, and with the subtle differences in meaning that exist between formally similar structures in the two languages. The solution which Dutch learners come up with, double *would* constructions, seems consistent with solutions to a number of other acquisition problems discussed elsewhere in the literature. Furthermore, it also resembles observable tendencies in the HCs of a number of standard and non-standard languages.

Recall that Dutch HCs may use either modal past tenses (preterite and pluperfect) or periphrastic conditionals with *zou(den)* + infinitive in HCs. We have seen that there are clear differences in distribution between the various structural possibilities permitted by Dutch, and I have claimed that these differences reflect grammatically encoded meaning distinctions in terms of the degree of speaker commitment to the realizability of the propositions in protasis and apodosis.

I have assumed that in Dutch HCs, the preterite expresses an *irrealis* condition in present and indefinite time-frames, not only on the basis of contextual clues, but also because of its unacceptability in HCs with future time adjuncts. But this is the modal meaning of the preterite, which tense form normally refers to *real* situations occurring in past time frames. Modal and non-modal meanings of the preterite therefore differ along two dimensions (hypotheticality and time-frame). As James points out:

> it is not normally the case that in order to learn where it is proper to use a past tense morpheme to indicate past time, what native speakers must do is memorise a list of specific constructions. But in the case where a past tense morpheme is being used to indicate the hypothetical, that is precisely what native speakers must do ... this means that the use of the morpheme in question ... to indicate past time and its use to indicate the hypothetical are not really parallel. The former use is normally regular and productive; the latter use is typically irregular and idiosyncratic. (James 1982:398)

Accordingly, I shall call the modal meaning of the past tense the *marked* meaning.

The pluperfect tense also has a normal reading (real, "past-in-the-past", Leech, 1971:42), and a marked, modal meaning (counterfactual, past). Unlike in the previous case, however, the semantic distance between the two meanings is principally along the hypotheticality dimension and is not as striking as in the case of the preterite.

Our data suggest that Dutch learners of English at advanced levels are unwilling to transfer the marked modal meanings of the Dutch past tenses to their formal English equivalents. If they did so, they would be imbuing the English past tenses with the same idiosyncratic meaning that they know is permitted in Dutch. This is a subtle form of crosslinguistic influence, in that the

L1's role is to constrain the form that the developing interlanguage may take rather than to provide a structure for copying over into the L2.

This reluctance to permit an equally marked structure in English is particularly understandable in the case of the preterite, because the mismatch between unmarked and marked meaning is greater here than in the case of the pluperfect. It is relevant to note that this reluctance to allow marked forms in L2 HCs may well be developmental, since Klein (1982), in a replication of Wekker, Kellerman and Hermans (1982) with less proficient Dutch school-age subjects, shows that structural transfer occurred much more frequently (particularly in the form of non-shifted $-/-$ in past HCs) than it did in the data from advanced learners described above (Wekker *et al.*, 1982).

Even though learners are unwilling to transfer the marked reading of the Dutch preterite and pluperfect to their English equivalents, they are, of course, still able to produce HCs, since Dutch provides the $+/+$ structure as an alternative. We have argued earlier that this latter structure is the default structure in Dutch. Once we accept that this is so, we see that advanced Dutch learners of English transfer the default structure to English, whatever they do in Dutch.

Thus Dutch learners of English sacrifice the grammatical distinction that Dutch makes between *potentialis* and *irrealis* conditionals in response to the structural ambiguity of the preterite. This sacrifice is not in fact particularly great, since as in other languages like English and French, the degree of commitment by the speaker to the falsity of the proposition expressed in the protasis can also be inferred from the context in which the HC is embedded, or from other knowledge sources. Thus the Dutch learner can effectively avoid the preterite in English HCs, reserving the periphrastic conditional tense as the sole means of marking hypothetical meaning in HCs.

Furthermore, this solution to the problem of how to form HCs in the L2 is, from a strictly communicative point of view, unlikely to engender negative feedback from native speakers of English (except of the metalinguistic sort in pedagogical environments), since the $+/+$ structure is unlikely to cause misunderstandings amongst native speakers. This fact, the fact that there are subtle meaning differences between the Dutch and English uses of the marked modal forms, and the reluctance on the part of the advanced learners to assign marked status to the English preterite would seem to conspire to keep the English input opaque.

Supporting evidence. The interpretation of the $+/+$ error made by Dutch learners thus rests on two assumptions: (a) learners will not use modal past tenses in English HCs because of their marked status, and (b) Dutch provides an alternative structure which expresses hypotheticality and is indifferent towards the *potentialis — irrealis* distinction. We must now look for evidence which supports this particular interpretation. There seem to be two sorts which are relevant. The first derives from acquisitional studies where learners react against structural ambiguity. The second derives from the examination of HCs in various languages where similar tendencies are apparent in non-acquisitional settings.

Evidence from first and second language acquisition. Dutch learners of English are not the only ones to make $+/+$ errors. Nemser (1974:57), for example, reports that many Hungarian learners "overtly indicate contingency in both the protasis and apodosis of conditional sentences" by inserting *would* in both clauses. Hebrew-speaking learners make the same error (Levenston, 1970:214), and it has also been reported for Czech (Vladimir Mach, personal communication), Finnish (Kari Sajavaara, personal communication), German (frequent personal observation), Polish (Waldemar Marton, personal communication) and Serbo-Croatian learners.

In all these cases, there are good structural reasons why the error should occur, since hypotheticality is marked explicitly in both clauses in all the relevant L1s. In Hungarian, for instance (Tompa, 1968:100–1), non-past HCs require the present conditional tense in both clauses, while past HCs require the perfect indicative plus a particle *volna* (historically the conditional form of the verb *to be*). Similarly, Hebrew and Polish require parallel marking in both clauses (viz. Hebrew *im hayita oved, hayita macliax* — "if you worked, you would succeed", Polish *gdybyś pracował odniósłbyś sukces* — "if you worked/ had worked, you would succeed/would have succeeded").

For our purposes, the most directly relevant study is the one reported by Trévise (1979). She found that her subjects, French first and second year university students of English, (1) had great difficulty in forming English HCs, (2) made $+/+$ errors when they did form them, and (3) in some cases altered correct $-/+$ HCs to incorrect $+/+$ in a subsequent editing phase. French is like English in not marking counterfactuality in HCs grammatically. The protasis requires an imperfect or pluperfect indicative, depending on the time frame, and the apodosis a corresponding conditional or conditional perfect (though see below). Thus French learners are also faced with the problem of coping with the modal meaning of what is formally a past tense in French and expressing it in English.

From a contrasting point of view, it is much more difficult to explain away Trévise's findings by an appeal to a structural description of French, since the standard language does not permit a double conditional structure. Instead, if a crosslinguistic explanation was insisted upon, one would have to invoke non-standard varieties of the language and show that it was these that influenced learners rather than the standard language. We return to this point below. In the literature of second language acquisition there is further evidence that learners will not transfer (or are reluctant to transfer) L1 features which they consider marked. This reluctance to resort to the L1 may be developmental, as I suggested above with respect to the Klein (1982) study, and may happen despite the nature of the target input. That is to say, even where the L2 and the L1 are equivalent, learners may behave as if they were not. (For a discussion of this phenomenon, see Kellerman, 1985.)

For instance, in studies of second language acquisition, Kellerman (e.g. 1982, 1986) showed that Dutch learners of English and German did not tolerate the same degree of polysemy in L2 lexical items as they knew existed in their L1 equivalents. Furthermore, the various meanings of the polysemous lexical items in Dutch were reallocated to other lexical structures in the L2 as a function of the perceived resemblance of those meanings to the *prototypical* (unmarked) meaning of the polysemous lexical items – the greater the distance from this prototype, the stronger the assumption by the learner of non-equivalence between the two languages, irrespective of the actual linguistic facts.

Similarly, Hoeks (1985) showed that Dutch learners translated polysemous Dutch nouns into English according to the semantic distance they perceived between them – the greater the distance, the more likely more than one translation equivalent would be sought, even if ultimately they could not find one. In the same vein, Ijaz (1985) found that learners of high proficiency from various linguistic backgrounds (principally German and Urdu) tended to transfer the prototypical meanings of L1 prepositions to their English equivalents, while less proficient ones assumed that L1 and L2 were semantically equivalent.

Gass and Ard (1984) studied Spanish and Japanese learners' responses to tense usage in English, and found that they were more likely to accept (and produce) prototypical meanings of tenses than secondary ones, even where, as in the case of Spanish, L1 and L2 overlapped. In all these second language cases, learners often assumed non-equivalence between L1 and L2 when there frequently was such equivalence. In first language acquisition, Karmiloff-Smith (1979) has shown that French-speaking children reanalyze structures with two meanings they had previously used in adult-like fashion so as to give each meaning a unique linguistic form. In doing this, they create a novel, if plausible, form for one of the meanings, retaining the original form exclusively for the other meaning. Later, these same children recombine both meanings into the original single form, and the novel form disappears.

Supporting evidence from other languages. I have claimed above that the preponderance of the + / + error in the English of Dutch learners comes about as a result of their unwillingness to assign modal meaning to past tense forms in the L2, since this is the marked meaning. In fact, although past tenses are widely used to express hypotheticality in the world's languages (James, 1982), we can also adduce evidence from a number of languages which shows that the tendency to disambiguate verb morphology in HCs is not unique to Dutch learners of English. Let us begin with Dutch.

(a) Clause order and verb morphology in Dutch

Despite the fact that Dutch allows past tenses of lexical verbs in both protasis and apodosis, native speakers often indicate a dislike of the past tense in an apodosis that has been preposed. Thus while

> (26) Als je zoiets zou doen, schopte ik je zo de trap af
> If you such-a-thing would do, I kicked-PRET you downstairs
> (If you did such a thing, I'd kick you downstairs)

is, as we have seen, perfectly acceptable to native speakers, the following is less so:

> (27) ?Ik schopte je zo de trap af als je zoiets zou doen (cf. Nieuwint, 1984)
> I kicked-PRET you downstairs, if you such-a-thing would do

Instead there is an expressed preference for the periphrastic conditional in a preposed apodosis, viz.

> (28) Ik zou je zo de trap afschoppen als je zoiets zou doen
> I would kick you downstairs if you such-a-thing would do

A perusal of the Nijmegen HC corpus (c. 700 sentences, as mentioned above) clearly supports native speaker intuitions on this point. The corpus shows that Dutch, like other languages, favors the order protasis-apodosis (Greenberg, 1963; Ford and Thompson, 1986; Comrie, 1986).[7] About 70 percent of HCs in our corpus have that order (450:192). However, when we analyze clause order by structure type (i.e. $+/+$, $-/+$, $-/-$, $+/-$), we find that, proportionately, the distribution of clause order is not evenly spread.

Of the 386 HCs with $/+$ apodoses in our corpus, only c. 60 percent have the order protasis-apodosis (233:153), while of the 158 HCs with $/-$ apodoses, as many as c. 84 percent have this order (133:25). This distribution is not sensitive to time frame. C. 59 percent of non-past (166:113) and c. 54 percent of past $/+$ apodoses (44:37) have this order; the comparable figures for $/-$ apodoses are c. 90 percent (26:3) and c. 82 percent (97:22).[8]

Comrie (1986) notes that in the world's languages the protasis is more usually overtly marked as non-factual than the apodosis (i.e. via a subordinating conjunction like *if*), which might be thought to explain why protases tend to precede apodoses. However, Comrie points out that this cannot be the whole story, since it would lead to the prediction that in those (few) languages where only the apodosis is explicitly marked for non-factuality, it should more frequently precede the protasis than in cases where it is not so marked. There is apparently no evidence in favor of this hypothesis.

In fact, in a language like Mandarin, the protasis must precede the apodosis, whether either, both, or neither is marked for hypotheticality.[9] As Comrie and others point out, and as we have already seen above, in English it is quite possible to have minatory/promissory conditionals without any explicit hypothetical marking, of the type *Laugh and the world laughs with you*, where no one would interpret the protasis as an injunction to act. Even if the change in verb forms was originally related to the avoidance of the momentary ambiguity between real and hypothetical meaning, it seems to have long been grammaticized (Comrie, 1986). Nevertheless it is difficult to see what else could be motivating the clear trend against preposed/− protases in our Dutch data if it is not the absence of specific grammatical "priming" of the modal meaning of the verb.

(b) Structural disambiguation in German HCs

Similarly, there is evidence in German that verb forms that are structurally ambiguous in HCs will be avoided. In HCs, German may either use the subjunctive or a periphrastic conditional with *würden + infinitive*. However, the subjunctive is avoided when this verb form is indistinguishable from the preterite.[10] In such cases the periphrastic conditional is preferred:

> (29) (a) Wenn es regnen würde, ... (If it rain would)
>   (b) ?Wenn es regnete, ... (If it rain-SUBJUNCTIVE)

On the other hand, if the subjunctive and past tense are not formally identical, then either the periphrastic conditional or subjunctive seem permissible:

> (30) (a) Wenn er kommen würde, ... (If he come would)
>   (b) Wenn er käme, ... (If he came-SUBJUNCTIVE)

Cf.

> (c) Wenn es regnete, kam er spät nach hause
>   (Whenever it rained-PRET, he would come-PRET home late)

(c) Evidence from French

As noted above, in standard French there is no structural correlate of +/+ in conditionals introduced by the subordinating conjunction *si*. Non-past HCs require the imperfect indicative in the protasis and the conditional in the apodosis, while past HCs require the pluperfect and the conditional perfect in the two clauses: *si j'avais le temps, je t'expliquerais/si j'avais eu le temps, je t'aurais expliqué*. However, in non-literary, informal French, where protasis and apodosis are simply juxtaposed or co-ordinated without *si*, the conditional tense is obligatory in both clauses, and the order must be protasis-apodosis:

(31) J'aurais le temps, je t'expliquerais (see also Posner, 1976)[11]

Furthermore, it has been observed that although clearly stigmatised (e.g. Grévisse, 1964:1081), the conditional tense does occur in *si*-protases in *le français populaire*. Interestingly in this respect, Claire Blanche-Benveniste (personal communication) has recorded that, in reading aloud, French children up to as late as ten years of age may spontaneously replace the imperfect or pluperfect tense of protases introduced by *si* with a conditional tense. Again we see that the standard language avoids past indicative tenses in protases where they are not preceded by a subordinator. That the conditional should appear in *si*-less clauses again suggests a response designed to obviate the structural ambiguity of past tense forms.

(d) Evidence from English

While standard descriptions of both British and American English insist that *would* cannot appear in the protases of HCs (except in one or two minor cases, e.g. where *would* is volitional), it is nevertheless not difficult to find contemporary and historical evidence for its existence. Non-standard usage is reputedly common in informal American speech and is occasionally detected in adult British speakers:

(32) I would have been much more happier if he wouldn't have head-butted me
     (Professional boxer, BBC Radio 4)

It should be pointed out, however, that the present author could not find one clear example of a *would* protasis in either the Brown or Lund-Oslo-Bergen English corpora.

However, examples of protases containing *would* or its Middle English equivalents may be attested as early as c. 1225 (Visser, 1963:1731):

(33) Her may me waiten for to slo; and *yf* he were brought of Liue. And mine
     children *wolden thriue*, Louerdings after me Of al Denemark mihten he be
     (They would wait for me to slay; and if they were killed and my children would
     thrive, princes after me of all Denmark might they be)

They are also attested among young American children (Kuczaj and Daly, 1979), although this might merely reflect the input:

(34) If you would have eated all that turkey, your tummy would have kersploded (age
     3.11)

A second non-standard variant in the protasis is common in both British and

American English. This is *intrusive have* (Fillmore, 1985), combined with '*d* in sentences like *If I'd've known you were coming, I'd've baked a cake.* In the spoken language, it does not seem stigmatized, though it is railed against by purists such as Fowler (1965).[12] In fact, Lambert (1983, cited by Fillmore, 1985) claims that the use of *intrusive have* in British English does not vary according to social class, and native speakers tend not to be aware of using it.

In American English it has long been recognised as very common (see Visser, 1973:2423 for sources). In England, examples may be found going back to c. 1400 (Visser, 1973:2425), where contrary to current practice, *would* did not appear in the apodosis either:

> (35) and (= if) I had natte have had that mony of William Barwell at that tyme, I had lost all my platte (1475–88)

Fillmore (1985) argues that *d'have* is not to be treated as a colloquial variant of the standard pluperfect, since one cannot say

> (36) *At that time I hadn't have opened your letter

as a variant of

> (37) At that time I hadn't opened your letter

or

> (38) *She telephoned me as soon as she'd've finished eating dinner

for

> (39) She telephoned me as soon as she'd finished eating dinner

Intrusive have can only be used now in the protases of past HCs or other clauses expressing hypotheticality, e.g. these contemporary (British) examples from Fillmore (1985) and elsewhere:

> (40) (a) If I'd've known Renoir was this popular, I would never have come – *Punch* cartoon
> (b) I wish I hadn't've said that
> (c) By the time you'd've noticed it, it'd've been too late

Thus Fillmore suggests that all the evidence points to the fact that *intrusive have* is an explicit marker of counterfactuality (a view shared by Visser, 1973:2424); for reasons explored earlier, it would be more accurate to call it an explicit marker of hypotheticality in a past time frame.

In all the above cases where HC morphology has been discussed, there seems to be evidence for a process of grammatical disambiguation of past tenses. While in established languages such tendencies cannot realistically be associated with ease-of-processing requirements, in the case of learners of English this is very likely to be the motivating force. We have seen that the same tendencies appear when learners are confronted with other structures with multiple meanings. The result of such disambiguation should be a structure with greater perceived isomorphism between form and meaning and a correspondingly smaller processing load for the learner. Since this tendency is discernible in a number of differing linguistic contexts, we may call it a natural tendency.

Morphological symmetry in protasis and apodosis

In the cases illustrated so far, there has been an inclination to reanalyze past tenses into other verb forms in HCs. It will not have escaped notice that the resultant change in the protasis frequently leads to morphological symmetry in the verb in protasis and apodosis. In fact there are many standard languages which require identical morphosyntactic constructions in the two clauses of a hypothetical conditional sentence.[13] Furthermore, in addition to the English, French, German and Dutch examples discussed above, there are other non-standard variants of languages not normally having symmetry where symmetry is, or is becoming, the norm.[14] Again we may speak of a natural tendency in languages.

As Posner (1976) and others have noted, many Romance varieties show morphological symmetry in protasis and apodosis (as was the case in Classical Latin). Posner states that it is actually the standard versions of these languages (and Catalan) that constitute the exception (though Rumanian does have symmetry). Symmetry is simply a pervasive phenomenon in Romance languages. Posner thus rejects crosslinguistic influence as the source of parallelism (in the form of si + -rais/-rais) in Canadian French (attributed to American English), in North African French (Spanish), or in Belgian French (Flemish). Similarly, says Posner, there is no need to attribute intrusive would in New York City English to Yiddish.

Now the appearance of morphological symmetry in HCs does not automatically entail the selection of one particular set of tenses rather than another (i.e. past tenses versus periphrastic conditionals or subjunctives). For instance, in addition to the conditional, some Italian dialects require their HCs to have two imperfect indicatives, and others imperfect subjunctives (Posner, 1976; Pountain, 1983; Harris, 1986). In any case, whatever the verb forms chosen, this preference for symmetry in the HCs of so many differing languages is striking. For Haiman (1986:221), the semantic symmetry of protasis and apodosis is reflected in their morphological symmetry.

Dutch and French learners of English show a similar trend towards verb–morphological symmetry. However, as will by now be obvious, a tendency towards symmetry alone is not sufficient "explanation" for the appearance of symmetrical structures noted in their English. If it were, we could equally well expect to find symmetrical structures with past tenses, but such structures, common enough in Dutch, are very rare among advanced Dutch learners, as we have seen. Thus, in the case of Dutch learners, the drive towards disambiguation takes precedence over the drive towards symmetry. The same could be said for French learners of English. However, in the case of Dutch learners, the presence of a "default" + / + with double *zouden* in Dutch may have a catalytic effect on their English; in the case of French, this is less clear.

That disambiguation leads to selection by the learner of a periphrastic conditional in English should not be surprising. Like *zouden* and *-rais*, *would* is an explicit marker of hypotheticality. + / + morphology is therefore simultaneously unambiguous and symmetrical; it is maximally semantically transparent (Slobin, 1977, 1980; Langacker, 1977; Naro, 1978; Kellerman, 1983; Andersen, 1984; Seuren and Wekker, 1986).

This leaves us with one problem. Why do Dutch learners on the whole find it easier to produce the desired English − / + HC in past environments than in non-past environments? That is, why do they move from the highly frequent Dutch − / − to English − / +, rather than to + / + ? After all, − / + is neither maximally transparent nor morphologically symmetrical.[15]

One possibility is that learners might feel less need to avoid the pluperfect in a past environment, because the modal meaning is closer to the non-modal meaning than is the case in non-past HCs. This might make the modal meaning of the English pluperfect more salient in the input, especially as, like Dutch, it will usually be interpreted as counterfactual. But this argument does not hold for the apodosis; the / + apodosis is normal in the L2 English of advanced learners, while the / − apodosis is the most common form in Dutch.

Perhaps the answer is really quite straightforward; these *are* advanced learners, and they do learn *something* about English HCs in all their years of study. It is the English protasis that is the locus of the acquisition problem, not the apodosis. The English apodosis requires *would* (or some other modal); it is therefore semantically transparent whether past or non-past, a fact which makes it salient and learnable.

Conclusion

In this chapter, I have proposed that Dutch learners of English produce double *would* structures such as *If I would be able to live all over again, I would be a gardener* in English HCs as a response to two tendencies. The first tendency is to avoid transferring the modal meaning of Dutch past tenses to English past tenses even though there is positive evidence for this in the input. Instead the modal meaning is reallocated to the explicitly hypothetical morpheme *would*, which is the equivalent of Dutch *zouden*. There is also evidence that under certain conditions even standard languages will avoid structurally ambiguous verb morphology in HCs. Similar attempts at disambiguation by learners are reported in other areas of the grammar in both the first and second language acquisition literature.

The outcome of the disambiguation process in many cases is a hypothetical conditional with symmetrical verb morphology in protasis and apodosis. This second tendency towards symmetry in HCs is to be found in the standard versions of many languages. It is also found in non-standard variants of those languages which do not normally permit it. Since learners of English from several language backgrounds also produce symmetrical HCs, these tendencies towards symmetry and towards structural disambiguation in learner language provide further evidence that interlanguages obey the same constraints as natural languages.

In the case of Dutch learners we see that the tendencies to disambiguate past tenses and to produce symmetrical morphology conspire to produce a characteristic error. While disambiguation of the past tense occurs in languages other than Dutch, and in non-Dutch learners of English, we should not ignore the fact that Dutch structure as perceived by the learner provides the environment in which these tendencies become apparent. There is therefore an interaction between natural tendencies and the native language.

The result of the interaction is a semantically transparent HC grammar which is simpler than both L1 and L2, in not using modal past tenses. Furthermore it is also simpler than Dutch in not making a morphological distinction between hypothetical and counterfactual. The reason why the +/+ error may fossilize may thus reside with the difficulty of overcoming these natural tendencies; however, the Dutch learner has also to discover that while English does have modal past tenses, their use in hypothetical conditionals is subtly different from the way they are used in Dutch. Such a suggestion, while entirely speculative at this stage and in no sense an explanation for fossilization, has an advantage over contrastive accounts in its appeal to the workings of languages in general.

Notes

I would like to thank Theo Bongaerts, Carlos Gussenhoven, Peter Jordens, Brian Wenk and Herman Wekker for comments on an earlier version of this paper.

1 Here are two examples. The first is taken from a recent book on computational linguistics: "If in a logical calculus a means *would* have to be built to establish their truth, one would have to create something that itself would be a model of the contents of the sentence ..." The second is from a report: "It would be unfortunate if our classification system *would* not enable us to break down the main types and investigate more superficial, formal, differences."

2 And of French, for that matter.
3 There are several types of conditionals. For a discussion, see Pountain (1983) and Traugott, ter Meulen, Reilly and Ferguson (1986).
4 Preposing the apodosis in English and Dutch also entails the obligatory absence of the correlative conjunction, viz. *Then the concert would be cancelled if it rained.
5 There are, of course, exceptions to this statement. The so-called "volitional" *would* is an obvious example. See, for instance, Nieuwint (1986).

Instead of the past tense or the pluperfect of a lexical verb, English highly hypothetical conditionals (HCs) may also allow a construction with *was/were to* or with *should*. These more formal and tentative types of HC (see Quirk, Greenbaum, Leech and Svartvik, 1985:1093–94) will not be considered here.

6 There may be some purely morphological factors affecting distribution which we have yet to investigate. In non-past time frames, the majority of verbs in −/ protases are highly frequent strong verbs with monosyllabic stems. In fact, seventeen such verbs or their derivatives accounted for c. 95 percent of the protases in −/+ and −/− sentences (*blijven, doen, gaan, hebben, komen, krijgen, kunnen, laten, liggen, moeten, mogen, rijden, staan, weten, worden, zeggen, zijn*); there were only five regular ones (*beschouwen, beweren, horen, leven, openen*).

However, there are fifty-eight different verbs in the protases of non-past +/+ HCs, including most of the above verbs, i.e. *doen, gaan, hebben, komen, krijgen, kunnen, laten, moeten, mogen, staan, worden, zeggen* and *zijn*. Together these latter verbs account for around 53 percent of all such +/ protases.

7 To be accurate, Greenberg, Ford and Thompson, and Comrie are dealing with conditional sentences of all types. Ford and Thompson's study is actually about frequencies of *if*-conditionals. However, this is unlikely to have any direct bearing on clause order. Of the 490 written conditional sentences they collected, 377 (77 percent) had the order protasis-apodosis; of the 406 spoken conditionals, 82 percent had this order.

8 Furthermore, when we consider "extraposed" HCs (cf. Pountain, 1983) where the apodosis contains a pronoun (usually subject or object of the clause) which refers to the whole protasis (e.g. *It would be nice if you could come*), the normal clause order is usually reversed. In our corpus there are 99 such extraposed HCs (c. 15 percent of the total); c. 76 percent of these HCs show the order apodosis-protasis (75:24).

The tendency not to prepose /− apodoses in HCs should be strongly apparent in extraposed HCs, since apodosis-protasis order is the norm. This is indeed the case. Of 153 /+ reversals, 68 are also extraposed (c. 44 percent); of the 25 /− reversals, a mere 3 (c. 12 percent) are also extraposed.

Given the state of our knowledge about the Dutch HC system, it is conceivable the differences between extraposed HCs and the rest are such that /− apodoses are excluded on grounds other than clause order. Certainly, the behavior of extraposed HCs is different from other HCs in some respects. We have mentioned that the order apodosis-protasis is the norm for extraposed HCs; furthermore, unlike ordinary HCs, extraposed HCs do not permit *dan* ("then") in the apodosis when this follows the protasis (*Als je zou kunnen komen dan zou het leuk zijn*).

However, even if we leave extraposed HCs out of consideration, the same trend against proposed /− apodoses remains. Approximately 27 percent of /+ apodoses precede their protases as against c. 14.5 percent of the /− apodoses.

9 Comrie (1986) notes that there are other languages where the protasis *must* precede the apodosis, such as Turkish and Ngiyambaa. In Dutch conditional–temporal sentences of the type *krijgt-ie de bal, scoort-ie* ("if he gets the ball, he scores") where there is no explicit subordinator marking conditionality, the first clause must be interpreted as the protasis. For a counterexample, see Comrie (1986:97). Haiman (1986:222) notes that apparent exceptions in English of the type *You're gonna kill yourself, you keep driving like that*, where the protasis follows the apodosis are also intonationally different from sentences where the protasis comes first.

10 The subjunctive is considered formal in any case and may be giving way to the periphrastic conditional in general. This does not alter the validity of the intuitions expressed here, however (Jürgen Meisel, personal communication). Norbert Dittmar (personal communication) adds that *regnete* in *Wenn es regnete – if it rained*, while correct, is more likely to be restricted to written language. He also adds that preference for the subjunctive or the periphrastic conditionals with *würden*, e.g. in cases where subjunctive and preterite do not coincide formally, may show regional variation.

11 Shana Poplack (personal communication) notes that forms like *j'avais le temps, je t'expliquerais* are produced by French-Canadians in addition to double conditionals.

12 Whether 'd is *would* or *had* is controversial. For discussion, see Visser (1973:2424) and Fillmore (1985).

Note in this respect the following quotation from James Joyce's *Dubliners* (Penguin Books, 1965:64): "He had a notion he was being had. He could imagine his friends talking of the affair and laughing. She *was* a little vulgar: sometimes she said: "I seen him" and "If I had've known". But what would grammar matter if he really loved her?"

13 In addition to those we have already mentioned (e.g. German, Dutch, Polish, Hebrew, etc.), we could also mention Russian, Latvian (Comrie, 1986), Rumanian (Mallinson, 1986:75–6), all of which may have conditional tenses in both clauses, and Ngiyambaa, an Australian language (Comrie, 1986). Haiman (1986:219–20) states that "many languages" (in addition to those just mentioned) have symmetrical verb forms in the two clauses of a HC. He names the following languages: Cebuano, certain New Guinea languages (Gende, Kobon, Daga, Maring), Pitta-Pitta (Australia) and Hausa.

14 For a relevant example, see Lavandera, 1975.

15 There are 196 Dutch — / — HCs in the experimental corpus in Wekker *et al.* (1982). C. 93 percent of these are past time. There are only 25 L2 — / — structures, of which 72 percent are past.

References

Akatsuka, N. (1986), Conditionals are discourse-bound. In Traugott, E., ter Meulen, A., Reilly, J. and Ferguson, C. (eds.), *On Conditionals*. Cambridge University Press.

Andersen, R. (1984), The one to one principle of interlanguage construction. *Language Learning* **34**. 77–95.

Comrie, B. (1986), Conditionals: a typology. In Traugott, E., ter Meulen, A., Reilly, J. and Ferguson, C. (eds.), *On Conditionals*. Cambridge University Press.

Davies, E. (1979), *On the Semantics of Syntax*. London: Croom Helm.

Dierikx, M. (1985), Dutch and English non-past counterfactuals. Unpublished M.A. thesis. Nijmegen University.

Fillmore, C. (1985), Syntactic intrusions and the notion of grammatical construction. *Berkeley Papers in Linguistics*.

Ford, C. and Thompson, S. (1986), Conditionals in discourse: a text-based study from English. In Traugott, E., ter Meulen, A., Reilly, J. and Ferguson, C. (eds.), *On Conditionals*. Cambridge University Press.

Fowler, H. (1965), *Dictionary of Modern English Usage*. Oxford University Press.

Gass, S. and Ard, J. (1984), Second language acquisition and the ontology of language universals. In Rutherford, W. (ed.), *Language Universals and Second Language Acquisition*. Amsterdam: John Benjamins.

Gass, S. and Selinker, L. (eds.) (1983), *Language Transfer in Language Learning*. Rowley, MA: Newbury House.

Geerts, G., Haserijn, W., de Rooij, J. and v.d. Toorn, M. (1984), *Algemene Nederlandse Spraakkunst*. Groningen: Wolters Noordhoff.

Greenberg, J. (1963), Some universals of grammar with particular reference to the order of meaningful elements. In Greenberg, J. (ed.), *Universals of Language*. Cambridge, MA: MIT Press.

Grévisse, M. (1964), *Le bon usage*. Gembloux: Editions G. Duculot.

Haiman, J. (1986), Constraints on the form and meaning of the protasis. In Traugott, E., ter Meulen, A., Reilly, J. and Ferguson, C. (eds.), *On Conditionals*. Cambridge University Press.

Harris, J. (1986), The historical development of *si*-clauses in Romance. In Traugott, E., ter Meulen, A., Reilly, J. and Ferguson, C. (eds.) *On Conditionals*. Cambridge University Press.

Hoeks, J. (1985), Transfer of homonymy and polysemy with special reference to Dutch and English. Unpublished M. A. thesis. Nijmegen University.

Ijaz, H. (1985), Native language and cognitive constraints on the meaning ascribed to select English spatial prepositions by advanced adult second language learners of English. Unpublished Ph.D. thesis. University of Toronto.

James, D. (1982), Past tense and hypotheticality: a crosslinguistic study. *Studies in Language* **6**. 375–403.

Karmiloff-Smith, A. (1979), *A Functional Approach to Child Language*. Cambridge University Press.

Kellerman, E. (1982), Predicting transferability from semantic space. *Studia Anglica Posnaniensia* **14**, 198–219.

  (1983), Now you see it, now you don't. In: Gass, S. and Selinker, L. (eds.), *Language Transfer in Language Learning*.

  (1985), If at first you *do* succeed ... In: Gass, S. and Madden, C. (eds.), *Input in Second Language Acquisition*. Rowley, MA: Newbury House.

  (1986), An eye for an eye: crosslinguistic constraints on the development of the L2 lexicon. In Kellerman, E. and Sharwood Smith, M. (eds.), *Crosslinguistic Influence in Second Language Acquisition*. Oxford: Pergamon Press.

Klein, A. (1982), Once a plus/plusser, always a plus/plusser? On conditionals. Unpublished term paper. University of Utrecht.

Klein, W. (1986), *Second Language Acquisition*. Cambridge University Press.

Kuczaj, S. and M. Daly, (1979), The development of hypothetical reference in the speech of young children. *Journal of Child Language* **6**, 563–579.

Lambert, V. (1983), The non-standard third conditional in English: a sociolinguistic study. Unpublished M.A. thesis. Reading University.

Langacker, R. (1977), Syntactic re-analysis. In Li, C. (ed.), *Mechanisms in Syntactic Change*. Austin: University of Texas Press.

Lavandera, B. (1975), Linguistic structure and sociolinguistic conditioning in the use of verbal endings in *si*-clauses in Buenos Aires Spanish. Unpublished Ph.D. dissertation. University of Pennsylvania.

Leech, G. (1971), *Meaning and the English Verb*. London: Longman.

Levenston, E. (1970), *English for Israelis*. Jerusalem: Israel Universities Press.

Mallinson, G. (1986), *Rumanian*. London: Croom Helm.

Naro, A. (1978), A study of the origins of pidginisation. *Language* **54**, 314–347.

Nemser, W. (1974), Approximative systems of foreign language learners. In Richards, J. (ed.), *Error Analysis*. London: Longman.

Nieuwint, P. (1984), Werkwoordstijden in nederlandse counterfactuals. *De Nieuwe Taalgids* **77**. 542–555.

  (1986), Present and future in conditional protases. *Linguistics* **24**, 371–392.

Posner, R. (1976), The relevance of comparative and historical data for the description and definition of a language. *York Papers in Linguistics* **6**, 75–87.

Pountain, C. (1983), *Structure and Transformations: the Romance Verb*. London: Croom Helm.

Quirk, R., Greenbaum, S., Leech, G. and Svartvik, J. (1985), *A Comprehensive Grammar of the English Language*. London: Longman.

Richards, J. (ed.) (1974), *Error Analysis*. London: Longman.

Scarcella, R. (1983), Discourse accent in second language performance. In Gass, S. and L. Selinker (eds.), *Language Transfer in Language Learning*. Rowley, MA: Newbury House.

Selinker, L. (1974), Interlanguage. In Richards, J. (ed.), *Error Analysis*. London: Longman.

Seuren, P. and Wekker, H. (1986), Semantic transparency as a factor in creole genesis. In Muysken, P. and Smith, N. (eds.), *Substrata Versus Universals in Creole Languages.* Amsterdam: John Benjamins.

Slobin, D. (1977), Language change in childhood and in history. In Macnamara, J. (ed.), *Language Learning and Thought.* London: Academic Press.

  (1980), The repeated path between transparency and opacity in language. In Bellugi, U. and Studdert-Kennedy, M. (eds.), *Signed and Spoken Language: Biological Constraints on Linguistic Form.* Weinheim: Verlag Chemie.

Tompa, J. (1968), *Ungarische Grammatik.* The Hague: Mouton.

Traugott, E., ter Meulen, A., Reilly, J. and Ferguson, C. (eds.) (1986), *On conditionals.* Cambridge University Press.

Trévise, A. (1979), Spécificité de l'énonciation didactique dans l'apprentissage de l'anglais par des étudiants francophones. *Encrages.* Numéro spéciale de linguistique appliquée. 44–52.

Van Es, G. and Van Caspel, P. (1975), *Syntaxis van het moderne Nederlands.* Reeks 1. Nr. 48. Archief voor de Nederlandse Syntaxis. Rijksuniversiteit Groningen. The Netherlands.

Visser, F. (1963), *A Historical Syntax of the English Language.* Part one. Leiden: E. J. Brill.

  (1973), *A Historical Syntax of the English Language.* Part three. Leiden: E. J. Brill.

Wekker, H., Kellerman, E. and Hermans, R. (1982), Trying to see the "would" for the trees. *Interlanguage Studies Bulletin* **6**. 22–55.

7. Spanish, Japanese and Chinese speakers' acquisition of English relative clauses: new evidence for the head-direction parameter[1]

SUZANNE FLYNN

Consistent with the general theme of this book, my purpose in this paper is to discuss system interaction in bilingualism. While many of the chapters focus on the normal and abnormal interaction of different aspects of language in speakers who have learned two or more languages simultaneously, I focus on the adult learner's acquisition of a second language, or sequential bilingualism in traditional terms. Within this context, I consider the relative contributions of past first language (L1) experience and processes independent of this in second language (L2) learning. I argue that the parameter-setting model of Universal Grammar (UG) hypothesized for L1 acquisition provides an explanatory framework within which to integrate these two components. In addition, I argue that this work can clarify our understanding of questions and issues related to normal and abnormal bilingual processing in much the same manner that investigations of this sort inform theories of L1 acquisition. In adult L2 learning we are dealing with sophisticated learners whose pragmatic and general cognitive abilities are for the most part fully developed. In both child L1 acquisition and in the simultaneous acquisition of two languages, we are often working with individuals who are at immature stages both in terms of their language abilities and in terms of their general pragmatic and cognitive development. If, in investigations of adult L2 learning, developmental patterns emerge that are also found in L1 acquisition, then these patterns cannot be attributed to impairments or deficits in general cognitive abilities alone, but might be argued to follow from properties that characterize the language faculty itself, as an independent domain of human cognition. In addition, if we find differences in these patterns among various L1 language groups learning a common L2, then these results could be argued to follow from the interaction of specific properties of the L1 and the L2 in the learning of the target language. Documenting these sets of patterns very precisely can provide new evidence with which to resolve issues surrounding current debates about domain specificity and properties of general cognition in language learning. They can also contribute essentially to our understanding of the interplay of these two components in functional bilinguals by allowing us, for example, to determine which aspects of a successful bilingual's language abilities are facilitated by general learning strategies and which are not. Finally, they can aid in our understanding of how, within this context, properties of two or more systems of language might interact at some level.

In this paper I will report results of an empirical study that demonstrate the importance of the role of the head–initial/head–final parameter in adult L2 acquisition of English. Original support for this model derived from an investigation of the head–direction parameter in adult L2 acquisition of null and pronoun anaphora in adverbial adjunct clauses. This paper extends this work to an investigation of bound variables in English restrictive relative clause structures (RRCs). In this paper, I will first summarize the results from previous studies; I will then report the new set of supporting data for the developing parameter-setting model of L2 acquisition.

Background

The general parameter-setting model of language and language acquisition assumed in this paper is a familiar one. Chomsky (1975, 1980, 1981, 1982, 1986a,b) has proposed this model in order to account for both the diversity of languages and for the rapid and uniform development of language among children on the basis of a fixed set of principles. As such, it is both a theory of the properties of grammars and a theory of the biological endowment for language with which all individuals are uniformly and uniquely endowed. As a theory of a domain specific faculty of human cognition, UG "provides a sensory system for the preliminary analysis of linguistic data and a schematism that determines quite narrowly a certain class of grammars" (Chomsky, 1975:12). Essentially, the mediation of UG in language learning restricts the infinite number of false leads that could be provided by random induction from unguided experience of surface data (Lust, 1986).

As a theory of grammars, UG attempts to provide "a system of principles, conditions, and rules that are elements or properties of all human languages, not merely by accident, but by necessity" (Chomsky, 1975:29). These rules and principles specified by UG should rule out an infinite set of grammars that do not conform to these fundamental properties. UG specifies those aspects of rules and principles that are uniformly attained in language but underdetermined by evidence. In addition, a number of these principles are associated with parameters. Parameters specify dimensions of structural variation across all languages. The values of these parameters are fixed by experience gained in the language learning process. Setting the parameters in one way or another will have a set of deductive consequences for the rest of the grammar. One such parameter is the head–initial/head–final parameter of X-bar theory (Stowell, 1981). Languages, in general, can be shown to differ with respect to the placement of a head (for example a noun in a noun phrase construction, and a verb in a verb phrase construction), in relation to its complements. In English, complements follow their heads such that we have noun–complement, verb–complement, etc. whereas in Japanese, complements precede their heads yielding complement–noun, complement–verb type structures. Setting the parameter in one way gets you English; setting the parameter in another way gets you Japanese.

In acquisition, the principles of UG initially constrain the range of possibilities logically allowed for language thereby restricting the possibilities for language learning. Setting the parameters of a language limits these possibilities even more.

UG and L2 acquisition

UG as a theory of acquisition characterizes L1 learning and does not make explicit predictions about L2 acquisition. However, if principles of UG do in fact characterize a language faculty that is biologically determined and that is necessary for the acquisition of an L1, then it seems quite reasonable to assume that principles of UG also play a role in L2 acquisition. Operating on just this assumption, I have attempted to construct a model of L2 learning that is consistent with a UG formulation of language and language learning. That is, one that accounts for L2 acquisition in terms of principles and parameters isolated in the L1 acquisition process (Flynn 1981, 1983a,b, 1984, 1985, 1987a, 1987b; Flynn and Espinal, 1985).

In this parameter-setting model, L2 learners are argued to use principles of syntactic organization isolated in L1 acquisition in the construction of the L2 grammar. Where principles involve parameters, L2 learners from the early stages of acquisition recognize differences in the values of these parameters between the L1 and the L2. In the cases in which the L1 and the L2 values differ, L2 acquisition is disrupted as learners must and do assign new values to cohere with the L2 grammar. Where the L1 and the L2 match, L2 learners can use this value in the construction of the L2 grammar. That is to say, L2 learners will not duplicate structures already available to them from their L1s. If these hypotheses are correct, we would expect two distinct patterns of acquisition. In the first case, the pattern corresponds to an early acquisition stage in English in which the learner is working out the basic structural configuration of the L1. In the second case, in which the L1 and the L2 match in head-direction, the developmental pattern should correspond to a later L1 stage of acquisition – one in which the learners have already established the basic structural configuration of the language and are now at a point at which they attempt to integrate this structure with the working out of the sentence level properties of the L2.

There are two important features of this model for L2 learning. First, L2 learners are claimed to use structural principles isolated in L1 acquisition in their construction of the L2 grammar. This aspect of the proposed model allows us to account for similarities between L1 and L2 acquisition that have been observed in the literature – a component of L2 learning captured by the Creative Construction (CC) model of Dulay and Burt (1974). Second, within this model, the L1 experience is important to the extent that it determines whether or not assignment of a new value for a structural parameter of language is necessary or not. That is, a match or mismatch in values of parameters associated with principles of UG determines whether or not L2 learners must assign a new value to principles to cohere with the L2. This aspect of the model allows us to account for the role of the L1 experience in L2 acquisition without invoking an astructural model of language transfer – an aspect of L2 learning captured by traditional Contrastive Analysis (CA) models of L2 acquisition (Fries, 1945; Lado, 1957).

The directionality principle in L1 acquisition

Empirical evidence in support of this model derived from several studies that investigated the role of the directionality principle in the adult L2 acquisition of English anaphora. This principle of directionality has been found to significantly characterize L1 acquisition. Evidence strongly suggests that young children are sensitive to their L1's structural configuration as determined by the head–initial/head–final parameter. For example, when young children learning English as their L1 produce subordinate clauses, they consistently place these clauses at the end of their main clause (Clark and Clark, 1977). It has been subsequently argued that children use this sensitivity to the head direction of their L1s to constrain their hypotheses about grammatical anaphora (see the discussion in Lust, 1986).[2] Children learning English show an early preference for forward over backward anaphora – a preference referred to as the forward directionality preference (see C. S. Chomsky, 1969; Goodluck, 1978, 1981; Lust, 1981, 1986; Lust, Solan, Flynn, Cross and Schuetz, 1986; Solan, 1977, 1978, 1983; Tavakolian, 1977). Children whose L1 is head–final prefer backward anaphora over forward anaphora. That is, in tests of elicited production, these children imitate sentences with backward anaphora correctly significantly more often than they do sentences with forward anaphora. In addition, analyses of natural speech samples for these children also indicate significantly more backward anaphora structures than forward anaphora structures (for Japanese see Lust, Wakayama, Hiraide, Snyder, and Bergmann, 1982; for Chinese see Lust and Chien, 1984; for Sinhalese, see Lust, de Abrew and Gair, forthcoming). These data from several languages provide important evidence that children's sensitivities to the configuration of their L1s significantly constrain their early development of critical aspects of grammatical anaphora.

In summary, the head–initial/head–final parameter is linguistically significant in grammars of natural languages and an important principle in the L1 acquisition of anaphora.

Summary of present investigations

In order to test the efficacy of the directionality principle in adult L2 acquisition, three groups of adults learning English as a second language (ESL) were tested: Spanish, Japanese and Chinese. These groups differ in terms of the match/mismatch in head direction to English, a head–initial language (see sentence 1). Spanish is head–initial, as shown in sentence 2 while Japanese and Chinese are head–final, as shown in sentences 3 and 4. In addition, Chinese was chosen not only because it is a head–final language but also because it matches English and Spanish in word order; it is SVO (Huang, 1982). Using Chinese speakers in this design allowed us to determine whether the effects isolated between the Spanish and Japanese speakers were due to differences in head direction alone or were principally due to differences in word order between the L1 and the L2. Results, as will be discussed below, confirm earlier reported findings with respect to the independence of word order and head direction (see an extended discussion in Flynn and Espinal, 1985).

> *English*
> (1) (The child [who is eating rice]) is crying.
> *Spanish*
> (2) (El niño [que come arroz]) llora.
> "The child who eats rice cries."
> *Japanese*
> (3) ([Gohan-o tabete-iru] ko-ga) naite-imasu.
> "Rice–object–eating is child–subject–crying is."
> *Chinese*
> (4) ([Na-ge zhen zai chi fan de] xiao hai zi) zai ku.
> That is eating rice–relative clause–little child is crying."

These speakers were tested in both their production and comprehension of complex sentences such as those exemplified in 5 and 6. These sentences differed in terms of pre- and post-posing of an adverbial subordinate clause, post-posed in 5, and pre-posed in 6. In addition, one half of the sentences involved a pronoun in *subject* position of the subordinate clause and one half did not involve any anaphor.[3]

The lexical items used in all the stimulus sentences in all tests were randomly chosen from a single list. In addition, attempts were made to keep all sentences pragmatically neutral in order that their meaning could not be astructurally determined.

(5) a The boss informed the owner when the worker entered the office.
   b The man answered the boss when he installed the television.
(6) a When the actor finished the book, the woman called the professor.
   b When he delivered the message, the actor questioned the lawyer.

Results of the elicited imitation test with these three groups of learners revealed two important findings. Firstly, results for the Spanish speakers (L1 = L2 in head direction) indicated a significant preference for sentences such as in 5b in which the antecedent preceded the pronoun. Results of amount correct demonstrated that these sentences were significantly easier to imitate than sentences such as in 6b in which the pronoun preceded the antecedent. The nature of the errors also supported this finding. For example, there were significantly more anaphora errors made on sentences with backwards anaphora than on sentences with forward anaphora. Sentences in 5a and 6a, without anaphora, did not show any significant differences in imitation, either overall or at any level. The learners imitated these sentences with equal ease.

Secondly, as hypothesized, the patterns for the Japanese and the Chinese speakers (L1 ≠ L2 in head direction) did not match the Spanish L2 learners. Specifically, there was no preference in imitation of sentences in 5b or 6b with either forward or backward anaphora. However, at the advanced level, Chinese and Japanese speakers indicated a preference for sentences which did not involve any pronoun anaphora but which did involve post-posed clauses. Japanese and Chinese speakers found sentences in 5a to be significantly easier to imitate than sentences in 6a. These results suggested that the Japanese and Chinese speakers did not simply perform worse than the Spanish speakers because of a mismatch in the head direction between the L1 and the L2 (Contrastive Analysis could have predicted this), but rather, that the Japanese and Chinese learners were attempting to organize the L2 around the head–initial configuration of English. At the advanced level, these results strongly suggest that these speakers had assigned a new value to the head–initial parameter in order that it match the L2 value. The preference for these post-posed sentence structures indicated that the Japanese and Chinese speakers were now attempting to construct the L2 grammar around the reset value of this head parameter. The nature of the errors for these two language groups additionally isolated head direction as a source of difficulty for the L2 learners and strongly suggested that L2 learners were sensitive to the head–initial structure of English.

From this initial set of results and others, I have argued for the relevance of a parameter setting model of UG and for the psychological reality of the specific principle investigated, the head–initial/head–final parameter and for its role in the directionality principle in L2 learning.

Focus of this paper

Given these results, a number of interesting predictions follow. For example, if sensitivity to the head–direction configuration is a general principle of acquisition, then one would expect to see its effects across several different types of constructions which involve head–complement configurations. Thus, in this paper I have extended this original work to investigate the role of the head–direction parameter in the acquisition of restrictive relative clauses (RRCs) in English. RRCs, in contrast to the original sentence structures tested, involve bound variables and the embedding of a subordinate clause under an NP (noun phrase) rather than an S (sentence), as with adjunct clauses. If the head–direction principle is general and characterizes acquisition in general, and if my claims about the L2 acquisition are correct, then we would expect, in a test with the same three groups of ESL learners, significant differences to emerge between the case in which the L1 and L2 match in head–direction (Spanish speakers learning English), and the case in which they do not (Japanese and Chinese speakers learning English).

Experimental design

The essential design of these studies tested the same three groups of adults learning English as a second language (Spanish, Japanese, and Chinese speakers) in their elicited production of four types of RRCs.

In the elicited production task, a learner is presented with a randomized set of sentence batteries. The experimenter gives orally, one at a time, a sentence from these batteries to the learner, who is then asked to repeat each sentence as presented. The basic assumption underlying the use of this task is that the active repetition of a stimulus sentence reflects input of the sentence to the learner's comprehension and productive systems, and the grammatical structure of the stimulus sentence is relevant to this processing. (For an extended discussion see Flynn, 1987a; Lust, Chin and Flynn, 1988.)

The four sentence types tested are shown in sentences 7–10. The sentences in 7 involved S (subject)/S (subject) relatives; the sentences in 8 involved

Table 7.1. *English as a second language proficiency level placement scores* (score range 0–50)

n = number of subjects tested
M = mean score.

Group	Low		Mid		High		Overall	
	n	M	n	M	n	M	n	M
Spanish	16	17.9	21	31.3	14	41.7	51	30.3
Japanese	7	20.3	25	30.8	21	42.5	53	31.2
Chinese	11	14.3	20	31.0	29	43.8	60	29.7
Overall	34	17.5	66	31.0	64	42.7	164	30.4

S/O (object) relatives; the sentences in 9 involved O/S relatives, and the sentences in 10 involved O/O relatives.[4] Each learner was presented with three tokens of each stimulus item. These sentences were administered in random order to each speaker for repetition.

> Samples of *stimulus sentences*
> S/S
> (7) The student who called the gentleman answered the policeman.
> S/O
> (8) The policeman who the student called greeted the businessman.
> O/S
> (9) The boss introduced the gentleman who questioned the lawyer.
> O/O
> (10) The diplomat questioned the gentleman who the student called.

Learners' knowledge of the lexical items used in the stimulus sentences was controlled. Prior to testing, each learner was given a bilingual list of all the words that were used in the stimulus sentences. That is to say, each speaker had a list of the words used in the stimulus sentences written in both their L1 (Spanish, Chinese, or Japanese) and the target L2 (English). Testing did not begin until each learner had demonstrated 100 percent understanding of the lexical items in English.

In addition, as in previous studies, all speakers were placed into one of three levels of English as a second language (ESL) ability, as established by a standardized ESL test, The Placement Test from the University of Michigan as shown in Table 7.1.[5]

Predictions for study

From the general hypotheses formulated concerning the role of the head–direction parameter in adult L2 acquisition of RRCs, the following set of predictions were generated for this study:

1 Imitation of sentences 7–10 should be significantly facilitated for the Spanish speakers but disrupted for the Japanese and Chinese speakers even when the three groups are equalized in basic ESL level as measured by the standardized test.

We would expect this result because these RRC sentences all involve embedding which in turn represents some form of head-complementation structure. Since the Spanish speakers' L1 head–direction .is initial, this head–complement organization in English follows their L1. This structural configuration should be available to these learners to consult in the development of the L2 grammar. On the other hand, the L1 for the Japanese and Chinese speakers' is head–final. As a result, I hypothesize that these speakers must revise principles of head–complementation when learning English. That is, Japanese and Chinese speakers must, as I argue, assign a new value to the head–direction parameter when acquiring English. Thus, the Japanese and Chinese speakers' acquisition of these sentences, as for adverbial clauses, should be significantly hindered by their need to assign a new value to this principle of organization for acquisition of this particular L2.

2 Errors made by the Spanish, Japanese and Chinese speakers should differ qualitatively. Japanese and Chinese learners should show critical difficulty with head–complement relations in this complex sentence formation. Spanish speakers should show less difficulty with this aspect of these structures.

3 If sensitivity to head direction is a general principle of acquisition, we should see evidence that these learners are working out the head–initial properties of English. Errors should be consistent with those found with children at early stages of the L1 acquisition of English.

Results

The results confirm my predictions. First, there were important overall differences between the Spanish and Japanese and Spanish and Chinese results but not between the Japanese and Chinese speakers in their production of each of the relative clause structures tested. These results hold even though these speakers were all equalized in ESL level.

Results summarized in Tables 7.2 to 7.5 show that the Spanish speakers imitated the sentence types tested significantly more successfully than the Japanese or Chinese speakers. The means for successful imitation for each group are shown in Table 7.2.[6]

Thus, the first prediction, facilitation in production of English embedding under an NP by ESL learners with a head–initial language and disruption of this production by ESL learners with a head–final language, was, in general confirmed.

Table 7.2. *Mean amount correct for each developmental level*
(Score range 0–3)

Language Group	SS	SO	OS	OO	Overall
Spanish					
Low	.63	.69	.38	.75	.61
Mid	2.19	1.33	1.00	1.76	1.57
High	2.57	1.93	1.50	2.20	2.05
Overall	1.80	1.32	.96	1.51	1.40
Japanese					
Low	.14	.00	.29	.14	.14
Mid	.64	.16	.20	.12	.28
High	1.28	.48	.90	.67	.83
Overall	.69	.21	.46	.31	.41
Chinese					
Low	.00	.09	.09	.09	.07
Mid	.55	.60	.55	.65	.59
High	1.27	1.66	1.14	1.69	1.44
Overall	.61	.78	.59	.81	.70

SS: *Subject–Subject relatives*
SO: *Subject–Object relatives*
OS: *Object–Subject relatives*
OO: *Object–Object relatives*

Table 7.3. *Lexical errors*
% of error (% of response)

Language group	Spanish	Japanese	Chinese
Low	23% (18%)	3% (2%)	5% (5%)
Mid	31% (15%)	11% (10%)	16% (13%)
High	47% (15%)	23% (17%)	30% (15%)
Overall	34% (16%)	12% (10%)	17% (11%)

The second prediction was also confirmed. Analysis of the errors confirmed a qualitative difference in the nature of the errors made by the two groups.

First of all, the errors that differentiated the three groups of ESL learners and accounted for the exceptional difficulty in the Japanese and Chinese groups were not lexical errors. In spite of the fact that the lexicons of Spanish and English are much more similar than for English, Japanese and Chinese, a greater number of lexical errors were made by Spanish speakers than by Japanese and Chinese speakers. This is shown in Table 7.3. An example of this sort of error is shown in 11.

(11) Stimulus: The policeman questioned the man who carried the baby.
     Response: The *gentleman* questioned the man who carried the baby.

126   *Suzanne Flynn*

Table 7.4. *Conversion to coordination*
% of two clause errors

Language group	Spanish	Japanese	Chinese
Low	20%	29%	16%
Mid	6%	13%	12%
High	3%	9%	7%
Overall	10%	17%	12%

Table 7.5. *One clause repetitions*
% of error (% of response)

Language group	Spanish	Japanese	Chinese
Low	30% (24%)	83% (79%)	66% (65%)
Mid	31% (14%)	45% (41%)	32% (26%)
High	20% (7%)	23% (18%)	25% (13%)
Overall	28% (15%)	43% (37%)	38% (27%)

In addition, errors which differentiated the two sets of learners and accounted for the lower success rate in the Japanese and Chinese speakers were primarily structural errors. For example, there are significantly more one clause repetitions for the Japanese and Chinese speakers than for the Spanish speakers. This is shown in Table 7.4 and exemplified in 12.

(12) Stimulus: The policeman questioned the man who carried the baby.
　　　Response: a The policeman questioned the man.
　　　Or: b Who carried the baby.

Also, of the two clause structural errors, there was a greater conversion of these sentence structures to coordinate sentence structures for the Japanese and Chinese speakers at the intermediate and advanced levels (where control of the two clause structure is evident) than for the Spanish speakers. This is shown in Table 7.5. Examples of this error are shown in 13.[7]

(13) Stimulus: The policeman questioned the man who carried the baby.
　　　Response: a The policeman questioned the man and carried the baby.
　　　　　　　b The policeman questioned the man and *the policeman* carried the baby.

A closer examination of the types of coordinate conversions made by the Japanese and Chinese speakers indicate that they all involved redundancy in the *subject*. For example, the RRCs were converted to coordinate sentences in which a redundant subject had been reduced as in 13a or to a coordinate sentence structure in which *subject* deletion would be possible. This is shown in 13b. This redundancy reduction is all in a forward direction. That is to say, the controller antecedes the deletion site. This pattern coheres with what young children learning English will do in early acquisition of English syntax (Lust, 1981) thus confirming our third prediction specified above. This conversion is especially noteworthy in that in order to do this, the meaning of the original sentence was changed, thus suggesting the primacy of structure over semantics in computing these sentences. In addition, these patterns exemplified by the Japanese and Chinese speakers correspond to English developmental patterns. Moreover, they suggest that these two groups of speakers are attempting to work out the properties of English and are not simply translating from their L1s. If they were simply matching the L1 to the L2, we would have expected patterns which matched L1 acquisition of these structures. That is, we would have expected the Japanese and Chinese speakers to convert the RRCs to coordinate sentence structures in which redundancy reduction goes backwards, i.e. deletion site to precede the controller (see discussion in Lust and Mangione, 1983).

Other forms of error also confirm a qualitative difference in the nature of the imitation between the head–initial speakers and the head–final speakers. The examples of imitation shown in sentences 14–16 indicate that the Japanese and Chinese speakers had particular difficulty establishing a head–complement and a head–anaphor relation which is required by the relative.

(14) Stimulus: The policeman questioned the man who carried the baby.
       Japanese response: Who question the man who question the baby.
(15) Spanish response: The policeman questioning the man who carried the baby.
(16) Stimulus: The lawyer who criticized the worker called the policeman.
       Chinese response: The lawyer who criticized the woman the lawyer called the policeman.

Consider the Japanese response in 14: Who question the man who question the baby. This reflects a structure that is not a head–complement structure but a series of juxtaposed questions. On the other hand, the Spanish error shown in 15 still involves a head–complement structure, the man who carried the baby, but errs in misrepresenting the tense of the main clause. In 16, the Chinese response does involve a head–complement structure, the lawyer who criticized the woman, but this complex NP is not embedded in the main clause; it is merely juxtaposed to another full sentence. This again suggests specific difficulty on the part of the Chinese ESL learner with the head–complementation structure, i.e. the embedding of English syntax.

Conclusions and discussion

The results summarized thus emerge in both L1 and L2 acquisition. How can we understand them? Given the controls exercised in the experimental studies, the results cannot be explained in terms of a lack of knowledge of the lexicon, task, or different ESL abilities.

We have basically three sets of learners at the same level of English ability yet two distinct patterns of acquisition emerge. At the most general level, these results suggest that adult L2 learners, like child L1 learners, are constrained in their mapping from the primary language data to the adult grammar. At a more specific level, these results suggest that adults are sensitive to differences in head-direction configurations between the L1 and the L2 and are constrained by a comparable set of linguistic principles observed in L1 learning in the acquisition of these structures. Where there is a match in parametric values for head–direction between the L1 and the L2, acquisition is facilitated; such a finding suggests that there is no need to assign a new value to the parameter set to match the L1 grammar. Where there isn't a match, a new value must be assigned to the parameter in question.

These data, along with others referred to in this chapter, provide important additional support for the parameter-setting model proposed by Flynn (1987a). This model, as briefly outlined above, allows one to account for both the role of the L1 experience in L2 acquisition and the role of principles independent of this experience. In this paper I have shown how Spanish, Japanese and Chinese speakers use the principle of head-direction isolated in L1 acquisition in adult L2 acquisition. I have also demonstrated the role of the L1 experience in this model.

In terms of system interaction in bilinguals, there are several ways in which these findings are relevant. First, these results isolate an important principle necessary to the acquisition of the L1 as well as the L2. This finding alone suggests that in the simultaneous acquisition of two languages we would expect to find that learners at early stages of acquisition establish the basic structural configuration as determined by the head–initial/head–final parameter for the languages they are learning. Second, given the two distinct patterns of acquisition exemplified in this paper, which I argue suggest that learners do not replicate structures where values of parameters match, we might also expect a similar process to hold in the simultaneous acquisition of two languages. That is, we might expect two distinct patterns of acquisition in the bilingual situation, one in which the two first languages matched in head-direction and one in which they did not. In the case in which they matched, we would expect that once the parameter is set for one language, it is also set for the second language. Problems for the learner in this case would have to do with keeping the lexicons distinct for each of these two languages. In the second case, learners would have to establish two distinct grammatical systems as well as two distinct lexical systems. That is to say (in contrast to the case in which the two languages' parameters match), once the value of a parameter is set for one language, it is not automatically set for the other language to be learned. In this case we might expect a slower rate of progress in acquisition for both languages when compared to the case in which both of the languages to be learned matched in parametric values. While these claims are highly speculative, they are empirically testable. Their confirmation could demonstrate one important way in which the study of L1 acquisition, adult L2 acquisition and simultaneous bilingual acquisition can be brought together.

Notes

1 The author wishes to thank Jack Carroll, and the editors of this book, Loraine Obler and Kenneth Hyltenstam, for their comments and suggestions for revisions. The author also wishes to thank the participants at the conference for their insightful questions, all of which helped in the re-thinking of many of the issues. A preliminary version of this paper was originally given at the Winter 1985 LSA meeting in Seattle, Washington. A preliminary report of these results is reported in Flynn, forthcoming (a).

2 Lust argues that children are sensitive to the Principal Branching Direction of their L1s. For a discussion of the correspondence between Principal Branching Direction and the head–initial/head–final parameter, see Flynn, 1987a; Flynn and Espinal, 1985.

3 In addition, all speakers were tested on adverbial adjunct clauses that involved null anaphors in *subject* position and on sentences that involved pre-posed clauses and a pronoun anaphor in subject position of the subordinate clause. For a complete discussion see Flynn, 1987a.

4 The first grammatical position refers to the grammatical function of the relativized NP in the main clause. The second grammatical position refers to the grammatical function of the NP in the subordinate clause.

5 The listening comprehension and the grammar sections of this test were used for placement (score range 0–50). See Flynn, 1987a for a detailed discussion of the derivation of these scores.

6 For the Spanish speakers there is an interaction of type that I will not pursue in this paper. I will, thus, summarize the four types of RRCs tested.

7 One reviewer suggested that the errors made by the Japanese and Chinese speakers might indicate lexical rather than structural problems with these sentences. If this were the case, we would have expected the errors to be random, i.e., to occur at many different places in the sentences as in the case with the Spanish speakers and not to emerge at just those points in the grammar that a head and a complement are instantiated.

References

Chomsky, C. S. (1969), *The Acquisition of Syntax in Children 5 to 10*. Cambridge, MA: MIT Press.

Chomsky, N. (1975), *Reflections on Language*. New York: Pantheon Press.

(1980), *Rules and Representations*. New York: Columbia University Press.

(1981), *Lectures on Government and Binding: The Pisa Lectures*. Dordrecht, Holland: Foris.

(1982), *Some Concepts and Consequences of the Theory of Government and Binding.* Cambridge, MA: MIT Press.

(1986a), *Knowledge of Language: Its Nature, Origin, and Use.* New York: Praeger Publishers.

(1986b), *Barriers.* Cambridge, MA: MIT Press.

Clark, H. and Clark, E. (1977), *Psychology and Language.* New York: Harcourt, Brace and Jovanovich.

Dulay, H. and Burt, M. (1974), A new perspective on the creative construction process in child second language acquisition. *Language Learning,* **24**, 253–278.

Flynn, S. (1981). The effects of first language branching direction on the acquisition of second language. In Harbert, W. and Herschensohn, J. (eds.), *Cornell Working Papers in Linguistics,* Ithaca, NY: Cornell University.

(1983a), *A Study of the Effects of Principal Branching Direction in Second Language Acquisition: The Generalization of a Parameter of Universal Grammar from First to Second Language Acquisition.* Unpublished Ph.D dissertation, Cornell University.

(1983b), Differences between first and second language acquisition: setting the parameters of Universal Grammar. In Rogers, D. and Sloboda, J. (eds.). *Acquisition of Symbolic Skills.* New York and London: 485–500. Plenum Press.

(1984), A Universal in L2 acquisition based on a PBD typology. In Eckman, F. (ed.). *Universals in Second Language Acquisition.* Rowley, MA: Newbury House.

(1985), Principled theories of second language acquisition. *Studies in Second Language Acquisition* **7**, 89–107.

(1987a), *A Parameter-Setting Model of L2 Acquisition: Experimental Studies in Anaphora.* Dordrecht, Holland: Reidel Press.

(1987b), Contrast and Construction in a Parameter-Setting Model of L2 Acquisition. *Language Learning.* **37**, 1, 19–62.

(forthcoming), Head-direction parameter in the acquisition of English relative clauses by adult speakers of Spanish and Japanese. In Gass, S. and Schachter, J. (eds.), *Second Language Acquisition: A Linguistic Perspective.* Cambridge University Press.

Flynn, S. and Espinal, I. (1985), The Head–Initial/Head–Final parameter in adult Chinese L2 acquisition of English. *Second Language Research* **1**, 93–117.

Fries, C. (1945), *Teaching English as a Foreign Language.* Ann Arbor: University of Michigan Press.

Goodluck, H. (1978), *Linguistic Principles in Children's Grammar of Complement Interpretation.* Unpublished Ph.D dissertation, UMass/Amherst.

(1981), Children's grammar of complement subject interpretation. In Tavakolian, S. (ed.), *Language Acquisition and Linguistic Theory.* Cambridge, MA: MIT Press.

Huang, J. (1982), *Logical Relations in Chinese and the Theory of Grammar.* Unpublished Ph.D dissertation, MIT.

Lado, R. (1957), *Linguistics Across Cultures.* Ann Arbor: University of Michigan Press.

Lust, B. (1981), Constraint on anaphora in child language: a prediction for a Universal. In Tavakolian, S. (ed.), *Language Acquisition and Linguistic Theory,* Cambridge, MA: MIT Press.

(1983), On the notion "Principal Branching Direction:" A parameter of Universal Grammar. In Otsu, Y., van Riemsdijk, H., Inoue, K., Kamio, A. and Kawasaki, N. (eds.), *Studies in Generative Grammar and Language Acquisition.* Monbusho Grant for Scientific Research, Tokyo, Japan.

(1986), Introduction. In Lust, B. (ed.). *Studies in the Acquisition of Anaphora, Vol. 1, Defining the Constraints.* Dordrecht: Reidel Press.

Lust, B. and Mangione, L. (1983), The principal branching direction parameter constraint in first language acquisition of anaphora. In *Proceedings of the 13th Annual Meeting of the Northeastern Linguistic Society.* Amherst, MA: University of Massachusetts.

Lust, B., Wakayama, T., Hiraide, H., Synder, H. and Bergmann, M. (1982), Comparative studies on the first language acquisition of Japanese and English: language universal and language specific constraints. Paper presented at the XIIIth International Congress of Linguists, Tokyo, Japan.

Lust, B. and Chien, Y. C. (1984), The structure of coordination in first language acquisition of Mandarin Chinese: Evidence for a Universal. *Cognition* **7**, 49–83.

Lust, B., Solan, L., Flynn, S., Cross, C. and Schuetz, E. (1986), A comparison of constraints on the acquisition of null and pronominal anaphora. In Lust, B. (ed.), *Studies in the Acquisition of Anaphora: Defining the Constraints, Vol. 1.* Dordrecht: Reidel Press.

Lust, B., Chien, Y. C. and Flynn, S. (1988), What children know: comparison of experimental methods for the study of first language acquisition. In Lust, B. (ed.), *Studies in the Acquisition of Anaphora: Defining the Constraints.* Dordrecht: Reidel Press.

Lust, B., de Abrew, K. and Gair, J. (in preparation). On the Acquisition of Sinhalese Anaphora.

Solan, L. (1977), On the interpretation of missing complement NPs. In *Occasional Papers.* Amherst, MA: University of Massachusetts.

(1978), *Anaphora in Child Language.* Unpublished Ph.D dissertation, UMass/Amherst.

(1983), *Pronominal Reference: Child Language and the Theory of Grammar.* Dordrecht: Reidel Press.

Stowell, T. (1981), *Origins of Phrase Structure.* Unpublished Ph.D dissertation, MIT.

Tavakolian, S. (1977), *Structural Principles in the Acquisition of Complex Sentences.* Unpublished Ph.D dissertation, UMass/Amherst.

8. Distinguishing language contact phenomena: evidence from Finnish–English bilingualism[1]

SHANA POPLACK, SUSAN WHEELER AND ANNELI WESTWOOD

The bilingual behavior which has provoked the most controversy in linguistics is undoubtedly intrasentential code-switching (CS). When two languages are to be used in a single sentence, various problems of incompatibility may arise. The most obvious derives from word-order differences – if a switch occurs at a boundary between two constituents which are ordered differently in the two languages, the resulting configuration will be ungrammatical by the standards of at least one. Another type of difficulty involves morphological disparity, as when a noun in one language must be inflected for case, where the other uses alternative means of accomplishing the same function. And there are many other problems having to do with subcategorization patterns, semantic differences, idiomatic constructions, etc.

It has been observed in systematic studies of bilingual communities that speakers tend to avoid these difficulties by eschewing switches at sites which would result in monolingually ungrammatical fragments. How is this accomplished? In earlier studies of Spanish–English bilingualism among Puerto Ricans in New York (Poplack, 1980, 1981; Sankoff and Poplack, 1981) we postulated the *equivalence constraint*, whereby switching is free to occur between any two sentence elements if they are normally ordered in the same way by the grammars of both languages involved, while prohibited elsewhere, as illustrated in (1).

(1) English: DET + N
    Spanish: DET + N

    CS: ENG DET + SP N
           SP   DET + ENG N

    English: ADJ + N
    Spanish: N + ADJ

CS: *ENG ADJ + SP N ⎫
        *SP ADJ + ENG N ⎪
        *ENG N   + SP ADJ ⎬ "crossovers"
        *SP N   + ENG ADJ⎭

Thus, for Puerto Rican bilinguals switching is permitted between a determiner of either language and a noun in the other but prohibited between a noun and an adjective because the result would be contrary to English word order, or between (most) adjectives and the noun, because this would be contrary to Spanish order.

Much has been written about the validity of this constraint, be it for Spanish–English or for other language pairs. A good deal of the work on bilingual discourse has made use of standard linguistic methodologies (e.g. informant elicitation, subjective reaction tests, introspection), yielding data which reflect indirectly (at best) actual language use in real-life situations. This is due in part to the unreliability of grammatical intuitions about bilingual syntax – a problem which is exacerbated in situations of social stigma – and in part to the fact that the study of isolated examples cannot distinguish between the systematic recurrent patterns of everyday interaction and other structures, albeit "acceptable" in some sense, which never or rarely occur.

The work we discuss here, in contrast, has been carried out using a sociolinguistic, or more specifically, *variationist* approach to the study of code-switching, conforming to a number of principles which have come to be associated with this paradigm. These include (1) the use of appropriate data, resulting from the study of language use in its natural context, (2) the principle of accountable reporting, which implies analysis of *all* of the relevant data, (3) the selection of informants to ensure representativeness, and the knowledge of what they represent, and (4) circumscription of the "variable context", i.e. defining the object of study (cf. among others, Labov, 1969, G. Sankoff, 1974).

It is not our claim that the equivalence constraint is uniformly pertinent to every bilingual community, even to those in which mixing of the two codes is frequent at the intrasentential level. A key aspect of New York Puerto Rican linguistic behavior is that intrasentential switching occurs in a smooth manner. Here, switches are usually *not* preceded or followed by hesitations or pauses, nor are switched items translations or repetitions of what went before. Contrary to some claims, no special local rhetorical effect is produced by the overwhelming majority of particular switches. The speaker does not draw attention to the fact that a language change has occurred, nor does the interlocutor have to acknowledge it, as illustrated in the examples in (2).

(2) a So you *todavía* haven't decided *lo que vas a hacer* next week. (01/135)[2]
"So you still haven't decided what you're going to do next week."

   b *Si tu eres puertorriqueño,* your father's a Puerto Rican, you should at least *de vez en cuando,* you know, *hablar español.* (34/25)
"If you're Puerto Rican, your father's a Puerto Rican, you should at least sometimes, you know, speak Spanish."

While such smooth intrasentential switching is not confined to Puerto Ricans – indeed, it is also characteristic of fluently bilingual Mexican–Americans (Pfaff 1979) – it may very well be relatively rare in other communities which are equally bilingual. For example, in a more recent, large-scale study (Poplack 1985), we examined the code-switching behavior of 120 bilingual speakers of French and English in the Ottawa-Hull region of Canada. Since French is typologically very similar to Spanish, patterns of code-switching in the two communities could be expected to be similar if not identical, if the structural properties of the languages involved were a key determining factor. However, the type of code-switching used in Ottawa-Hull is dramatically different from that attested among the Puerto Ricans. Only a minuscule proportion of the French–English switches are genuinely intra-sentential. Instead of weaving the two languages smoothly together at imperceptible switch points, French speakers draw attention to the switch by any one of a number of discourse devices, for example metalinguistic commentary, repetition or translation, English bracketing. Virtually every switch serves a rhetorical purpose, whereas for the Puerto Ricans, the smooth switching style is itself a speech mode emblematic of community identity. Indeed, in order for the switch to accomplish its purpose in the French community, it must be highlighted, i.e. salient, and should not pass unnoticed, as can be observed from the examples in (3). One byproduct of this flagging is the interruption of the speech flow at the code-switch point, effectively circumventing a grammaticality requirement, or rendering one unnecessary.

(3) a Je m'adresse en français, pis s'il dit *"I'm sorry",* ben là je recommence en anglais. (MM/3254)
"I begin in French and if he says, "I'm sorry", well then I start over in English."

   b Mais je te gage par exemple que ... excuse mon anglais, mais les *odds* sont là. (CD/716)
"But I bet you that ... excuse my English, but the odds are there."

   c Je suis un peu trop anglicisé, anglifié, *anglicized.* (GF/1361)
"I'm a little too anglicized, anglified, anglicized."

Thus, while the linguistic configuration involved is typologically very similar in the two communities, as indeed are many aspects of their sociological situations, and while they both make plentiful use of code-switching, the syntactic constraint obtaining in one is largely irrelevant to the other, because of the different discourse functions that code-switching serves in each.

It is thus apparent that not only is code-switching structured differently from community to community, but not all data on switching constitutes acceptable evidence regarding the operation of syntactic constraints. Ungrammaticality is indeed avoided in the French–English context, but this is only a trivial consequence of the flagging of switches. We return to the distinction between smooth and flagged code-switching in our discussion of Finnish–English bilingualism below.

Typological differences between language pairs

The studies of Puerto Ricans and Franco-Ontarians (as indeed is the case with the majority of work on code-switching) have involved pairs of typologically similar languages. It has often been claimed that though the equivalence constraint is an intuitively natural way to account for code-switching behavior in languages which already share many surface similarities, it founders in typologically different structures (e.g. Bentahila and Davies, 1983; Prince and Pintzuk, 1983; Bokamba, 1985; Nishimura, 1985). The research we report here is part of a larger project, directed by D. Sankoff, examining code-switching phenomena in communities specifically chosen according to pre-determined typological differences in the code-switched pairs.

At one level, the propensity toward code-switching (versus borrowing, for example) is typologically determined. We noted earlier that the Spanish–English case may be an extreme one. Code-switching is copious, transitions are smooth, and it occurs at all permissible code-switch boundaries, of which there are of course many, given the similarities between the languages. Major code-switching sites are between subject NP + VP, V and object NP, preposition + NP, internal to the NP, internal to the PP, around coordinate and subordinate conjunctions, etc. In typologically *different* languages, word order incongruence renders code-switching more problematic because the resulting code-switched sentences risk violating the patterns of one or both languages. In moving from the Spanish–English situation to one where English co-exists with a strongly SOV and/or case-marked language, for example, many permissible switch boundaries are lost.

We propose in this paper to test the validity of the equivalence constraint on the basis of data on Finnish–English bilingualism, comparing a postpositional with a prepositional language, but where no other major word order difference obtains, as illustrated in (4).[3]

(4) **Spanish (French)   English**
    SVO   SVO
    PREP   PREP
    N + ADJ   ADJ + N

Finnish	English
SVO	SVO
POST., CASE	PREP
ADJ+N	ADJ+N

Finnish, unlike English, has a rich system of obligatory morphological case-marking for each of 15 nominal cases. These are used to fulfill subject, direct object, genitive and partitive functions, and in expressions of location and direction, time, instrument, and manner (e.g. Karlsson, 1983), functions which are carried out in English by prepositions or word order. Given the analytic nature of English, the equivalence constraint makes strong predictions about where intrasentential code-switching within this language pair should not occur. If we nonetheless find English-origin material in the "prohibited" switch sites, we may conclude that (1) either the proposed constraint does not account adequately for the data, or (2) the data involved are not code-switches.

Circumscribing the variable context

Once we have established that speakers are indeed alternating between languages in a smooth, unflagged way, we must circumscribe the variable context, i.e. determine whether the other-language material under investigation in fact constitutes a code-switch, or rather, represents some other manifestation of language contact. On the synchronic level, it is often impossible, in a given sentence, to tell whether a genuine switch has taken place, particularly at the level of single-word incorporations, which may be ambiguous as to their status as code-switch or loanword. Borrowing as a process differs radically from code-switching, and failure to separate data on the two phenomena can only obscure the conditioning of each.

The traditional characterization of an established loanword is an L_2 item, phonologically, morphologically and syntactically integrated into host-language discourse, which is both recurrent in the speech of an individual and widespread in the community. Thus, for the same Puerto Rican data, our working hypothesis was that an English-origin word in an otherwise Spanish context that did not satisfy these criteria would only occur in English monolingual discourse or in code-switches from Spanish to English. In general, however, borrowing is a much more productive process and is not bound by all of these constraints. In particular, the social characteristics of recurrence and dispersion need not be satisfied. This type of borrowing has been called *nonce* borrowing (Weinreich, 1953, cf. also Poplack, Sankoff and Miller, 1988). Distinguishing loanwords from code-switches when this process is prevalent is even more delicate.

In this paper we address this problem by proposing and testing a consistent framework for distinguishing code-switching from borrowing, making use of quantitative distributional methods. We will show that the morphological and syntactic role of a nonce borrowing is equivalent to that of an established loanword, which is in turn identical to its host-language counterpart, and in this, the two contrast with code-switching. It will be our claim that nonce borrowing is particularly productive in Finnish–English bilingualism, out-weighing code-switching by a factor of at least 5:1, and this may well be the case for typologically different language pairs in general.

Data and methods

In keeping with the variationist quest for appropriate data, the materials on which this study is based consist of natural tape-recorded conversations between eight first-generation Finnish women and Westwood, a core in-group member of the local Finnish community. Data were collected using standard social network techniques. All informants are fluent native speakers of Finnish who migrated to Canada as adults, although their time of residence in the country varies from 13 to 55 years. Six are also highly proficient in English; indeed, for all but one, English is currently the preferred language in most domains of social interaction, with the notable exception of the friendship network in which Westwood is linked to them, whose meetings are at least partially motivated by the desire to speak Finnish and participate in Finnish culture.

The base language of these conversations is Finnish, but they contain liberal incorporations from English. All of the latter were extracted from the corpus and initially categorized according to whether or not they represented unambiguous code-switches, i.e. multi-word fragments which are lexically, syntactically and morphologically English, as in the italicized portions in (5).

(5) Niin siellä oli tuota, kätilö   joka oli *head of the district who has*
    so   there was *filler* midwife-n.[4] who was

  not practiced for twenty years, and there she was sillä oli   se vauva
                                                      it-ad. was it baby-n.

  kädessä. (19b/326)
  arms-in.

  "So there was um, the midwife who was head of the district who has not practiced for twenty years, and there she was, she had the baby in her arms."

The overwhelming majority of English-origin material in the corpus, however, consists of single nouns, which we have said may equally well represent instances of borrowing as of code-switching. We may make use of the morphological criterion of obligatory case-marking in Finnish[5] to determine whether these items are in fact behaving like their counterparts in that language, as would be expected if they were loanwords.[6] Accordingly, we noted for each the case it would require were the sentence entirely in Finnish, and whether that case was in fact marked, as in (6). Not all of the nouns requiring inflection by Finnish rules actually received it, as may be seen in (7), and these were noted as well.

(6) Misis K. oli *housekeeper*ina. (9a/126)
    was   -es.
    "Mrs K. was the housekeeper."

(7) Mä laitoin   oikein ison   semmosen *aluminum pan-ø* lihapullia. (10a/368)
    I   made-1p. really big-g. such-g.   [g.] meatballs-p.
    "I made a really big, like aluminum pan of meatballs."

In keeping with the distinction drawn above between flagged and smooth code-switching, we also noted the presence of various discourse phenomena in the environment of the English-origin items which might indicate poor integration into host-language discourse. Included here were perceptible pauses, as in (8), and false starts, as in (9), preceding or following the noun in question, and the presence of material repeating, translating or explaining the English-origin form, as in (10).

(8) Mitä sä   haluat   se ... *lunch*iks?" (16a/096)
    what you want-2p.   it   -tr.
    "What do you want for ... lunch?"

(9) Kakskytviis dollaria viikko **ruoka**- *room and board-ø* (10a/204)
    Twenty five dollar-p. week-n. food-
    "Twenty-five dollars a week for food- room and board."

(10) Ne lapset   tuli ja pyys **kirjoja**, *books.*
     they children-n. came and begged books-p.
     "The children came and begged for books, books."

We also noted the occurrence of what we refer to as *flags*, forms preceding the borrowed word, which in some sense bracket or highlight it, thereby calling attention to its presence. Forms functioning in this way include *sellainen, semmo(i)nen, tuollainen, t(u)ommo(i)nen* "such, like that", *tällainen, tämmö(i)nen* "like this, of this sort", *niin kuin, kuin* "like", as well as English *you know*.

Throughout the discourse the interlocutor frequently appeared to be ratifying the fact that the speaker had switched languages: to signal either comprehension, acknowledgment or acceptance of the fact that a loanword had been used. Interjections expressing agreement such as *joo, ya, niin, uh huh* were considered possible ratification markers.

Finally, although Finnish does not make use of articles *per se*, initial

Table 8.1. *Distribution of English incorporations in Finnish discourse*

intrasentential code-switches	tags/interjections	single nouns[7]
12.9% (154)[8]	18.8% (225)	68.2% (813)

examination of our data suggested that demonstratives (e.g. *tämä* "this", *tuo* "that", *nämä* "these", *nuo* "those", *se* "it", "that", *ne* "they"), declinable indefinite pronouns (e.g. *joku* "someone" and *jokin* "something") and the numeral *yksi* "one" were being used much like English determiners, possibly to carry the inflection missing from the loanword, or in some other way signal English usage (cf. also Lehtinen, 1966:175). An example of this use of Finnish "determiners" may be found in (11).

(11) Ne   aloitti **sen** *union-ø* (2a/231)
They started it-g.
"They started the union."

Of course all of these markers can, in principle, occur just as well in monolingual Finnish discourse as in the environment of English-origin incorporations. To assess the extent to which the latter were actually behaving like their Finnish counterparts, we compare rates of inflection, flagging and determiner usage with those for an equal number (N = 803) of native Finnish nouns in the corpus.

An accountable report on the data

Table 8.1 summarizes the distribution of incorporations from English in the corpus. We note first that less than 20 percent of the incorporations from English are made up by tags, a freely moveable category with no syntactic relation to the rest of the sentence, as in (12).

(12) a Mutta en   mä viitinyt, *no way!* (9b/134)
But   not-1p I bothered
"But I'm not bothered, no way!"
  b Jäi   pois työstä. *Thank God!* (2a/232)
left-she away job-el.
"She left the job. Thank God!"

This is a relatively small number when compared with, for example, the New York Puerto Rican community, among whom tag-switching was found to be a device used by non-fluent bilinguals, allowing them to engage in the code-switching mode without having to respect a grammaticality requirement

Table 8.2. *Distribution of unambiguous code-switch types*

	N	%
Comp + S	95	62
V + (Object) NP	25	16
(Subject) NP + VP	10	6
Dem + N	9	6
Adj/adv + N	11	7
V + Infinitive	4	3
Totals	154	100

(Poplack, 1980). Here, however, tag-switching is by no means the domain of non-fluent bilinguals. For the least English-proficient speakers in the sample, such switches do not exceed 6 percent of the incorporations from English, proportions which are comparable to those found for the most proficient in that language (Wheeler, 1987). Indeed, it is clear that tag-switching is simply not a common strategy among these speakers.

We mentioned earlier that the equivalence constraint makes strong predictions as to where intrasentential code-switching between Finnish and English should *not* occur. Finnish is postpositional, case-marked, and makes little or no use of determiners. When juxtaposed with English, potential switch sites within what corresponds to an English PP, and in most cases, to an NP (both found elsewhere to be favored switch sites) are forfeited. Thus, it is not surprising that intrasentential code-switching is also infrequent, not exceeding 13 percent of the data. We first examine the relatively clear cases of switching involving multi-word fragments of English, including English function words where appropriate and never containing Finnish function words or morphology (Table 8.2). The largest fraction consists of English sentences embedded by means of the complementizer *että* within a Finnish matrix sentence, as in (13). The next largest group involves English material in post-verbal NPs in object position, as in (14). The remainder all occur at syntactic boundaries where English and Finnish show congruent word order as well: for example between subject NP and VP, as in (15).

(13) Sano että tulla   tänne että *I'm very sick.* (16b/412)
say that come-inf. here that
"Tell [them] to come here, that I'm very sick."

(14) Mun vanhin on- nyt alkaa *part-time nursing in*
my oldest is   now starts
intensive care. (10b/237)
"My oldest is- is now starting part-time nursing in intensive care."

(15) Sen tuota titteli *was abolished.* (2a/236)
it-g. filler title-n.
"Her title was abolished."

On the other hand, switches at sites prohibited by the equivalence constraint do not occur. Thus, there are no switches involving (1) negative particles, (2) following English prepositions, (3) preceding Finnish postpositions, (4) following Finnish preposed, question-marked verbs, or (5) in the vicinity of inverted English WH-interrogative structures. We have seen from Table 8.1, however, that only a small proportion of the English-origin material is contained in intrasentential switches. The overwhelming majority (68 percent) consists of single nouns or compounds within otherwise entirely Finnish utterances, largely occurring in precisely the contexts proscribed by the equivalence constraint. This leads us to question whether they are in fact code-switches, or some other manifestation of language contact.

Nominals

We have given an informal account of the equivalence constraint. This constraint is difficult to formalize, but this has recently been done mathematically by Sankoff and Mainville (1986a, 1986b) for a particular class of grammars. What are the consequences of this formalization for the present discussion?

We first illustrate the predictions of the equivalence constraint with potential switches involving an English preposition and a case-marked noun (of either native Finnish or English-origin), organized according to the four principles in (16). For the moment we set aside the limited class of Finnish prepositions and ignore the presence or absence of the determiner.

(16) Predictions of Principle I: *no crossovers*
  a *E prep + F noun
  b *E noun + F case-marker
  c *F noun + E prep
  d *F case-marker + E noun

    Predictions of Principle II: *monolingual grammaticality*
  a *F case-marker + F noun
  b *E noun + E prep

    Predictions of Principle III: *no omissions*
  a *lone E noun (no E prep, no F case-marker)
  b *bare F noun (no E prep, no F case-marker)

    Predictions of Principle IV: *no repetitions*
  a *E prep + F noun + F case-marker
  b *E prep + E noun + F case-marker

The predictions of Principle I are that no English preposition should precede or follow a Finnish noun, nor should a Finnish case-marker precede or follow an English noun. Principle II predicts the obvious restrictions against a Finnish case-marker followed by a Finnish noun or an English noun followed by an

English preposition. Principle III proscribes a lone English noun (i.e. with no preposition), or a bare (i.e. non-case-marked) Finnish noun, and Principle IV excludes any combination of English preposition and Finnish case-marker in the vicinity of the noun, i.e. "portmanteau" constructions, or copy-translations.[9]

All of these predictions are verified in our corpus, except for Ib and IIIa (given in bold face in 16), where we find massive exceptions involving English nouns in ungrammatical constructions according to English rules, either with or without Finnish case-marking. We return to these exceptions below. First we examine another set of constructions corresponding to English NPs which would require an article according to English grammar.[10] What does the equivalence constraint predict for these structures (17)?

(17) Predictions of Principle I: *no crossovers*
    a *E det + F noun
    b *E noun + F case-marker

    Predictions of Principle II: *monolingual grammaticality*
    a *E noun + E det
    b *F case marker + F noun

    Predictions of Principle III: *no omissions*
    a *lone E noun (no E det, no F case-marker)
    b *bare F noun (no E det, no F case-marker)

    Predictions of Principle IV: *no repetitions*
    a *E det + F noun + F case-marker
    b *E det + E noun + F case-marker

Principle I prohibits a switch between an English determiner and a Finnish noun; principle II, a series of intenally ungrammatical combinations; principle III prohibits a lone English noun (i.e. without a determiner) or a non-case-marked Finnish noun; and principle IV, copy translations.

How do these predictions actually hold up in our Finnish–English bilingual data? Again we find the same sort of massive exceptions as in the previous analysis (Ib and IIIa), namely English-origin nouns with Finnish case-markers as in (18), and English nouns with no case-marker but without the required article (19).

(18) Näitä   kaks, kolme *bypass*ia sillä   on. (11a/399)
    these-p. two   three   -p. he-ad. is
    "He has two, three bypasses".
(19) Mä sanoin   että mä menen *interview-ø*. (10a/134)
    I   said-1p. that I   go-1p.
    "I said that I'm going to an interview".

In sum, a large proportion of the English-origin material in our corpus apparently cannot be accounted for by the equivalence constraint. The fact that most of these words carry the correct Finnish case-marking suggests, however, that they are not code-switches at all, but result from nonce

Table 8.3. *Rates of case-marking of English-origin nouns by case, as compared with Larmouth's characterization of their degree of boundness*

Case	Degree of boundness (Larmouth 1974)	% case-marking	Totals
Nominative	strong	100%[11]	370
"True" Genitive	strong	94%	16
Ablative (L)	strong	sparse data	1
Elative (L)	moderate	88%	17
Illative (L)	moderate	72%	61
Adessive (L)	moderate	10%	20
Inessive (L)	moderate	68%	121
Partitive	weak	46%	134
Allative (L)	weak	33%	6
Accusative	weak	n/a[12]	—
Translative	—	36%	11
Essive	—	33%	6

borrowing, a process which (unlike the relatively restricted set of established borrowings) applies to the entire English nominal lexicon.

Recall, however, that Finnish case-marking is *obligatory*, and indeed appears categorically on all of the native Finnish nouns in our corpus. Yet a good proportion of the English nouns under discussion (21 percent) do not carry this marking. A recent analysis of nonce borrowing from English into Tamil (Sankoff, Poplack and Vanniarajan, 1986), an SOV language which is also postpositional with case-marking, but where case-marking is *optional*, showed that the distribution of case-marking on English-origin nouns quantitatively paralleled that for native Tamil nouns. How can the discrepancy between the Finnish and English-origin nouns be explained?

Variability in case-marking of both Finnish (Lehtinen, 1966; Larmouth, 1974) and English (Lehtinen, 1966) nouns is not unknown amongst transplanted Finns, and has been ascribed to contact and convergence with English. In an attempt to explain this phenomenon in the Finnish of three successive generations of Minnesota-born Finns, Larmouth hypothesized that case-markers were most likely to be deleted in contexts where (1) they are least strongly bound to the noun, and (2) they have the greatest degree of semantic transparency. Table 8.3 compares the rates of case-marking on English-origin nouns by case in our corpus with Larmouth's characterization of their degree of boundness.

Despite sparse data in some of the contexts, the overall distribution of case-marking in our material appears to support his model. Moreover, the partitive, arguably the most semantically transparent of the Finnish cases, can be seen to be marked less than any other case occurring frequently enough to rule out

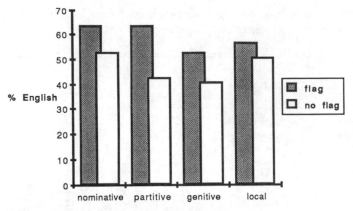

Figure 8.1. Percentage of all nouns which are English, in the presence or absence of a flag

statistical fluctuation. Compare this with the local (marked (L) in Table 8.3) cases, whose omission would likely involve misinterpretation on the part of the hearer, and which all show moderate to high rates of marker presence. However, when we examine the ranking of case-marking for each individual in the sample, we find that no two speakers manifest an identical or even similar ordering. The wide intra-individual variability casts doubt on Larmouth's explanation.

Moreover, Larmouth's hypothesis does not explain why this variability should affect only the *English-origin* nouns in our corpus. Let us now examine these data in more detail. We note first that the presence of English-origin material in Finnish sentences tends to be associated with an unusually high rate of certain discourse phenomena. For example, there is a good deal of what we have referred to as functional flagging, as in the French–English code-switching described earlier. Many English-origin nouns are preceded by discourse markers such as *semmonen* "such" and *niin kuin* "like", as in (20), which in some instances seem to be entirely confined to a signaling function.

(20) a Hän ois   **niin kuin** *programme*ri. (22b/097)
        he   would be like   -n.
        "He would be like a programmer."
     b Rupesin   pitämään **semmosta** *rooming house*a. (15b/136)
        started-1p. to keep   such-p.   -p.
        "I started to keep a rooming house."
     c Ne   on ihan **niin kuin semmosia** *temper tantrum*. (27b/261)
        They is quite like   such-pl.-p.
        "They are quite like, like temper tantrums."

This may be seen in Figure 8.1, which shows that English nouns occur far more frequently after flags than do their Finnish counterparts, and this holds, regardless of the case of the noun.

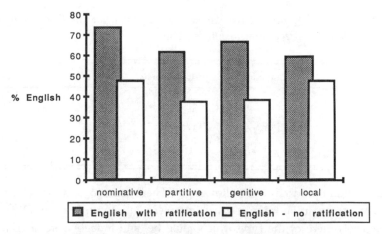

Figure 8.2. Percent of nouns which are marked, by case, in the environment of ratification

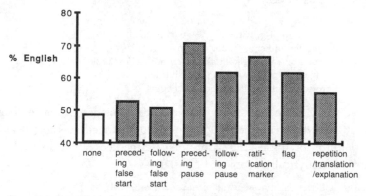

Figure 8.3. Percentage of nouns which are English in the environment of various discourse features

Another discourse phenomenon we analyzed was the use of ratification markers (e.g. *yes, uh huh, joo, niin*) on the part of the interlocutor. These were, of course, quite frequent throughout the conversations amongst all participants, but especially so immediately following English nouns. Figure 8.2 shows that in all cases, English-origin material occurs more frequently than native Finnish in the environment of these ratification markers.

Indeed, it is apparent from Figure 8.3 that of all the discourse phenomena examined, at least three seem to be clearly associated with the presence of English material: a perceptible preceding pause, a ratification marker on the part of the interlocutor, and a flag.

We now return to the massive exceptions to the predictions of the equivalence constraint outlined above. We first examine those constituents in our data which correspond to English prepositional phrases and in which the

Table 8.4. *Relationship between flagging and case-marking of English-origin nouns requiring a preposition in English*

	+Case marker	−Case marker
%		
Flag/	40%	68%
Pause/	(63/158)	(53/78)
Ratification		
Marker		

noun or noun phrase is of English origin. There are 246 of these which would require a preposition if the construction were entirely in English. Of these, 10 (4 percent) were of the type which could be, and indeed were, accompanied by a member of the limited class of Finnish prepositions, as in (21), or a postposition, as in (22).

> (21) Jos mä lasken sen **ilman** *contract*ia tänne sisälle ... (11b/172)
>   if I let-1p. it-g. without   -p. here in-al.
>   "If I let him in here without a contract ..."
> (22) Kaurapuuron saa *haggi*ksen **sisään** työntää. (25b/242)
>   porridge-g. can   -g. into   stuff-inf.
>   "Porridge can be stuffed inside the haggis."

These were all case-marked and can be considered nonce loans. The distribution of the remaining 236 cases is summarized in Table 8.4.

Two thirds of these (158/236) are case-marked nonce loans (as in 23), leaving 78 analytically problematic instances.

> (23) Mä kerran lähetin sen tuonne *dry cleaner*iin. (29b/397)
>   I once sent-1p. it-g. there-al.   -il.
>   "I once sent it to the dry cleaners there."

Note, however, that these tend to be problematic for the speaker and/or hearer as well, since there is a dramatic increase (to 68 percent) in the rate of discourse marking of the caseless nouns. Even the 10 percent of remaining nouns which are neither case-marked nor flagged are mostly accompanied by some other discourse marker than those counted in Table 8.4 (e.g. a following false start or pause). We may thus treat the set of caseless nouns as either flagged, non-smooth single-word switches, or in some instances, as poorly integrated nonce borrowings.

While the equivalence constraint correctly predicts the absence of switches after an English preposition, it also predicts that there *should* be some switches before prepositional phrases. In comparing the behavior of multi-word English sentence fragments (i.e. unambiguous code-switches) with that of nonce loans in this regard (Table 8.5), we find that, among the former, there are 25

Table 8.5. *Distribution of English prepositions before nonce loans, at code-switch boundaries and within code-switched fragments*

	Before nonce loans	At switch boundary	Within switch
Presence of preposition	0% (0/236)	64% (16/25)	98% (39/40)

Table 8.6. *Relationship between flagging and case-marking of English-origin nouns requiring a determiner in English*

	+Case marker	−Case marker
% Flag/ Pause/ Ratification Marker	38% (63/168)	66% (50/75)

instances of constructions which require an initial preposition at the switch point, and this is actually present in two thirds of the cases. Any missing prepositions tend to be flagged, suggesting some difficulty in constructing the switch boundary, rather than speakers' lack of English competence, as in (24).

(24) Se oli kai   neljä vai oliko   se viis vuotta sitten siellä **kuin**
     She was maybe four or was-int. it five year-p. then there like

   nursing home-ø (16b/145)
          [in.]
   "She was maybe four or was she five years there like [in a] nursing home."

Prepositions which are required *internal* to English discourse, in contrast, are virtually always present, while in the vicinity of nonce loans, they are categorically absent.

We may now examine the nominal constructions which would require a determiner were they entirely in English. No such determiners actually occurred, except as required internal to multi-word English fragments. Table 8.6 shows the distribution of case-marking and discourse flagging of the single noun items.[13]

This enlarged set of nouns shows the same increased discourse flagging of

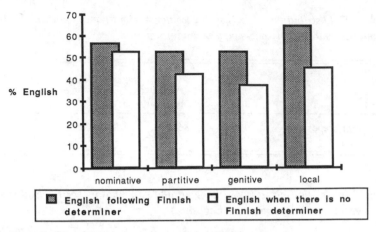

Figure 8.4. Use of Finnish determiners preceding English nouns

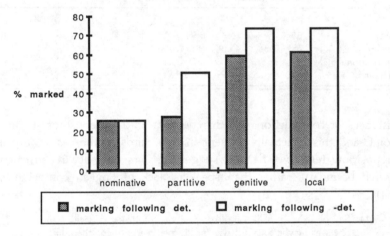

Figure 8.5. Rates of case-marking on English-origin nominals following a Finnish determiner

caseless items, confirming our view that most are nonce borrowings. There is some reason to believe that many of the remainder should be considered as code-switches.

Of the small number of nouns which are neither flagged nor case-marked, 68 percent (17/25) are preceded by what we have called a Finnish "determiner", (for example demonstratives *se* "it/this", *tama* "this", *tuo* "that", and (in the local cases), the adverbs of place *siellä*, *tuolla* "there" and *täällä* "here"). We see from Figure 8.4 that these are particularly frequent in the environment of English nouns, where in many instances they may no longer convey a specific marked demonstrative (or locative) value, but simply one of definiteness (cf. also Lehtinen, 1966). The figure shows that in all cases,

Table 8.7. *Distribution of English determiners before nonce loans, at switch boundaries and within code-switched fragments*

	Before nonce loans	At switch boundary	Within English fragments
Presence of Determiner:			
Finnish	42%	48%	0%
	(101/243)	(14/29)	(0/56)
English	0%	17%	86%
	(0/243)	(5/29)	(48/56)

English nouns occur more frequently following a Finnish determiner than not. Moreover, the nouns following these determiners are less likely to be marked (in all cases but the nominative) than those which appear without a determiner (see Figure 8.5).[14]

This leads us to suggest that many of these tokens are in fact code-switches and not borrowings, and that the determiners are serving a flagging, or switch-signaling function.

As previously, we now compare this with the behavior of determiners in unambiguous English sequences, as in Table 8.7.

Nonce loans are accompanied by a Finnish determiner less than half the time, with the proportion of determiner presence rising to 66 percent when a noun requiring a determiner by English rules occurs at a switch boundary. Of course, none of the latter is case-marked. The determiner may either be English (17 percent) or Finnish (48 percent), depending on the switch site (between preceding category and noun phrase, or between determiner and noun phrase). However, when English noun phrases occur *internal* to English discourse, a full 86 percent (48/56) of those requiring English determiners have them, in accordance with English grammar.

Discussion

Our analysis has revealed three separate lines of evidence supporting the distinction between code-switching and borrowing:

(1) There is a total lack of inflection on nouns within English stretches which are clear cases of code-switching, contrasting with a strong tendency (79 percent) to inflect the borrowed English nouns we have been considering.

(2) There is appropriate usage of English prepositions and determiners in unambiguous code-switches to English, contrasting with their total absence in the environment of English nouns occurring within otherwise Finnish utterances.

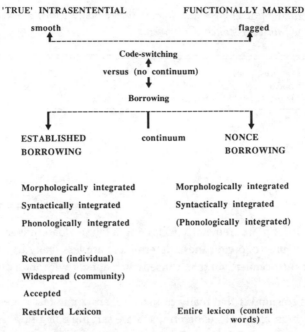

Figure 8.6. Characterization of code-switching and borrowing

(3) There is a significant trend towards complementary distribution of inflections and discourse flagging signals: less than 5 percent of the English nouns requiring inflection in Finnish (N = 443) failed to show either a case-marker or a flag.

We can thus identify most of these nouns as nonce borrowings. The remainder – the caseless nouns – may be treated as flagged, non-smooth single-word switches. Specialization of Finnish "determiners" before English origin nouns appears to be functioning as another switch-signaling device. Recall that the functional flagging in the typologically similar French–English pair was a way of calling attention to the switches, and rendered a grammaticality requirement irrelevant. In the Finnish–English materials, flagging is associated with *production* difficulties, despite the fact that all our informants are fluent first-generation speakers of Finnish, as well as being proficient in English. This is because these speakers do not belong to a bilingual community in which *either* nonce borrowing *or* code-switching (whether smooth as in the Spanish–English and Tamil–English [Sankoff, Poplack and Vanniarajan, 1986] cases, or flagged as in the French–English case) is a discourse *mode*. These speakers use English in most interactions and domains, for example with children, spouse and co-workers, and virtually only have occasion to use Finnish when participating in the particular Finnish-speaking network in which we recorded them. These results confirm our suggestion that the morphological and syntactic role of nonce borrowing is identical to that of established loanwords, which in turn reflect the grammatical patterns of the host-language. In this, both contrast with code-switches, which retain source-language morphology and syntax, as illustrated in Fig. 8.6.

It must be stressed that all of the empirically studied communities to which we have referred manifest very different patterns of bilingual behavior, despite the fact that in each we can attest at least some smooth code-switching, at least some nonce borrowing, and at least some flagging. Nevertheless, it would be injudicious to consider the highly-flagged French–English material as the optimum data for the study of smooth code-switching. Nor is the Spanish–English situation, with its ease of switching, the most suitable context in which to analyze nonce borrowing.

However, once we have established that the social role of language mixing is propitious to the smooth integration of elements of both codes, typological considerations are predictive of the types of mixture. Similar typologies are conducive to code-switching, while conflicting typologies are more likely to result in nonce borrowing. And since all these phenomena occur to at least some degree in all the communities, the overwhelming nature of these patterns could never have been distinguished without systematic quantitative analysis of natural performance data.

Notes

1 The generous support of the Social Science and Humanities Research Council of Canada to Poplack for the project "Sociolinguistic aspects of language contact in the Ottawa-Hull region", and to D. Sankoff for the project "Code-switching constraints in typologically different language pairs" is gratefully acknowledged. Earlier versions of parts of this paper were presented at NWAVE XIII (1984), the VI International Conference of Nordic and General Linguistics (1986) and the IX Meeting of the American Association for Applied Linguistics (1986). We thank David Sankoff for his contributions to the analysis and interpretation of the materials, Doug Walker for careful comments on the manuscript, and Marguerite Trudel-Maggiore for her expert preparation of the text. This chapter is reprinted from The Nordic Languages and Modern Linguistics 6, edited by P. Lilius and M. Saari. Helsinki University Press: 33–56 (1987).
2 Codes identify speaker and utterance.
3 Word order is actually relatively free in Finnish, variation serving mainly to alter the focus of the sentence. The unmarked order, however, is SVO.
4 The following abbreviations are used throughout in the glosses of Finnish cases: n. = nominative, g. = genitive, p. = partitive, in. = inessive, el. = elative, il. = illative, ad. = adessive, ab. = ablative, al. = allative, tr. = translative, ess. = essive, ø = zero morpheme, int. = interrogative, pl. = plural, inf. = infinitive. Grammatical persons are designated 1p., 2p., etc.
5 In all cases but the nominative singular, which receives a null mark.
6 Readers familiar with the *free morpheme* constraint (Poplack, 1980; 1981), which prohibits a *code-switch* between a bound and a free morpheme of different languages, will note that nonce borrowing occurs *without* any change of code on the morphological and syntactic levels.

7 The only other single lexical items of English origin found in the corpus were a small number (< 7 percent) of adjectives and verbs (< 2 percent), which we do not include in this analysis.

8 An additional 163 occurrences originally coded as intrasentential code-switches were in fact examples of reported direct speech, as in the following example.

Lääkäri   sano   että *"when you go to Finland, no funerals"*, ja   mä sanoin
doctor-n. said-3p. that   and I   said-1p.
"Okay, no funerals". (291/065)
"The doctor said 'when you go to Finland, no funerals', and I said, 'Okay, no funerals'."

These all satisfy the equivalence constraint since both languages have the same structure for reporting speech. Switching for this purpose is a well-documented discourse device (e.g. Gumperz, 1982; Poplack, 1985) and, indeed, accounts for the majority of the switches used by some of the speakers in our sample.

9 Such examples are in fact attested, but contra Nishimura (1985), they are exceedingly rare. We found two cases in our data:

Mutta se oli *kidney*stä *to* aort**aan**. (11a/337)
but   it was   -el.   -il.
"But it was from the kidney to the aorta (to)."

Ja   sitten...uh missä hän n--**at** yliopisto**ssa** otti...   niin kuin
and then   where she n--   university-in. took-3p. like
art history. (11a/252)
"And then...uh where did she-- at university (at) she took...like art history."

10 Note that these data contain, as a subset, the NPs contained in the structures corresponding to English prepositional phrases discussed above, but include in addition, many others corresponding to English subjects and direct objects which also require case-marking according to Finnish rules.

11 For the nominative singular, which in standard Finnish takes a null mark, we considered bare English nouns to be "marked" for case, i.e. to follow native-language patterns. Of course, it has been widely reported (e.g. Lehtinen, 1966; Karttunen, 1977; Martin, 1981; Virtaranta, 1981) that many consonant-final nouns borrowed into Finnish take a vocalic ending (e.g. *jobi* "job", *kaara* "car"), which serves as a stem for further case-marking. However, since consonant-final nouns occur natively in Finnish with no such vowel addition, we are reluctant to consider the 72 percent of consonant-final English-origin singular nominal stems in our data as failing to show obligatory case-marking, particularly since this rate far exceeds the incidence of case-absence found for any other case (Table 8.3). Such an inflated rate would be particularly curious in view of the fact that the nominative is by far the most frequently used case in the data. We suggest that the optional presence of the stem vowel serves as a phonological marker of loanword integration. This would explain its relatively sparse occurrence in our data, which contain both established and nonce borrowings.

12 Because our data were analyzed according to morphological case rather than syntactic function, the figures for the accusative case are contained in the calculations for the nominative and genitive, and thus cannot readily be brought to bear on Larmouth's claim.

13 Nominative contexts have been excluded from this calculation.

14 "Marking" for the nominative case in this instance refers to the previously mentioned addition of the stem vowel to consonant-final English nouns. The fact that there is no difference between marking rates in the two contexts, in contrast with the other cases, lends support to our suggestion (endnote 11) that addition of the stem vowel is a phonological integration device rather than specifically a marker of case.

References

Bentahila, A. and Davies, E. (1983), The syntax of Arabic-French code-switching. *Lingua* **59**, 301–330.

Bokamba, E. G. (1985), Code mixing, language variation, and linguistic theory: evidence from Bantu languages. Paper presented at the 16th Annual Conference on African Linguistics.

Gumperz, J. (1982), Conversational code-switching. In his *Discourse Strategies*. Cambridge University Press.

Karlsson, F. (1983), *Finnish Grammar*. Helsinki: Werner Söderström Osakeyhtiö.

Karttunen, F. (1977), Finnish in America: A case study in mono-generational language change. In Blount, B. G. and Sanches, M. (eds.), *Sociocultural Dimensions of Language Change*. New York: Academic Press.

Labov, W. (1969), Contraction, deletion and inherent variability of the English copula. *Language* **45:4**, 715–762.

(1971), Some principles of linguistic methodology. *Language in Society* **1**, 97–120.

Larmouth, D. W. (1974), Differential interference in American Finnish cases. *Language* **50:2**, 356–366.

Lehtinen, M. (1966), Analysis of a Finnish-English Bilingual Corpus. Ph.D. Dissertation, Indiana University.

Martin, M. L. (1981), Finnish as a means of communication in Thunder Bay. In Karni, M. G. (ed.), *Finnish Diaspora I: Canada, South America, Africa, Australia and Sweden*. The Multicultural History Society of Ontario, Toronto. Papers of the Finn Forum Conference, Toronto, Nov. 1979.

Nishimura, M. (1985), Intrasentential code-switching in Japanese and English. Ph.D. Dissertation, University of Pennsylvania.

Pfaff, C. W. (1979), Constraints on language mixing: intrasentential code-switching and borrowing in Spanish/English. *Language* **55:2**, 291–318.

Poplack, S. (1980), "Sometimes I'll start a sentence in Spanish y termino en español": Toward a typology of code-switching. *Linguistics* **18:7/8**, 581–618.

(1981), Syntactic structure and social function of code-switching. In: Duran, R. (ed.), *Latino Discourse and Communicative Behavior*. New Jersey: Ablex Publishing Corporation. Pp. 169–184.

(1985), Contrasting patterns of code-switching in two communities. In Warkentyne, H. J. (ed.), *Proceedings of the Fifth International Conference on Methods in Dialectology*, University of Victoria Press: pp. 363–385.

Poplack, S., Sankoff, D. and Miller, C. (1988), The social correlates and linguistic processes of lexical borrowing and assimilation. *Linguistics* **26:1**, 47–104.

Prince, E. F. and Pintzuk, S. (1983), Bilingual code-switching and the open/closed class distinction. Unpublished manuscript.

Sankoff, D. and Mainville, S. (1986a), Un modèle de l'alternance de langue sous la contrainte d'équivalence. *Revue québécoise de linguistique* **15:2**, 233–246.

(1986b), Code-switching of context-free grammars. *Theoretical Linguistics* **13**. 1/2:75–90.

Sankoff, D. and Poplack, S. (1981), A formal grammar for code-switching. *Papers in Linguistics* **14:1**, 3–46.

Sankoff, D., Poplack, S. and Vanniarajan, S. (1986), The case of the nonce loan in Tamil. Centre de recherche de mathématiques appliquées, Technical Report No. 1348. University of Montreal: Montreal.

Sankoff, G. (1974), A quantitative paradigm for the study of communicative competence. In Bauman, R. and Sherzer, J. (eds.), *Explorations in the Ethnography of Speaking*. Cambridge University Press.

Virtaranta, P. (1981), Finnish dialects in America: some experiences and problems. In Karni,

M. G. (ed.), *Finnish Diaspora II: United States*. The Multicultural History Society of Ontario, Toronto. Papers of the Finn Forum Conference, Toronto, Nov. 1979.

Weinreich, U. (1953), *Languages in Contact*. The Hague: Mouton.

Wheeler, S. (1987), Code-switching and Borrowing in a Finnish-English Bilingual Situation. M.A. Thesis. University of Ottawa.

9. The boustrophedal brain: Laterality and dyslexia in bi-directional readers

LORAINE K. OBLER

Introduction

Today most, but not all, of the languages of the world are read from left to right. Historically, however, we know that sizable populations have read from right to left, as readers of Hebrew, Arabic, Persian, and Urdu do today. In the early stages of development of Greek writing, reading was in boustrophedon, reading alternately lines from left to right and then right to left, the way some modern day computers' printers print. Historically Chinese and Japanese are read in columns from up to down starting in the upper *right* hand side of the page; only in the modern era has a horizontal direction been preferred. That remains right to left in Taiwan, but has become left to right in the People's Republic of China and in Japan.

Should the thought cross one's mind that reading left to right is more "natural" because most people read that way today, it bears remembering that for centuries after the seventh and eighth century spread of Islamic civilization, the vast majority of the literate world was reading its languages from right to left. Most obviously in the case of modern Chinese there are cultural and political factors that interact in determining reading direction as well.

Laterality studies of bi-directional readers

Before we turn to the cases of reading disturbance in bi-directional readers, it is worth reviewing the laterality literature on healthy bi-directional readers. This research has virtually all been carried out with the Hebrew script and English, testing readers of either Hebrew or Yiddish.

The question that researchers into laterality via tachistoscopic methods posed first in the early 1950s was: to what extent does reading direction contribute to lateral dominance? Since virtually all the early tachistoscopic studies were done using left to right languages such as English, it was conceivable that the results which showed right visual field effect for language had more to do with eye scanning than with the true laterality for language which had been inferred from aphasia after left brain damage.

Reading direction, it should be pointed out, actually involves scanning in both directions. There is the single scan to the beginning of a line, which is then followed by saccadic – or interval – scanning in the direction of reading. Different brain mechanisms are involved in each of these scanning activities. We may assume that the frontal eye field of the hemisphere contralateral to the direction of scan is predominantly active during the scanning to the beginning of a line, and it is probably the case that bilateral brainstem areas are engaged in saccading along the direction of reading.

In order to test the extent to which reading scan could be disengaged from "true" laterality for language, one might present materials vertically rather than horizontally (which a number of investigators have done), with the expected decrease in laterality, but this poses a very "unnatural" i.e. unpracticed task. Mishkin and Forgays (1952) tested the extent of interaction of reading direction and laterality by testing a sample of 19 bilingual subjects on both English and Yidddish words. Their subjects' performance on English words showed 40 percent greater recognition from the right visual field as compared to the left visual field, whereas for Yiddish words, recognition was 25 percent greater for words in the left visual field as compared to the right visual field. This difference for English was significant, whereas the difference for Yiddish was not. A simple prediction that language dominance for any language would be manifested by a right visual field effect was not borne out. Reading scan direction was clearly a potential additional factor.

The subjects in Mishkin and Forgays' experiment, they acknowledged, were not as fluent in their reading of Yiddish as in English; perhaps this had had an effect. Orbach (1952) sought to correct this by running a similar experiment using highly skilled Yiddish readers. Orbach also took into account the age of acquisition of reading of each language. As with the study by Mishkin and Forgays, with English words there was a strong right visual field effect. With Yiddish words, by contrast, subjects who learned English first showed a right visual field effect, whereas subjects who learned Yiddish first showed a left visual field effect, both significant effects. It appeared that there was something about Yiddish which made it more bilaterally represented than English, especially for people who learned it young.

By 1967, Orbach had considered the vast variety of factors which might be interacting to show this difference between the languages. For him these included not only direction of reading, but also what he called the "lack of distinctiveness" of Hebrew letters (no empirical demonstration was given, however). He also claimed that in English the beginning letters of a word are more crucial for appreciating it than they are in Hebrew (p. 128). In addition, he correctly observed that Hebrew readers (unlike, *mutatis mutandis*, English readers) regularly read other left to right languages, and moreover have practice within Hebrew of reading numerals from left to right. The study Orbach carried out in 1967 was quite similar to his previous one in that he presented English and Hebrew words tachistoscopically to bilingual native Hebrew readers. As before, he found no laterality effect with Hebrew words, but a significant right visual field effect on the English words, for the right-handers. In this study he also tested left-handers and found an interaction between laterality as measured by the tachistoscopic paradigm, and handedness. Thus, scanning direction alone was not the explanation for the difference between the two languages; rather he concluded that a combination of "directional scanning, selective attention, cerebral dominance and structural factors all influence the left–right recognition differential."

In the meantime, Barton, Goodglass, and Shai (1965) had made one obvious manipulation to eliminate reading scan direction by testing native readers of Hebrew, who were in the United States for advanced schooling, on Hebrew and English words presented vertically. With vertical presentation they found a significant right visual field effect for both languages.

When we applied this manipulation with our colleague Gaziel (Albert and Obler, 1978), we actually obtained a left visual field effect for vertical presentation of English words in our right-handed Americans, who spoke and read English better than Hebrew, but knew both languages. Indeed, we realize that vertical presentation as a rule minimized differences among our 3 groups. (In addition to the native English speakers who knew some Hebrew, we had balanced bilinguals and native Hebrew speakers who knew some English; for the purposes of this experiment only right handers were tested.) We concluded that measurements of true language dominance by vertical presentation were problematic.

We also presented reading materials horizontally in the two languages and did not see a consistent reverse pattern of field effect for Hebrew and English. From Barton, Goodglass, and Shai, one must conclude that visual scanning contributes to an "apparent change in laterality for Hebrew reading"; from our study we conclude that reading scan alone cannot fully account for laterality patterns.

A recent contribution to this literature is Tramer, Butler and Mewhort, 1985. They presented a series of 6 English or 6 Hebrew letters to the left or right visual fields of 6 right-handed highly competent bilinguals – 3 females and 3 males. Subjects were instructed to recall as many letters as possible, either in a left to right direction, in right to left, or in alphabetic order. By a correctness measure, order of report was not a significant variable, nor was visual field alone a significant variable. The significant interaction was between visual field and language whereby English letters produced a right visual field effect and Hebrew letters produced a left visual field effect. The authors conclude that cerebral laterality had no effect; only reading scan direction did. This is particularly surprising, the authors acknowledge, because the letter strings never composed words or even approximated them. Moreover the Hebrew and English strings were randomly intermixed, so the subjects could not plan scanning direction in advance. Rather, something about the letters themselves seems to have induced the effect.

On the basis of this series of studies (and we have been able to find none published on languages other than Hebrew and Yiddish) we conclude that reading scan direction contributes to an *apparent* laterality in tachistoscopic testing. In addition, the extent to which a language is well known and practiced also seems to have an effect on limiting it to the left hemisphere. (See also Silverberg, Bentin, Gaziel, Obler, and Albert, 1979 in this regard.)

Possible manifestations of dyslexia in bilingual readers

The critical symptom of letter-by-letter dyslexia is that the patient reads a word by identifying the letters, either overtly or covertly and can only read the word after identifying the individual letters. Obviously this will only be successful in a language which has an orthographic script consisting of letters. Thus, if one knew how to read one language whose orthography used letters and one language that used ideographs, such as Chinese, one would be expected to be a letter-by-letter reader only in English. Note that letter-by-letter reading is often associated with a hand movement of tracing the letters out. Interestingly, such a phenomenon has been reported for a Chinese–English aphasic with dyslexia (Lyman, Kwan and Chao, 1938). So we may have been too hasty in assuming that letter-by-letter alexia cannot exist in Chinese. Needless to say, it depends on how rigid one wants to be in defining it; we understand that the underlying deficit is the same in both languages, and the compensatory strategy is the same, but can obviously be used more in an alphabetic language than in one with an ideographic system.

Suppose we were to find a bilingual who read two languages whose orthography consisted of letters, and the patient was a letter-by-letter reader in one but not the other. In that case we would less likely assume that it was structural differences in the language which accounted for this behavior, but look for explanations on the basis of how the languages had been learned. For example, if in learning to read language A, spelling had been stressed, while in learning to read language B, whole word identification had been stressed, or if the patient's job had involved substantial spelling in language A, but not in language B (e.g. s/he was a typist in language A or a composer of language A dictionaries), it is at least conceivable that in reading language B post-morbidly, the letter-by-letter strategy would be unavailable (or less available) to the patient. Frankly, if this were to happen, I would expect to see a fairly quick transfer of the decoding strategy so that the patient could read language B as well as language A.

Patients with phonological dyslexia make visually-motivated errors in reading; that is, they will respond with a word which has some, but not all, letters in common with the targeted word. In principle, such an error is possible in alphabetic orthographies, syllabic orthographies, and ideographic orthographies, although one would expect that the error in the first two would be phonologically closer than with the ideographic words; that is to say, if one confused elements of an ideograph in Chinese, one would often produce a word that sounds substantially different from the target word. Indeed, since such an error might be considered a semantic error, and since, in the standard cognitive neuropsychological classification of dyslexias, the phonological dyslexic does not make semantic errors, categorizing a reader of Chinese as a phonological dyslexic could cause some confusion.

In the unlikely event that it was possible to construct non-words in both languages where the dyslexic patient had difficulty reading them in only one language, we would be forced to look for differential learning or usage patterns of the two languages. That is to say, it is conceivable that the patient had learned or used one language in a primarily phonological decoding pattern, and thus was still able to do it, even for non-words, but had learned and/or used the other language predominantly through the word recognition mode, and therefore decoding of non-words would have been slower pre-morbidly and then quite difficult after brain damage.

Surface dyslexia involves loss of whole-word recognition; grapheme-to-grapheme rules are spared however, so patients perform much better in reading aloud regularly spelled words than irregular words. Moreover, when they read words aloud, they make regularization errors. Clearly, for a bilingual patient to be able to manifest this kind of dyslexia, it is necessary that the orthographic systems of language A or B have a phonological script and both regularly and irregularly spelled words. Such a phenomenon, for example, could not be obtained in Spanish, as Coltheart (1982) pointed out and demonstrated with the patient who made no errors on irregular words in Spanish because there are no irregular words. If the orthography is not a phonologically encoded one, as is the case for the ideographic languages, such errors cannot occur.

If one were to see a patient who read two languages which did have both regular and irregular words, say English and French, and this patient evidenced surface dyslexia in language A but not in language B, one would have to infer that a route through the lexicon was available for language B but not language A. This is conceivable if one learned to read language A solely in order to be able to read it aloud (for example, if A was a religious language for which one did not know the meaning of the individual words) while one learned to read language B for meaning.

Misunderstanding of homophones can occur in languages that have a one-to-one grapheme-to-morpheme system, but a one-to-more-than-one phoneme-to-grapheme system. Coltheart's (1982) Spanish speaker made errors of defining Spanish words on the basis of their homophones; thus indicating via this secondary characteristic that the subject was indeed a surface dyslexic in Spanish as well as in English. Confusing the meaning of written homophones can also occur in ideographic languages, as Coltheart points out.

Finally, consider the component symptoms of deep dyslexia. The definitional symptom for deep dyslexia is the making of semantic errors (e.g. reading *orchestra* for *symphony*). It must be possible to make semantic errors in all languages. If a patient were to display semantic errors in one language but not another, we would have to assume that s/he had different lexical organizations for the two language systems, whereby the connection between semantics and the phonological output lexicon functioned correctly in one language, but not in the other. This could be due to learning to read one language apart from meaning. In traditional bilingualism terminology, it is possible that a coordinate bilingual would be more likely to have such a differential lexical system than would a compound bilingual. It is unclear to us how such a phenomenon might be based on language-specific factors.

Derivational errors are a concomitant symptom in deep dyslexia. These are of interest to the linguist because they pertain less to orthography and more to the structure of the actual language in question. Indeed, there are languages such as Chinese that do not construct words through derivation, and others which do to greater (e.g. Hebrew and Arabic) and lesser (e.g. English) degrees. Thus, it is conceivable that a patient would make derivational errors in language A but not in language B simply because language B did not use derivational affixes. It is also possible that the derivational system in language A is substantially more complex than the system in language B. If A's derivational morphology is more complex, this could result in more intricate neuronal "wiring" in which case it would be less susceptible to deficit with alexia. Alternately because derivational morphology occurred more frequently in A, in any spontaneous reading the deficits would be substantially more noticeable in language A.

Functor reading is impaired in deep dyslexia. No doubt this characteristic is related to the production of derivational errors discussed above and to the fact that most deep dyslexics are Broca's aphasics, with tendencies towards agrammatism. Here again we may easily postulate differences among languages, knowing that some (e.g. Thai) rely heavily on functors, whereas others (e.g. Turkish) rely more heavily on inflectional affixes for such syntactic functions as verb tense and aspect.

If, as Coltheart's school would posit, derivational errors but not inflectional errors occur in the monolingual dyslexic, then we may expect the dyslexic reader of language A, which has many functors and few inflections, to be substantially more impaired than the reader of language B, which relies on inflections to indicate those syntactic functions indicated by functors in language A. We will investigate this further in discussing our Hebrew–English dyslexic below.

Brain damage in bi-directional readers

If true laterality is affected by the practice effect, one might expect a paradoxical finding in cases of aphasia resulting from left-hemisphere lesions whereby the *less* known language for reading would be better preserved after an aphasia-producing accident. That is true in 2 of the 4 aphasia cases I will talk about (and 4 of the 11 cases of brain-damage I will review). Moreover, the literature on brain damage as it interacts with bi-directional readers suggests a weak tendency to deficit in the language which is read from right-to-left.

Seven cases of bilingual or polyglot aphasics who read a right-to-left language can be found in the literature. We have very little information on four of them, so I will treat them summarily. The first is case 6 reported by L'Hermitte and colleagues (1966). It is the case of an Egyptian-born Jew who was schooled in Arabic, as well as French, Hebrew and English. While his extensive left-sided lesion may have influenced his reading in all languages, it would appear that he was only tested in French and in Spanish, and in those languages his spelling was equally impaired. So, we have no data about his abilities to read in his right-to-left languages.

Nair and Virmani (1973) mention two patients who lost their abilities to read right-to-left languages. In one it was Persian which was lost and in the other patient it was Urdu. Interestingly, of the 33 polyglots Nair and Virmani tested, only these two, who had right-to-left languages, appear to have had differential loss of capacity in their languages; the other 31 had a similar disturbance in both languages. About the first patient we have no further information. About the second, we can presume that Urdu was a native language, since the patient was a physics professor who used English primarily in his professional life and had not used Urdu much in recent years. Thus, this case might contradict the hypothesis based on the laterality studies that the less well known or practiced language was *more* likely to recover after aphasia. However, since the patient learned that language first, it may support a modification of this thesis, namely that a language which is less well known due to later learning would be the first to return due to right hemisphere participation.

That hypothesis, however, would appear to be contradicted by case number 79 of Obler and Albert in Albert and Obler (1978). It is the case of a young left-handed woman whose mother tongue was Hebrew and who had immigrated as an adolescent to England where she became quite fluent in English. However, she returned to Israel and used predominantly Hebrew at the age of 18 until she was in an automobile accident at 20, resulting in bilateral frontal lesions. Her verbal comprehension for the two languages was equal when she was tested three weeks after the accident, but she made substantial reversal errors when writing English. On one day she would left-right reverse the individual letters as she was writing her name; on another when asked to write the alphabet in English she wrote each letter correctly but starting from the right side of the page. She did not make such errors in Hebrew. So her less well known and later learned language, English, was not better preserved.

At this point it is worth inserting the case reported by Streifler and Hofman (1976), since that also involved left-right reversal in reading as well as writing, but only for Hebrew and not for the patient's native language. However, since there was no frank aphasia in this case, I do not count this case among the aphasics. This is the case of a 47 year old woman who was apparently ambidexterous, as were her father and her son. The woman was a native speaker of Polish, but learned to read Hebrew first at the age of 4 for religious purposes. In young adulthood she immigrated to Israel where Hebrew was the language she used daily.

After a minor automobile accident resulting in a slight brain concussion, the patient had no aphasic disturbance except that when asked to write in Hebrew she wrote in mirror fashion. Moreover, she was able to read mirror-reversed Hebrew but not standardly presented Hebrew. In contrast, she read Latin characters well in the standard orientation, but was unable to read them in mirror presentation.

Because there appeared to be some other cognitive and subcortical changes in this woman (in particular because she lost her calculating ability which was necessary for her work and demonstrated much left-right reversal in her everyday activities), the authors speculated that there might be organic impairment, but since they were unable to find it they at first suspected this woman of hysteria. In the published draft of the paper, however, they were more prepared to admit a possible interaction between bilateral pathology and an earlier unusual brain organization related to the ambidexterity of her family. Why this should apply only to Hebrew, the language she first learned to read, and not to Polish, is entirely unclear. For our purposes we must conclude that reading scan direction does appear to have contributed to the deficit in this case. My suspicion is that there is some non-linguistic phenomenon, related to motoric "knowing" that languages may be written and read both from left to right and from right to left which is confusing both this patient and that of Obler and Albert.

The three more extensively reported aphasia cases are all reported by Halpern (1941, 1949, 1950). The first is the case of a young German man whose handedness is not noted, who had read and written Hebrew for religious purposes as a child. Moreover, he had spoken it a bit, as well as German, after he came to Palestine at the age of 20, but then was wounded in his left temporal lobe at the age of 22. This patient read (and spoke) more fluently and correctly in Hebrew than he did in German for the 8 months after the injury. He learned to read both Hebrew and German in childhood, so age of acquisition cannot be the crucial factor. Halpern explicitly states that German had been his dominant language at the time of the injury, so this case does support the hypothesis that a less well-known language is better recovered. Moreover, this case contradicts the speculative rule that the right-to-left language is worse after brain injury.

A second case reported in Halpern, 1949, is that of a left-hander with a right-sided lesion. This young man was a native speaker and reader of Russian, who had learned to read and write Hebrew at the age of eight. He had immigrated to Palestine at the age of 14, where he started to read Hebrew. At the age of 36 he was wounded in the right temporal lobe. The patient evidenced a sensory aphasia in Hebrew, and in reading and writing he omitted and "confused" letters. In Russian, however, he was unable to speak or read and write at all.

The third case Halpern reported is that of a converted left-hander whose native language was English. He had learned to read religious Hebrew at the age of 7 and then immigrated at the age of 20 to Palestine. He had a left parietal temporal wound at the age of 42 resulting in a sensory aphasia with acalculia, as well as alexia and agraphia. Initially, only his English returned, but after the first 2 months the patient worked very hard on his Hebrew and was able to recover it, particularly in the written modalities, until it was better than his English.

Lest it appear that differential alexia is the rule with readers of at least one left-to-right orthography and at least one right-to-left orthography, we must include the case reported by Sroka, Solsi and Bornstein, 1973. They reported the case of a patient with alexia without agraphia, equally in both Hebrew and English. The patient is probably a right-hander since at this late date left-handedness should have been mentioned had it occurred. Her native language was Slovakian and in addition to English she had learned German in high school and then Hebrew when she immigrated to Israel after high school.

Her lesion resulted from an arterior venous malformation of the left posterior cerebral artery and was in the left occipital subcortical region of the lingual and fusiform gyri. In the earliest stages, the patient could not read in any of her languages. As her reading returned, the authors report that she was equally impaired in all languages. Interestingly, she did make some left-right confusions, for example in English confusing p and q or b and d.

When given six letter words, the patient read the beginnings of them better. This probably interacted with her ability to read short words better than long words in all languages.

She was clearly using both analytic and whole word strategies, as is evident from the fact that, at times, she could get elements of a word correct but not the whole word. At other times, when she was tested with Hebrew words in which a letter or an inflection was deliberately missing, the patient would spontaneously read the word as if it included that letter or inflection.

To summarize on the basis of the 6 aphasia cases on which we have any information at all (I exclude the L'Hermitte *et al.* case), we have 4 in which the left-to-right language was initially better preserved for reading and 2 in which the right-to-left language was better preserved. So, as with the laterality studies, reading direction does not seem to be crucial for systematically predicting brain organization for reading. As to the hypothesis, generated on the basis of the experimental tests of laterality, that the less well-known language might be better preserved, at least 4 of the 6 cases contradict it. Two of these cases, however, are left-handers, as is Halpern's third case, for whom English returned best first, but was then overtaken by Hebrew. We must recognize that this set of aphasic patients does not have a normal distribution of handedness, and may not, therefore, be representative of the larger polyglot aphasia population. Certainly, the bilingual lateralization experiments were virtually all conducted on right-handers, except for that of Orbach (1967) who did find more bilateral representation of language for left-handers.

One final study worth mentioning is that of reading-triggered epilepsy reported by Stevens in 1957. The case of interest to us is his case number three, of a 24 year old woman whose handedness is not mentioned. Reading of any sort triggered her epileptic attacks, but reading of Hebrew, which she had learned for religious purposes, precipitated the attacks substantially faster than reading of English. Even if the attacks were not full-fledged, they were evident from an EEG recording:

Reading English at various sizes of print under varying conditions of illumination failed to produce dysrhythmia in the electroencephalogram. However when the patient was given Hebrew to read, a crescendo of spike discharges was promptly precipitated, eventuating in jaw twitching followed by a feeling of warmth and then of being dazed, until finally she was unable to continue the reading.

But we cannot jump to the conclusion that it was reading direction which differentially triggered the attacks, since reading music was more like reading Hebrew for her than was reading English, and of course music is read from left-to-right. In this case we might be tempted to argue that it is the less well known languages – Hebrew and music – that are more problematic. Of course this is directly contradictory to the expectation that less well-known symbol systems would be more likely to be spared through bilateral representation, even though we are not considering frank aphasia here.

Developmental dyslexia in bi-directional readers

Critchley (1970) reports, unfortunately too briefly, on four cases of developmental dyslexia in Near Easterners. The examples he gives are all in the writing rather than the reading modality. His assessment is that the three cases of Arabic–English dyslexics all made errors in both writing and spelling in both languages, as did his Hebrew–English dyslexic in both the reading and writing modalities. The Hebrew–English speaker, it is worth noting, had her "preferred direction of automatic gaze" from right to left.

By my analysis, the extended example Critchley gives of one $14\frac{1}{2}$ year old Arabic–English dyslexic male shows substantially different sorts of errors in the two languages. In English the boy makes the following errors:

(1) Addition and omission of punctuation
(2) Omission of letters, as in *pleas* for *please*
(3) Lack of space between words, as in *Whenyou*
(4) Reversals of letter order in the word *recieve* for *receive*
(5) Space between words where there should be none: *Any way*
(6) Substitution of one unusual letter for another: *whaw* for *way*
(7) Substitution of one morphological ending consistently for another: *starter* for *started* twice in one letter
(8) An l to r substitution which is presumably phonologically motivated: *frute* for *flute*
(9) A semantic paragraphia, phonologically motivated: *by* for *buy*
(10) A visually motivated literal paraphasia: *tike* for *like*
(11) Confusion of a contraction: *I do nont* for *I don't*
(12) Substitution of a phonologically close word: *Ones* for *Once*
(13) A learned rule mislearned, in *pesical* for *physical*
(14) m to n in *nath* for *math*
(15) Functor class substitution: *with* for *will*.

In Arabic, by contrast, there are as many errors, but the errors are much more frequently ones of confusing one letter for another: that is, they are visually motivated errors. There are also orthographic errors wherein this boy displaces dots and bars; in English such misplacements might be seen as punctuation errors but in Arabic they convert one letter into another. It is worth noting, however, that there is no indication that these differences between the two languages in this dyslexic (or either of the other two Arabic–English speakers referred to whose materials were not included in the text) have to do with reading scan direction.

Case study of a bilingual dyslexic

The final bilingual dyslexic I will discuss was tested twice by Dr. Eva Baharav when she was a student with me in Boston in 1983.

M.Y. was born in Israel to German speaking parents in 1940. As was common among immigrants at the time, her parents insisted on speaking Hebrew in the home. Nevertheless, M.Y. reported that she understands German reasonably well, but speaks it minimally. At the age of 6 she started to study Hebrew reading and writing. At the age of 10 she started studying English in school through a written and oral method, and at the age of 11 she spent several months in the United States, which, she reported, familiarized her with English.

At the age of 19, she married an American with whom she spoke English and with whom, when we tested her at the age of 43, she continued to speak English. Between the ages of 19 and 29 she lived in America and spoke and wrote English almost exclusively, at home and in her work as a nurses' aide. At the age of 29, she returned to Israel for another 10 years during which time she continued to speak English with her husband and children. However, at this time she would speak Hebrew with neighbors. At the age of 39, she returned to the United States and used English almost exclusively. She then studied for a high school degree in English, and had training in basic reading skills which, she reported, focused her successfully on slowing down and grasping the meaning of what was read. When we tested her in 1983, she was enrolled in college, studying the social sciences.

As to her history of dyslexia, it was apparently so severe in Hebrew that from an early age her step-father treated her as though she were retarded. A physician concurred with this diagnosis and recommended special schooling; however, her mother believed her to be normal and sent her to a private school. There, although M.Y. did well socially, she performed quite poorly in educational activities. She recalled that she had periods of time when she would "block out" what was going on around her, when she was required to read, or when someone tried to explain something to her. Even at the age of 43 she felt she has these episodes of "block out" when under academic pressure.

From the neurological point of view, it is worth mentioning that M.Y. herself is left-handed and her son (but also her husband) are left-handed. However, both her parents are right-handed and her other child, a daughter, is right-handed. The son, moreover, has reading disorders which may be less severe than M.Y.'s were, since they have been treated in school, and she reports "he is dealing with them."

M.Y. recognizes that she omits word endings when she reads in English, "especially with long words." M.Y. also recognizes that she reverses numbers, for example reading 69 as 96, and that she confuses certain letters which have one phonemic representation in Hebrew and another in English, in particular N a grapheme which is pronounced as an /m/ in Hebrew. She also stated that she has trouble following orders given her in rapid succession, and that she has problems using the terms *left* and *right* in both languages. She can, however, read maps successfully and orients herself well in the environment.

In the initial test session, Dr. Baharav gave M.Y. two texts to read in English and four in Hebrew (two voweled and two non-voweled since daily Hebrew is read without most vowels indicated, although religious texts and children's books are voweled as a rule). On the second testing, she was given word lists varying for word length, frequency, voweledness, prefixes and word compounds and functor/substantive word category.

In reading text aloud, the presence or absence of voweling in Hebrew made virtually no difference to M.Y., but in both languages, the difficulty of the text made a difference. By a gross count of percent of words containing errors, M.Y. made more errors in English (34.5 percent) when reading aloud a scientific passage than she did when reading a sixth grade story (13 percent). In Hebrew she made 15 percent errors reading a non-voweled adult novel, 15 percent errors reading the Bible which is voweled, and 11 percent errors reading a non-voweled newspaper. When reading a voweled poem, however, she made 37 percent errors.

By far the most frequent errors in the reading of English text, as she reported, were errors of inflectional endings. On three occasions her errors consisted of substitutions (e.g. *curtailed* for *curtails*, *features* for *featuring*, *closest* for *closer*). On most occasions she deleted endings (e.g. *limited* to *limit*, *times* to *time*, *notice* to *note*).

The next most frequent category was a substitution of one word for a visually similar word. In most instances both words were functors:

thus to *those*
they to *the*
indeed to *needed*
odd to *add*
though to *through*
sure to *swear*

In another category of errors, she was apparently trying to sound out words she did not recognize. (Note that the word-initial segments were most likely to be correct.)

opaque to *opi-ekyu*
focal to *focim*
numerosity to *numerisity*
potential to *potentiyal*
predetermined to *predeterminates*
semantics to *semininc*
lexical to *laxion*
linguistic to *linguistig*
algorithmic to *alego … ratmic* (long pause in middle of word)
syntactic to *tictic*

In only one instance did she recognize a word and give it in the Hebrew translation. This was with the name *Ruth*, which she read as *Ruti*, a common translation equivalent to the Hebrew name. This might be considered a semantic error of the sort deep dyslexics make. The only other related example in our corpus was in the compound word list, where she read *schoolyard* as /shul/, no, schoolyard, *shul* being the Yiddish word for *synagogue*.

In Hebrew, to our surprise and in contrast to English, there were very few errors of word endings, including inflectional endings on text reading. Indeed, by a gross analysis of where errors occurred in the word, only 2.7 percent of the English errors occurred in the first syllable as opposed to 34.4 percent in Hebrew; by contrast, 70.2 percent of the errors were made at the end of the word in English, and only 17.2 percent in Hebrew, and there were substantially more errors in the middle of the word (48.2 percent) in Hebrew than in English (27 percent). These results can be seen in Table 9.1.

Note that in Hebrew as in English, however, word-initial consonants were almost invariably correct. The vast majority of error productions in Hebrew were non-words; in English this type of error was substantially smaller. Thus we must note there are two forms of what might be considered visually motivated errors; in English these are, in about two-thirds of the cases, accounted for by the loss of inflectional endings; in Hebrew they are accounted for by an incorrect production of the vowels, regardless of whether the text was voweled or non-voweled, and an incorrect choice was made of a consonant phoneme due to a diacritic error (e.g. reading שׂ/s/ for שׁ/š/).

Table 9.1 *Location of M.Y.'s reading errors*

	Beginning of word	Middle of word	End of word
English	2.7%	27.0%	70.2%
Hebrew	34.4%	48.2%	17.2%

One way we tested the degree to which reading scan direction might cause the word-ending difference between Hebrew and English, was to perform further qualitative analysis on the word-ending errors in English. In English we can consider separately the derivational suffixes and the inflectional suffixes. Out of a total of 38 derivational suffixes, M.Y. erred on only one (2 percent); out of a total of 32 inflectional suffixes, she erred on sixteen (50 percent). This strongly suggests it is a linguistic factor rather than a reading-scan direction factor which is operating.

Moreover, this was not explainable by inflectional affixing. In the Hebrew corpora, there were 185 instances of prefixes (55 the definite article, 30 verb related, 100 appended prefixes). M.Y. committed only 14 prefix errors (7 percent) out of which 9 affected the definite article, and 5 were the result of the wrong vowel choice for the functor (note that with functors the consonant is much more crucially semantic than the vowel). In English, there were no productive prefixes in the texts, so we cannot compare prefixes and suffixes directly.

Two striking findings come out of the initial analysis of text reading: (1) M.Y. makes errors on inflectional suffixes in English (and hardly on derivational ones), whereas she does not in the equivalent material in Hebrew, and (2) her reading errors in Hebrew are substantially more likely to result in non-words than they are in English.

Next, we attempted to pit morphology against reading direction. When we tested prefixes, suffixes and compounds more systematically in word lists in both languages at the second testing, we found errors equally on the first and second half of compound words in both languages. In Hebrew, again, M.Y. made minimal errors on both prefixes and suffixes; in English she made errors on words with the prefix re- (but not with *un-*, *non-* or *anti*). Interestingly, her errors were not on the prefix itself:

> *reunite* to *reunit*
> *reappear* to *repair*
> *renegotiate* to *regenegotate*
> *reeducate* to *reducate*
> *reassure* to *reshure*

As to the errors on text suffixes made in English but not in Hebrew, the simplest explanation might be a right visual field neglect, but this we ruled out with the standard neurological line-crossing tests in the second testing. Another explanation would be the fact that M.Y. learned English well at a fairly late age, and may not have mastered equal proficiency in the language; in such a case, as I know well from experience, inflectional endings are less likely to be well mastered than, say, lexical items or prominent word-frame structures. One might argue that the difficulty with affixes in English might be the result of learning the language from the age of 10, which meant it was more weakly represented in M.Y.'s brain. This explanation seems unlikely, however, because not only did M.Y. consider herself fluent in both languages, and have no accent in either language, she also reported using English more, particularly in school where literacy tasks are quite frequent. Also, in Hebrew her errors would often result in non-words, whereas in English her errors never did, a further indication that her control of English was at least as good as, and probably better than, her control of Hebrew.

The most interesting explanation would be that it is a language-specific effect we see manifested in M.Y.'s differential dyslexic disorder. It is not the differential orthographies *per se* that are engendering the differential dyslexia pattern, but rather the different processing status of the written word morphology in Hebrew. From the point of view of English, Hebrew has a substantially more complex morphological system. Hebrew has a root system whereby three consonants form a root which is associated with a meaning or range of meanings, and on the basis of which patterns of vowels or vowels-plus-consonants can be added for derivational purposes, whereas English uses suffixes for deriving nouns (such as *-ity*, *-tion*, etc.) Hebrew uses what Dressler (personal communication) calls *transfixes*, which interleave with the roots. Hebrew does use affixes as well, in particular to mark tense, number, and gender – moreover compared to English it has a productive prefix as well as suffix system. In addition, Hebrew, like English, does have functors that are, as a rule, orthographically independent units.

In the strong form of Grodzinsky's (1984) argument, it is impossible for a Hebrew-speaking agrammatic patient to produce a non-word via omission of an inflectional or derivational affix, unlike the agrammatic in other languages that do not include such a system. The difficulty with Grodzinsky's argument is that Hebrew does also have prefixal and suffixal affixes for gender, number, and tense on verbs, so it would still be possible to omit or substitute for these, even if transfixed morphology would be conceptually impossible to delete. Because M.Y. makes 7 percent errors on prefixes in Hebrew, but fewer than 1 percent on suffixes, we will simply have to assume that the transfixing of the verb-related patterns on roots is so pervasive that it influences the processing of the affixes as well. This would account for the fact that the errors in Hebrew are errors of substitution, whereas those in English are omissions. If this schema is correct, then we must conclude that M.Y.'s dyslexia provides an instance in which the specific languages learned by a bilingual require, or at least engender, differential processing.

With this case we are again challenged to sort out the effects that reading direction, age of acquisition, familiarity with the language, and language structure may have. Were the direction one reads each language the crucial factor, we might expect to see errors on word endings in Hebrew as well as English, but we do not. Were some sort of left dominance for language to bias the side of the word on which errors were made, we would expect errors at word beginnings in Hebrew, since we find them at word endings in English. In Hebrew we do find some errors at word beginnings, but even more word medially. At best we might argue *post hoc* that M.Y. has a weak left hemisphere language dominance, which results in fragility in reading the right side of words. In English this results in the omission of inflected endings for which the saliency of word beginnings in Hebrew compensates. However, more strictly linguistic factors cannot be ruled out in her case. Clearly, the patient has different strategies in reading the two languages, since she produces so many more non-words in Hebrew. Thus we are left to fall back on an interactionist theory. Cerebral dominance for language processing is no doubt important in dyslexia, but an interaction with reading scan direction cannot be ruled out. Nor can a number of other factors which are illustrated in the cases reviewed in this paper, such as acquisitional parameters and linguistic effects.

Acknowledgments

I would like to thank M. P. O'Connor for editorial help as well as information about the history of orthography, and Martin Albert for information about brain bases of scanning. My thanks also go to Eva Barahav who recognized the importance of M.Y.'s case when she met her, and was involved in all stages of testing M.Y. Portions of this paper were presented at the 1985 IALP Aphasia Committee meeting in Belgium.

References

Albert, M. L. and Obler, L. (1978), *The Bilingual Brain: Neuropsychological and Neurolinguistic Aspects of Bilingualism*. New York: Academic Press.

Barton, M., Goodglass, H. and Shai, A. (1965), Differential recognition of tachistoscopically presented English and Hebrew words in right and left visual fields. *Perceptual and Motor Skills*, **21**, 431–437.

Coltheart, M. (1982), The psycholinguistic analysis of acquired dyslexia: some illustrations. *Philosophical Transactions of the Royal Society of London*, B298, 151–164.

Critchley, M. (1970), *The Dyslexic Child*, second edition, Springfield, Illinois: C. Thomas.

Grodzinsky, Y. (1984), The syntactic characterization of agrammatism. *Cognition*, **16**, 99–120.

Halpern, L. (1941), Beitrag zur Restitution der Aphasie bei Polyglotten im Hinblick auf das Hebraeische. *Schweizer Archiv für Neurologie und Psychiatrie*, **47**, 150–154.

(1949), La langue hébraïque dans la restitution de l'aphasie sensorielle chez les polyglottes. Semaine des Hôpitaux de Paris, **58**, 2473–2476.

(1950), Observations on sensory aphasia and its restitution in a Hebrew polyglot. *Monatschrift für Psychiatrie und Neurologie*, **119**, 156–173.

L'Hermitte, R., Hécaen, H., Dubois, J., Culioli, A. and Tabouret-Keller, A. (1966), Le problème de l'aphasie des polyglottes: remarques sur quelques observations. *Neuropsychologia*, **4**, 315–329.

Lyman, R., Kwan, S. and Chao, W. (1938), Left occipito-parietal brain tumor. *The Chinese Medical Journal*, **57**, 491–516.

Mishkin, M. and Forgays, D. (1952), Word recognition as a function of retinal locus. *Journal of Experimental Psychology*, **43**, 43–48.

Nair, K. R. and Virmani, V. (1973), Speech and language disturbances in hemiplegics. *Indian Journal of Medical Research*, **61**, 1395–1403.

Obler, L. K. (1984), Dyslexia in bilinguals. In Malatesha, R. N. and Whitaker, H. A. (eds.), *Dyslexia: A Global Issue*, The Hague: Nijhoff (an expanded version was presented at the NATO conference of the same name, in Maratea, Italy in October 1982).

Orbach, J. (1952), Retinal locus as a factor in the recognition of visually perceived words. *American Journal of Psychology*, **65**, 555–562.

(1967), Retinal locus as a factor in the recognition of visually perceived words. Visual fields as a function of cerebral dominance and reading habits. *Neuropsychologia*, **5**, 127–134.

Silverberg, R., Bentin, S., Gaziel, T., Obler, L. and Albert, M. (1979), Shift of visual field preference for English words in native Hebrew speakers. *Brain and Language*, **8**, 184–190.

Sroka, H., Solsi, P. and Bornstein, B. (1973), Alexia without agraphia with complete recovery. *Confina Neurologica*, **35**, 167–176.

Stevens, H. (1957), Reading epilepsy. *New England Journal of Medicine*, **257**, 165–170.

Streifler, M. and Hofman, S. (1976), Sinistrad mirror writing and reading after brain concussion in a bi-systemic (oriento-occidental) polyglot. *Cortex*, **12**, 356–364.

Tramer, O., Butter, B. and Mewhort, D. J. K. (1985), Evidence for scanning with unilateral visual presentation of letters. *Brain and Language*, **25**, 1–18.

10. Deterioration and creativity in childhood bilingualism

HERBERT SELIGER

Introduction

"The easiest for me is to open both faucets and let the two languages flow together."

While this paper will discuss aspects of first language attrition in a child bilingual, the above statement by an adult bilingual in the process of losing her first language is relevant, since this paper will examine what happens when the bilingual allows both "faucets" to be open and both languages to flow together.

The problem confronting the researcher in bilingualism and first language attrition is to explain how traffic is directed when two language grammars are melded and allowed to intermix. What principles seem to be governing the movement of rules from one language to the other and what determines which factors become changed in the host language and what remains?

It will be hypothesized that the process of language attrition is motivated by a principle of REDUNDANCY REDUCTION by which the bilingual's L1 grammar is reduced to a parsimonious set of linguistic and cognitive rules.

> REDUNDANCY REDUCTION PRINCIPLE: If both languages contain a rule which serves the same semantic function, that version of the rule which is formally less complex and has a wider linguistic distribution (i.e. can be used in a greater variety of linguistic environments) will replace the more complex more narrowly distributed rule.

That is, in the case of L1 attrition, simpler, more widely distributed rules from L2 will replace those from L1. We know that when a language is acquired, it is not acquired all at once but in stages. Consider now the converse of language acquisition, the divesting of a language ability previously acquired. In a sense, we are speaking of the development of "linguistic incompetence" and the movement by stages from grammar to semi-grammar (Gleitman and Gleitman, 1970), from native speaker competence to an interlanguage of the first language.

Consider also that this divesting of language ability is not a sudden occurrence or one which happens as the result of an accident, a stroke or disease. Rather, it takes place in the context of normal bilingualism so that while one language appears to be dying, the other, existing in the same mind, appears to be thriving.

In previous research on first language attrition (Seliger, 1977 and 1980), it was suggested that a metaphorical and symbiotic relationship exists between languages in contact at both the societal level and within the mind of the individual bilingual speaker. In the case of the individual bilingual, the first or "host" language and the second or "guest" language may develop a variety of possible relationships which will be discussed below. However, what is clear is that since nature does not suffer vacuums or voids, where one exists linguistically, an available language will fill it. With the exception of the so-called "balanced bilingual", languages within individuals are usually in competition for space and dominance.

An additional aspect of first language attrition is that what is lost is not a conceptual ability so much as the ability to give linguistic formulation to those concepts already attained. For example, having already acquired the function and form of relativization, what would a speaker do if the semantic function were retained but the rules for formation of relatives impaired?

This paper will describe the findings in a case study of first language loss with a normal bilingual child. The title implies that language attrition or loss in the context of bilingualism does not result simply in deterioration and shrinking of language ability, but also in the creation of forms which are unique to the first language of the speaker. As will be noted below, the language performance of the attrited speaker is clearly deviant from that of both the fully developed native speaker of that language and the developing monolingual child.

Theoretical questions raised by language attrition

Several important theoretical questions are raised by the study of first language attrition:

1. What causes the bilingual to lose control of selected aspects of the first language? While this chapter will not discuss the causes for first language attrition which appear to reside in the sociolinguistic conditions of bilingualism, of related interest is the question of why language attrition

appears to be *selective*. That is, why are some aspects of the language affected and not others? Lexical attrition appears to be a function of the domains of use for the two languages of the bilingual. However, it would be difficult to demonstrate a functional reason for the loss of syntactic rules such as those for the formation of relative clauses when they are replaced by rules for the same construction from the second language. By the same token, it is difficult to explain why some rules are not affected at all by attrition while others are lost or replaced through transfer from L2 or the creation of new unique forms in L1.

2. What processes, either universal or language-specific, are involved in the dissolution of first language abilities? Given current assumptions about the universality of linguistic and cognitive abilities related to language acquisition, it is only reasonable to assume that similar assumptions may be made about the processes involved in the dissolution of language ability. In the case of first language attrition, it is clear that an additional confounding factor is the fact that two languages exist in the mind of the speaker and that the speaker is more advanced cognitively. This suggests that both universal and language-specific sources must be examined for first language attrition and that while universal factors are involved, the direction and type of attrition may be related to factors such as language typology.

3. What can be learned from language attrition about the two languages in contact? The effects of language attrition over time can reveal interesting aspects of language relationships from a linguistic perspective. For example, given that each of the languages of the bilingual contains rules for a particular sentence type, will both rules be maintained or will one predominate? What factors, linguistic or psycholinguistic, will determine which rules in each of the two languages are maintained and which are lost? Is there a primary direction of influence? Are some languages more affected by contact than others? What affects differences in the permeability or robustness of different types of rules in language contact?

Possible configurations of the bilingual's languages

Several possible configurations are possible to describe the relationships between the different languages which the bilingual speaks. These configurations are shown in Table 10.1.

1. L1 and L2 co-exist and the bilingual maintains native-like fluency in both. This has been referred to as "balanced bilingualism".
2. L1 remains dominant and L2 is relegated to clearly defined functions for the bilingual, such as work or religious ritual. This configuration is common for adult

Table 10.1 *Configurations of the bilingual's languages*

1.	L1	>	<	L2
2.	L1	>		L2
3.	L1	<		L2
4.	Ł1	<		L2

immigrants who acquire anything from a rudimentary version of L2 to a higher level of proficiency depending on the functions which L2 must fulfill. However, even where a high level of L2 proficiency is not achieved, some attrition in the lexicon of the adult bilingual may be evident (Seliger, 1977).

3. L2 becomes dominant. Evidence for L2 dominance can be found in the phonology, lexicon and syntax of L1. Where there is a reduction in the ability to retrieve elements from the L1 grammar, L2 elements are often substituted. At this stage, comprehension does not appear to be impaired, but the ability to judge the grammaticality of deviant utterances in L1 may be affected. This third configuration is the area of study for first language attrition.
4. L2 displaces L1 so that little or no ability in L1 remains. This phenomenon is found in early sequential childhood bilingualism.

What are the mixing patterns of the bilingual's languages?

Given the fact that two or more languages co-exist in the mind of the bilingual, what are the possible patterns of interaction between the two languages in terms of the bilingual's relative ability to maintain the integrity and autonomy of the two languages? It would appear that there are three possible answers to this question:

1. The bilingual is able to maintain the two languages autonomously. In this case, little or no mixing takes place between the two languages; each is assigned a clearly defined sociolinguistic role and domain. (Fishman, 1971)
2. The bilingual may mix the languages consciously or unconsciously depending on external factors such as the language repertoires of the other interlocutors, contextual stimuli, or the acceptability of mixed varieties as a social norm. (Pfaff, 1979)
3. In the case of language attrition, the bilingual may lose a sense of what is grammatical for one or both of the languages and not be able to control the mixing of the two. That is, the bilingual may not be aware of the transfer and mixing of elements from one language to another and the creation of new forms in the "host" language.

Language attrition may be characterized as an example of language mixing in which the two systems are mixed inappropriately at some level. For example, the syntax of L2 might be used while speaking L1. The speaker may be unable to perform judgments of grammaticality and may use deviant forms in sociolinguistic environments in which code mixing would not be appropriate.

Background and methodology

The specific case of first language attrition to be reported is of an English–Hebrew bilingual child, S, who immigrated to Israel from the U.S.A. at the beginning of her seventh year. She was studied for the first time from the beginning of her ninth year for approximately ten months, with samples of language taken approximately every three to four weeks. Further samples of language performance were collected again during her tenth and eleventh years.

Upon arriving in Israel, the family switched to speaking Hebrew in order to facilitate the children's adjustment. According to her mother, S did not speak Hebrew at the time of immigration.

Three types of data have been collected from S:

1. Natural speech data which were recorded during the period described above every three to four weeks.
2. Responses on metalinguistic tests of judgment,
3. Elicited performance.

Natural speech samples

The natural speech samples were elicited in tape-recorded sessions in which the researcher sat alone with S who was asked to tell a story, relate what was happening in school, or make small talk. Each session lasted approximately twenty to thirty minutes. The informant was aware that she was being recorded but was not cognizant of the purpose of the recording. She was also informed from the beginning that the researcher did not speak Hebrew. Utterances showing attrition which occurred when the recorder was not on, were also noted by the researcher.

Metalinguistic tests

The metalinguistic tests which were administered in the second year of the study, were developed on the basis of deviant utterances which were produced during S's free discourse. These same tests were also administered to two groups, each containing six monolinguals aged six and nine, to confirm that errors found for S were not part of the normal performance of 5.5 to 6.5 year-olds, the age at which S immigrated nor of nine-year-olds, the age at which the data were collected from S.

The metalinguistic tests consisted of sentences for judgment or completion. In the cases where the subject judged a correct sentence as unacceptable or "bad", she was asked if she could improve it or make it more acceptable. These changes were noted next to the stimulus sentence and became the data termed "sentence improvement".

Findings

The data to be discussed here will be limited to S's relative clause performance. Three aspects will be discussed:

1. Errors in free discourse.
2. Acceptability judgments on metalinguistic tests.
3. Elicited production on a "sentence improvement" task. (Monolinguals were also asked to perform this task.)

Hebrew Relative Clauses It is first necessary to discuss briefly the rules for relative clauses in Hebrew which are relevant to the data to be discussed. (For a more comprehensive discussion, see Berman, 1978 and Hayon, 1969.)

1. Hebrew, like English, is right branching. Hebrew relatives are placed immediately after the head noun (phrase).
2. While modern Hebrew is SVO, word order is more flexible than in English.
3. The common relative marker *še–* is used regardless of the type of relative. It does not function as a relative pronoun but rather signals the subordinate status of the sentence to which it is attached.
4. Pronominal referents are copied in the relative clause except in subject position where they are optional.
5. Pronominal objects of prepositions are bound to prepositions. Prepositions are not stranded.
6. Unmarked word order of relative clauses is the same as in simple sentences. Elements are not fronted or moved as in English *for the purposes of relativization*. Reordering of word order is found in adult Hebrew primarily for the purposes of emphasis or topicalization.

Performance in free discourse

The utterances below were culled from tapes recorded during the first year of the study.

1. So I tell it to the girl thats (sic) was sitting next to me.
2. We're learning at a story that its name is...
3. ...the girl that it was her present...
4. So the girl that get the present she went to told the teacher.
5. I going to tell you a different thing that everyone likes it.
6. The school gives the girl that she has the birthday...

They show that S has developed the following rules for English relatives:

1. *That* appears to be preferred as the all-purpose relative.
2. S uses both the filled and the unfilled subject position, (*that* + subject pronoun) and (*that* − subject pronoun) respectively. Hebrew allows this option, English does not. See sentences 1, 4, and 6. (See also below.)

3. Pronominal referents are retained in non-subject positions which would be consistent with Hebrew. (Sentences 2, 3, 5, and 6)

S's performance in natural discourse in English (L1) shows clear evidence of the effect of Hebrew (L2).

Performance on metalinguistic judgment and sentence improvement

As stated above, the metalinguistic tests were developed on the basis of error patterns which appeared in the free discourse performance of the informant. In order to limit the scope of this paper, only S's performance on the relative clause tests will be discussed.

The responses of S and the monolinguals to the stimulus sentences are shown below. In the responses, a = stimulus sentence; b = S's improvement after rejection; c and d = 5.5 to 6.5 year-old monolingual improvement of stimulus.

7a. There is the man who I talked to you about him.
7b. There is the man that I talked with you about him.
7c. There is the man who I talked to you about.

8a. The man who the dog bit him is angry.
8b. The man that the dog bit him is angry.
8c. The man who the dog bit is angry.

9a. The man the dog bit is sick.
9b. The man that the dog bited is sick.
9c. The man who the dog bit is sick.
9d. The dog bit the man and now he is sick.

10a. The game which is more fun is in my room.
10b. The game that is funner is in my room.
10c. The game which is in my room is more fun.

11a. The girl who I am taller than her lives on my street.
11b. The girl that I am taller than her lives on my street.
11c. The girl that I am taller than lives on the street.
11d. The girl who lives on my block is taller than me.

12a. The cat scratched the man who was sleeping under the tree.
12b. The cat scratched the man that was sleeping under the tree.
12c. The cat pushed the man who was sleeping under the tree.

13a. I saw the boy whose name I don't remember.
13b. I saw the boy that I don't remember his name.
13c. I saw the boy and I don't remember his name.

14a. The girl who she is my friend is short.
14b. The girl that is my friend is short.
14c. The girl who is my friend is short.

These are representative responses from the twenty-five item test and are consistent with S's free discourse performance described above. Sentence 12c is an example of a change produced by a native speaker who did not focus on the syntactic form of the sentence. This can often happen when young subjects are asked to decide whether a sentence is "good" or how they might make it better if the sentence is unacceptable to them.

Two aspects of S's performance will be discussed from the data shown in sentences 7 to 14: simplification of the relativizer and copying or non-deletion of the referent pronoun. It is important to note that, in contrast to borrowing, the simplification of the relativizer allows for a change in the *formal* status of the relative clause in English from a subordinate to an independent clause with the attached relative marker. In other words, *that* has assimilated the role of *še–* in Hebrew (see discussion above). This change may be seen as a possible precursor to the emergence of coordinate or conjoined sentences in place of relative clauses.

1. *Simplification of the relativizer.* A review of the improvement sentences (the b. member of each set) produced by S shows that the set of relative pronouns has been reduced from *who, which, whose,* and *that* to *that*. It is interesting to note that in all of the elicited improvement sentences, the informant specifically corrected for the relativizer rather than accept others and did not reject these sentences on the basis of other grammatical problems present.

What appears to be happening, in addition to a simplification of the set of relative pronouns, is a shift in the *formal* status of the relative morpheme from that of pronoun to that of relativizer similar to the role and status of *še–* in Hebrew. This change of status for *that* combined with pronominal copy also changes the status of the subordinate relative clause to that of a sentence with a subordinating morpheme similar to Hebrew, as in sentence 15.

> 15. haiš šehakelev našax oto koes.
>   "the man *that*-the-dog bit him (is) angry"

As in Hebrew, S's dominant language, *that* has changed from being a relative pronoun to becoming the marker for the relative.

As noted above, the same metalinguistic tests, judgment and improvement, were administered to monolingual native speakers of English within two age groups: 5.5 to 6.5 and 8.5 to 9.5. It is not unusual for monolinguals to prefer *that* as an all purpose relative pronoun. However, it is clear from their sentence improvement responses (7c through 14c), that *that* is still regarded as a relative pronoun as well as a subordinator. None of the monolinguals rejected ungrammatical sentences in the judgment test because of the relativizer, as appears to be the case from S's sentence improvements.

In sentence 9, the deleted relative pronoun is inserted by both S and the monolinguals. The sentences in 9c and 9d show two different solutions suggested by the monolinguals. One is to insert the missing relative; the second solution is to simplify the relative sentence by changing it to a conjoined sentence as was done in 13c. While in her free discourse S shows a tendency to produce many run-on conjoined sentences, she did not change any of the test sentences in conjoined sentences.

S's improvement of sentence 14 conforms to Hebrew rules for relativization. She changes *who* to *that* and also deletes the redundant pronoun. The unmarked or more common form in Hebrew relativization is the unfilled subject position. Because of the clitic system of Hebrew, the subject of the verb need not be expressed as a pronominal. In tense marked verbs, it is expressed as a suffix (past) or a prefix (future).

Non-deletion of the referent pronoun

Hebrew, with the exception of the subject position discussed above, retains or copies the pronoun in the relative clause. This is abundantly clear in S's attrited grammar of English relative clauses both in her free discourse sentences and in her metalinguistic judgments and sentence improvements. It is clear from S's performance that she is applying the Hebrew rules for relative clauses and has lost the ability to distinguish those rules appropriate for English from those appropriate for Hebrew.

Discussion

An explanation of S's attrited relative clause grammar of English should try to relate both the simplification of the relative marker *that* and the transfer of pronominal copy to an underlying psycholinguistic principle which can explain what is transferred and what is lost.

At the beginning of this study, an adult language attrition informant was quoted as saying that the easiest for her was to allow both languages to flow together in what may be referred to as the OPEN FAUCET STRATEGY of bilingual processing. While it may appear to bilinguals that this is what they are doing in the process of speaking one language while allowing elements of a second language to intermix, such an explanation is unsatisfactory. It is clearly not the case that both languages simply flow together without some kind of control from within the respective grammars themselves. That is, in order to understand first language attrition in the context of bilingualism, it is necessary to understand whether cognitive or linguistic principles decide what survives and what is lost in the contributing languages. Why are some elements of the first language more permeable to loss and displacement by elements from L2, while others remain relatively unaffected?

It is also clear from an examination of S's relative clause grammar of English, that functional or sociolinguistic explanations related to such parameters as frequency of use, utility or cultural salience will not suffice. There is no reason to suppose that simplification of the relative and pronominal copy are in any way sociolinguistic phenomena.

The Redundancy Reduction Principle

At the beginning of this paper, it was suggested that the grammatical changes seen in S's grammar could be explained by postulating a principle which states that in the case where L2 becomes the dominant language of the bilingual and there is attrition in L1, those rules that serve the same semantic function but which are simpler linguistically, will displace similar but more complex rules in L1. This is the Redundancy Reduction Principle.

A corollary to this principle might be: transfer from L2 those rules that are similar and can be utilized to serve multiple functions in L1 while lessening the burden on memory to retain less generalizable rules. In S's case, it is not just that the set of relative clause pronouns was reduced to *that* but that the status of *that* was changed from relative pronoun to relativizing morpheme similar to the status and function of *še–* in Hebrew. The additional retention of pronominal copy further changes the formal status of the relative clause from that of a subordinate clause to that of an independent clause attached to a subordinating morpheme. For example,

> 7b. There is the man that I talked with you about him.

contains a relative clause which results from the Redundancy Reduction Principle. *That* functions as a marker for the relative clause but the clause without *that* may be formally classified as an independent sentence because it still contains the referent pronoun. This rule for relativization is more parsimonious because it allows that same clause structure to be used in conjoined sentences. That is, attrition has led to the creation of a new, more broadly based rule for relativization.

In a situation in which the bilingual's competence in L1 is gradually eroding, S's transfer of Hebrew rules for relativization to English results in the following:

1. Relativization can still be expressed by embedding the clause in the same position as in English.
2. Maintenance of a simpler sentence structure for the relative clause, as in Hebrew, eliminates the need to retain rules associated with fronting, stranding and pronominal deletion associated with English.
3. The set of relative pronouns can be replaced by an all-purpose marker which can

serve as relativizer when the pronoun is copied, the relativizer + subject pronoun when in the subject position for the relative clause, and as a complementizer in non-relative clause complement sentences.

These changes allow the bilingual to maintain both languages to varying degrees, by combining elements from L1 and L2 and arriving at a more parsimonious grammar. As stated, this is achieved by reducing a redundancy perceived by the bilingual to exist in the combined set of the grammars of the two languages. It presupposes, of course, that the bilingual ceases to perceive the two grammars as being autonomous and independent of each other.

Hyltenstam (1984), investigating the role of typological markedness in acquisition (not *attrition*), has suggested that such strategies as pronominal copy serve to reduce the psycholinguistic processing load in cases where the first language of the learner may not relativize positions low on proposed universal hierarchies, such as that suggested by Keenan and Comrie (1977). In the case of second language acquisition, as opposed to first language attrition, these arguments are more likely to be valid because another linguistic system does not exist in the mind of the incipient bilingual. Arguments may be found to support either a transfer explanation or a linguistic universal explanation in acquisition. However, while it may be stated that attrition may also be explained on the basis of linguistic universals, these universals are most likely filtered through linguistic systems already existing in the bilingual's linguistic repertoire. Basing explanations on the bilingual's demonstrated accessibility to both linguistic systems would provide a more parsimonious and direct explanation. However, this does not mean that further research will not reveal evidence that other explanations are also viable. As it has been shown that both universal and language-specific transfer explanations are valid in the case of acquisition, it would not be surprising to find this true also for attrition.

Are there stages to attrition?

Hamburger and Crain (1982) claim that it should be possible to see the precursors of relative clause acquisition in the language performance of the child acquiring relatives before the actual appearance of relatives in the child's speech. By the same token it should be possible to see early indicators of first language attrition or dissolution in the types of sentences produced by the speaker which in turn lead to a break-down in grammatical ability and later production. This is possible because first language attrition in the context of bilingualism is not the result of sudden trauma but the incremental effect of a particular bilingual context.

In S's language these precursor stages might be manifested in the following ways:

1. Since, as we have seen, S's relative clause rules have given the formerly subordinate relative the status of relativizer + independent clause, the next stage might show a predilection for conjoined sentences and a drop in the frequency and variety of relatives, as is shown in the following sentence found in S's free discourse data -

    15. Once upon a time, there was a girl and she did soup.

2. On metalinguistic tests, S's sentence improvements might tend toward simplification of relatives much as younger monolinguals did in 9d above.

The reduction of relatives to conjoined sentences would be consistent with the principle of redundancy reduction since more or less the same meaning could be expressed. In addition, the same basic syntactic mechanism available for relatives is available for conjoining in Hebrew. In the case of conjoined sentences, a conjoining morpheme *ve–* is attached to the sentence to be conjoined just as *še–* is attached to the sentence to be given relative status.

Of course an argument can be made that since the bilingual is utilizing a transfer strategy to maintain rules lost from L1 through attrition, there may be no further deterioration in relative clause rules in English, since they are supported by the transfer of rules from the second language. Only longitudinal studies of many such cases may be able to clarify this issue.

References

Berman, Ruth Aronson (1978), *Modern Hebrew Structure*. Tel Aviv: University Publishing Projects.

Fishman, Joshua A. (1971), *Sociolinguistics*. Rowley, MA: Newbury House Publishers.

Gleitman, Lila and Henry (1970), *Phrase and Paraphrase*. New York: Academic Press.

Hamburger, Henry and Crain, Stephen (1982), Relative acquisition. In: Stan A. Kuczaj II (ed.), *Language Development: Volume 1 – Syntax and Semantics*. Hillsdale, New Jersey: Erlbaum.

Hayon, Yehiel (1969), *Relativization in Hebrew: A Transformational Approach*. Ph.D. dissertation, University of Texas, Austin.

Hyltenstam, Kenneth (1984), The use of typological markedness conditions as predictors in second language acquisition: The case of pronominal copies in relative clauses. In Roger W. Andersen (ed.), *Second Languages*. Rowley, MA: Newbury House.

Keenan, E. L. and Comrie, B. (1977), Noun phrase accessibility and universal grammar. *Linguistic Inquiry*, **8**: 63–99.

Pfaff, Carol W. (1979), Constraints on language mixing: Intra-sentential code-switching and borrowing, *Language*. **55**:2, 291–318.

Seliger, Herbert W. (1977), Biological analogs for language contact situations. *International Review of Applied Linguistics*, No. 2.

(1980), Interlanguage II: What happens to the first language of second language learners? Unpublished paper. National TESOL Convention, San Francisco.

11. Crosslinguistic influence in language loss

MICHAEL A. SHARWOOD SMITH

This chapter will deal with the problems involved in the investigation of language loss (or language "attrition" as it is often called: see Lambert and Freed, 1982) with special reference to "crosslinguistic influence" (CLI). CLI is a term adopted in an earlier paper on language loss (Sharwood Smith, 1983a) and discussed fully in Sharwood Smith and Kellerman (1986). It is a psycholinguistic term referring to the influence on the learner which one language system he or she possesses may have on another language system. This is irrespective of whether the language system is a mature language or whether it is in a developmental stage or fossilized before attaining maturity. The term is meant to cover more than the word "transfer" and includes borrowings, influence on L1 from L2, avoidance of transfer, etc. In other words, it covers a fairly wide range of phenomena (see Sharwood Smith and Kellerman, 1986). As far as CLI in an attrition context is concerned, the attraction of language loss studies for the present writer dates from about the time when he supervised a Utrecht-based project carried out by Galbraith and Van Vlerken on adverbial placement amongst young native-speakers of English resident in the Netherlands, which showed how language loss was not simply confined to situations where the language under "attack" was a low-prestige language and/or where native-speaker input was no longer available to the speaker (see Van Vlerken, 1980; Galbraith, 1981; Sharwood Smith, 1983a, 1983b). The data seemed to indicate not only that this was a phenomenon that occurred much more widely than was generally thought, but also that it might be worth looking at the more "learner-internal" aspects of language loss and not focus on the external conditions as purely sociolinguistic studies would do. One of the most obvious learner-internal factors was indeed L2 influence on L1 and the project results indicated that this manifested itself in interesting ways.

The more general characteristics of language loss will now be considered and how they might be fitted in to a model of language acquisition and, in particular, how certain attempts to create frameworks for attrition research might help in our understanding of how crosslinguistic influence may affect the rate and manner of loss.

In one striking way, language loss looks like the opposite of language acquisition. The most obvious metaphors we would look for here are ones that signified "diminution" versus "expansion" and "simplification" versus "complexification". The notion that acquisition and loss are related, but opposed, takes very clear shape in Roman Jakobson's regression hypothesis where he claims that the developmental sequences in acquisition are the mirror image of sequences in aphasic loss (Jakobson, 1941, 1968). Although aphasia might be considered a special case of language loss, the regression hypothesis could easily be extended to all forms of language change understood as "loss" or "attrition" (cf. Freed, 1982). Note that in second language research the fact that a first language might be "lost" in reverse order brings with it the implication that there will be no CLI-based explanation for developmental sequences; since CLI could not possibly have operated in the monolingual acquisition of the L1, it can hardly be claimed to operate in its loss. In actual fact, there seems to be little or no hard evidence in favor of the regression hypothesis, in any pure form at least, which leaves the door open for CLI-based accounts in many areas of language loss.

Another way in which loss can be contrasted with acquisition is if one were to adopt what Carroll might have regarded as a "properly" behaviorist contrastive analysis hypothesis (Carroll, 1968) namely, rather loosely expressed, the claim that the acquiring of new habits leads to the extinction of habits associated with a related task. Hence, to the extent that language loss takes place in contexts where the loser is acquiring or using another linguistic system, then the habits of that system will lead to the extinction of the other system. Again, and happily enough, there seems to be no evidence that the acquisition of an L2 inevitably leads to the extinction of the L1 (although there may be some curious peripheral effects even in a foreign language teaching context).

In 1982, there appeared the first book of readings on language loss in a second language research context, edited by Richard Lambert and Barbara Freed and containing papers from a conference on this theme at the University of Pennsylvania in 1980. In the appendix there is a summary of previous research, mostly work done in the seventies, which is interesting but sparse. Since that time, there have been signs that this area of research has been developing fast (as the other papers in this volume clearly show; see also papers in Weltens, de Bot and van Els, 1986). The Lambert and Freed collection suggests that there are a great number of very different ways in which language loss research can be conducted, just as the very phenomenon itself requires differentiation into loss amongst normals as opposed to the various types of aphasic loss (cf. Obler, 1982). Loss can be studied in its sociocultural context, a classic study being the investigation of "language death" where Nancy Dorian looked at a community of speakers of East Sutherland Gaelic in North-Eastern Scotland, and the researcher can also look at the effects of attitude and motivation on retention of the language in question. The researcher can also look at some political aspects, for example the effect of deliberately seeking to maintain or discourage a minority language in a given community. The topic can also be looked at from a pedagogical point of view, i.e. in terms of what might be done to "remedy" loss in the individual. Here, the focus will be on the more purely psycholinguistic aspects (see Sharwood Smith, 1983a, 1983b).

A psycholinguistic study of loss naturally requires some sort of theoretical framework for looking at the learner-internal characteristics of language change within the individual. One useful dichotomy, which has a fairly long tradition in psychology in one form or other, is the distinction between knowledge structures and the way that knowledge is processed in real time. This dichotomy surfaces in Chomsky's competence-performance distinction and has more recently been re-expressed as the distinction between competence and control (see the discussion in Sharwood Smith, 1986). As far as loss is concerned, one then has to ask the question to what extent the learner has lost control of still-existent knowledge and to what extent the knowledge has itself changed or dissipated so that there is nothing to access. Competence will be used here in the Chomskyan sense, and, specifically where grammar is concerned (rather than, say, pragmatic knowledge) it will be assumed accordingly to develop, at least in an acquisitional context, within the constraints that Chomsky bundles together under the term "UG" (universal grammar) and which are hypothesized to be part of man's biological endowment (see Chomsky, 1965). Also, it should be noted that a "modular" approach to linguistic ability is being used here in the sense that processes of loss, like processes of acquisition, may operate quite differently according to which module is undergoing change; for example, to take two basic linguistic systems which may be treated in modular fashion, grammatical attrition may need to have a quite different theoretical account than, say, pragmatic attrition and it would be wrong to assume *a priori* that processes like transfer or regularization or simplification – whatever that may mean – will apply in anything like the same way.

Another useful framework for looking at language development in loss as well as acquisition may be found in Karmiloff-Smith's recent proposals for studying first language acquisition in which, briefly stated, she sees development as following three phases, and potentially a fourth (Karmiloff-

Smith, 1985). The first phase is data-driven in which the learner masters the components of a task but without much overall organization. The second phase involves the imposition of organization of the separate components but in a manner which may often conflict with the evidence provided by the language to which the learner is exposed: i.e. it is not data-driven but rather "input-oblique" (see Kellerman, 1984 and Kellerman and Sharwood Smith, 1986). The third phase involves the readjustment of this organization in the light of evidence in the input, and the fourth "optional" phase involves the construction of metalinguistic knowledge, i.e. knowledge accessible to conscious inspection by the learner, about the area of language in question. This notion of three- (or four-)phase development has more directly to do with the development of competence rather than with the processing control aspects of knowledge referred to above.

One thing should be clear about language attrition research (and this seems to be a matter of general agreement amongst researchers nowadays), namely that loss should be regarded as an integral part of language acquisition studies as a whole. This is clear if we regard language loss as a special instance of what I called "competence change" – change, that is, which is not *convergent* on some norm furnished over a period of time by exposure to native-speaker data. Language change in an attrition situation clearly involves competence change that *diverges* from this norm. However, given the previous assumption that competence change can take place independently of the presence of input from the external environment, as in Karmiloff-Smith's second phase of acquisition, for example, then divergent competence change can be driven or channeled just like convergent competence change by processes and principles of internal construction such as UG and, indeed, by input from within, i.e. CLI. In fact, many phenomena observed in language loss can only be explained by resorting to the idea of internal reorganisation since the new forms that are developed – and we can speak of "development" in loss – are not, as Seliger demonstrates in this volume, necessarily available in the exposure. Indeed, if they are available – if language losers "learn" forms from other losers more advanced than they are, and these deviant forms in the input are noticed by those less advanced losers and incorporated into new versions of the old system – then loss looks even more like a form of acquisition. So, one way or the other, developing competence in loss and developing competence in acquisition can be seen as related processes.

Finally, in considering matters from the competence perspective, at least, one might wonder whether "losses" are at issue or whether they are more aptly described as "gains". In some cases, new deviant forms seem to bring an enrichment of the language, especially where the "diverger" introduces "other language" elements, i.e. resorts to CLI, which create possibilities of expression which were not there in the original version of the language possessed by the speaker. This phenomenon also takes place in acquisitional scenarios as well. Karmiloff-Smith documents the acquisition of L1 French where we get children creating surface forms to distinguish different meanings that are expressed by a *single* form in adult French. Thus "un" meaning either the indefinite article "a" or the numeral "one" becomes "un" in the first case and "un de" in the second, in the child's developing French grammar. In an L1 acquisitional scenario the child becomes more sensitive to adult input eventually and readjusts the grammar, just as one might imagine a language loser would do in a re-acquisition scenario, as when returning to the community of native speakers of the language being lost. Where there is no re-acquisition, presumably the "enriched" grammar may stabilize. Note, that if one were to encounter such enrichment, one would have a ready-made set of hypotheses to test concerning the origin of the enrichment. If the L2 contained the richer system, CLI might be hypothesised: L2 input has triggered the change. If, however, the L2 contains no such structures, then one can appeal to the same reorganisational principles as observed in acquisition. Seliger (1984) in fact has an example of a Hebrew-L1/English-L2 bilingual who produced a Hebrew sentence with preposition-stranding (not permissible in Hebrew): **ma at medaberet al* instead of *al ma at medaberet*. As Seliger comments, this may be adduced as evidence of an expansion of the L1 system if the speaker now has both the stranded and non-stranded versions in his or her new competence. In such cases, L2 input, or rather intake into the L1 system, seems to be the most likely candidate for explaining the loss phenomenon. Interestingly enough, Berman and Olshtain document examples from the speech of English–Hebrew bilingual children, whose L1-English has developed what looks like an avoidance of stranded constructions as in *He doesn't know to who belongs* and the odd if not completely deviant *He's thinking about with what they can play* (see Berman and Olshtain, 1983). In this case, we can talk about a reduction of the system since the stranded alternatives would seem to have been lost.

So far, only competence has been at issue. However, in accordance with the Competence-Control model, one has to distinguish between divergent change in competence and divergent change in on-line processing control mechanisms. This kind of distinction is a familiar one in aphasic and other language pathology studies. For example, Berndt and Caramazza discuss "peripheral" and "central" deficits (Berndt and Caramazza, 1980:229). Central deficits will manifest themselves in the continuing presence of deviant structures under all conditions, whereas peripheral deficits will show variability. In cases of language loss (non-pathological divergence) it is worth asking to what extent the failure of an "ex-native speaker" to show as steady an adherence to the native standard as comparable native-speakers (given the normal incidence and type of performance slips) is the result of competence change or a change in the way competence is controlled. In other words, native competence may still be intact but the mechanisms for manipulating competence on-line have undergone some change. Seliger's preposition-stranding example is a case in point. He notes first, before considering the competence-based explanation, that the structure could be the result of a diminution in L1 processing ability. Note that, as was stressed in Bialystok and Sharwood Smith (1985), "control" involves not only access and retrieval but also integration. Thus, we can imagine a situation where, say, a non-deviant item was indeed retrieved – perhaps alongside some equivalent L2 candidate or some equivalent new L2-*influenced* candidate – but the non-deviant candidate was discarded at the integration stage: in other words, the native form is dumped half-way and never sees the light of day. Alternatively, it may emerge in performance *after* a self-correct procedure is carried out by the speaker.

In principle, subjects in a loss situation can demonstrate their possession of native competence by various means, including self-correction and also the selection and rejection of test items exemplifying standard and deviant forms respectively. If the Hebrew speaker mentioned in Seliger's example can consistently self-correct or is able, in an intuitional judgment test, successfully to select only non-stranded Hebrew structures and reject all stranded versions, we may assume that his or her production of *ma at medaberet al*, with stranding, was a matter of control: a relexicalized English structure was chosen by way of a control strategy. The same case could, of course, be made for the Berman-Olshtain example: if *who it belongs to* is accepted and if *thinking about with what they could play* were judged unlikely or incorrect, then, again, a control-based explanation can be appealed to.

The Andersen/Preston framework

Competence-control-based interpretations of language attrition phenomena can still admit a wide variety of theoretical positions. Roger Andersen (1982) provided a fairly complex framework of assumptions and hypotheses based on various different types of research findings to date. These were subsequently modified by Preston (Preston, 1982).

Preston tried to separate out more clearly three distinct key notions:

(1) Attrition *sites,*
(2) *Processes* of attrition and
(3) *Results* of attrition.

In other words, any theory of language loss should detail separately the likely sites of high or low attrition, the processes by which attrition takes place and, finally, the results of processes operating with respect to the various sites. In actual fact, most or all of Andersen's and Preston's categories of process relate most obviously to competence change. The "results" look ambiguous: in principle, at least, some results may come about mainly or solely because of the operation of some processing (control) principle whereas others may come about because of some principle of knowledge (competence) development. Of course, only a developed theory of competence and control could allow a satisfactory specification of results along these lines. For the moment the problem should be recognized in principle.

In Preston's formulation, there are 13 sites or areas of "high attrition likelihood". They are repeated here with a few comments:

(1) Inexperienced items (e.g. lexical items to which the speaker is simply no longer exposed or no longer uses)
(2) Marked items (Note that a precise definition of markedness is required here)
(3) Low-frequency items
(4) Uncommon items
(5) Unique items (items and distinctions in L1 that simply do not exist in L2)
(6) Low functional-load items
(7) Categorical items (i.e. there is variation where there once was a fixed categorical rule)
(8) Low information-load items
(9) Items learned last
(10) Opaque items (e.g. "vet" versus "animal doctor")
(11) Synonymous items (in a pair, one item goes)
(12) Bound items (attrition seems to involve preferential treatment for free forms over bound forms)
(13) Irregularities

Preston also points out that it is not stated in such a list how categories interact. For example, in the case of 3 and 13, he notes that languages support a great deal of irregularity in areas of high frequency. Presumably, these are empirical questions which such a framework can make available to us for further research.

The *processes* of attrition discussed by Andersen amount to ten in number. They are, as itemized by Preston (p. 76), the following:

(1) Analysis (use of free forms rather than bound forms)
(2) Collapse (alternative structures fuse into one or are replaced by a new single structure)
(3) Overgeneralization (extension of a system)
(4) Regularization (creating regularity where there was irregularity, whether or not the model is a regular form in the original system)
(5) Transfer (this term seems to be restricted to morphosyntax but presumably extends at least to phonology)
(6) Borrowing (this term is only discussed by Andersen in connection with lexical items)
(7) Innovation (only lexical in Andersen's discussion)

(8) Paraphrase (more paraphrase needed to compensate for loss of expressive power in the system

(9) Circumlocution (more circumlocution needed to compensate for loss of expressive power in the system)

(10) Avoidance (the subject avoids situations, abandons messages, etc. due to loss of expressive power)

As just mentioned above, we can immediately see in this list of processes a prevarication (at least in terms of the Competence-Control model) between competence change processes and on-line processing control. To what degree, for example, is transfer an emergency strategy when there is processing overload and to what degree is it developmental – the influence of previous knowledge (competence) on new knowledge. There is also a shady area where either purely linguistic processes are at issue like regularization, or extralinguistic processes or processes that can be related in part at least to the discourse level, like avoidance. In other words, the categories cut across modules: it may be useful to try and redefine the framework for a particular model of the combined (language) knowledge system.

Processes (6) to (10) in particular, perhaps (5) to (10), can be categorized as compensatory strategies; not surprisingly they are taken over from Tarone's framework of communication strategies (Tarone, 1980).

Handling communicative situations in a systematic way may lead to competence change, of course, but there are processes which may be independent of language use in this direct and obvious way. Preston, in fact, wisely cuts out compensation and avoidance and reduces Andersen's list of processes to:

(1) Overgeneralization (intra-system)
(2) Transfer (inter-system)
(3) Analysis
(4) Forgetting (items vanish without trace)

Preston then presents the third list, i.e. "results", as follows:

(1) Fewer items
(2) Less variety
(3) Fewer distinctions
(4) Variation
(5) Agrammaticality
(6) Analyticity
(7) Ambiguity

As mentioned above, the result categories are still ambiguous as regards their psycholinguistic basis. In other words they describe the product (observable behavior) of processes which have not been itemized with the particular psycholinguistic dimensions in question here. At the same time, they definitely impose further order on the Andersen taxonomy.

The conspiracy framework

In Sharwood Smith (1983b) a number of factors which had been outlined in earlier papers were reconsidered and a list of twelve factors were proposed as a preliminary step towards a psycholinguistically motivated research programme. These factors seemed, again on the basis of the kind of phenomena already observed in data corpora, to be worth investigating. In other words, the list was not a replacement of such taxonomies as discussed above, but rather constituted a different way of focusing a language loss investigation. More specifically, the factors under consideration were ones that might conspire to facilitate or inhibit divergent change, i.e. *loss*. The basic idea was that it might be useful to think in terms of a number of properties obtaining in a given situation which might attract deviation from the standard, either in competence terms or in terms of processing control. The idea behind this was that if one could take a subset of forms within a given area of language (considering the L1 and L2 of the subject in question as well as the conditions of use), one might be able to select relevant factors from the list and categorize given test items in terms of those factors, drawing up a matrix whereby each test item would get a + or a − for presence or absence of one of those factors. Hence item X might have three "loss-inducing" properties and item Y would have only one. Therefore, one would hypothesize X to exhibit more frequent and/or earlier divergence from the native-speaker norm than item Y. A number of statistical tests such as multiple regression and factor analysis (cf. McLaughlin, 1980) could be applied in the analysis of the results of such investigations. Of course this procedure could also be applied to factors in Andersen's sites, as listed by Preston (see above).

The 12 factors (in Sharwood Smith, 1983b) were as follows:

(1) Typological proximity
(2) Structural similarity
(3) Cross-linguistic support
(4) Iconicity
(5) Familiarity
(6) Coding efficiency
(7) Comprehensibility
(8) Solidarity
(9) Input sensitivity
(10) Associative triggering
(11) Semantic enrichment
(12) Ludic potential.

Typological proximity

To take these one by one, the first factor, *typological proximity*, relates to Kellerman's notion of "psychotypology" (Kellerman 1983). Various experiments based in Nijmegen as well as elsewhere have indicated that learners have their own personal "intuitions" about how language systems relate to each other and what in any system is more or less "transferable", the standard example being those particularly idiosyncratic aspects of the lexicon which we call "idiomatic". If learners tend to regard idioms as relatively untransferable, *ceteris paribus* in acquisition, it would be interesting to see if they are relatively reluctant to admit them into their L1 from an L2. In Kellerman's experiments it seems that psychotypology is conceived as a conspiracy between inherent non-transferability such as possessed by idioms, bound forms, etc., and a crosslinguistic computation which rates a particular L1 and a particular L2 as being a specific distance apart. In fact, this may be a modular computation in that different modules of the language system may be rated at different distances apart. For example, either as a first assumption or as a result of exposure to new data, the learner may rate basic word order (say phrase structure configurations) as being distant while at the same time perceiving (or coming to perceive) the lexicon as being close. Hence CLI will occur frequently at the lexical level but not in that particular part of the grammar. One example of this could be Polish and Dutch which differ grammatically but much less so at the semantic and idiomatic end of the lexicon. From the present writer's observations from acquisition at least, it appears that perceived similarity sometimes, where such a degree of similarity was originally not at all expected, leads to a CLI-based strategy in this particular area of the language, while having no such effect on other areas. If there is no negative evidence, the learner incorporates the idiom, or whatever, into the lexicon. In attrition terms, he or she would tend to restructure the L1 under the influence of the L2 at an early stage where the language *in toto* or the linguistic areas concerned were perceived to be typologically proximate, and at a late stage where the systems were felt to be distant from one another. So, here we would have not only a process from the Andersen/Preston list, but psycholinguistic explanation for the process, since a list of processes does not tell you how and when they operate.

Structural similarity

Structural similarity can be listed separately in the sense that within the framework of psychotypology, certain forms may be more prone to CLI by reason of their structural similarity than others that are less similar. Thus we find one informant, a native speaker of English in Holland, saying things like *I'll set the tea* (from Dutch: *de thee zetten* instead of *I'll lay the table for tea* and another saying *cope* meaning *buy* (from Dutch *kopen*) as in *I'll cope the car* and *overdrive* meaning *exaggerate* from Dutch: *overdrijven*) as in *You mustn't overdrive*. In all these case an existent word in the standard native speaker lexicon is assigned a different meaning on the basis of a matching with a structurally similar L2 word (see Sharwood Smith, 1983b).

Crosslinguistic support

Crosslinguistic support may enhance transferability in that two languages may possess something in common, making it more transferable into a third language. In a sense this is a psychotypological universal in that the learner or loser is, as it were, saying this item is common to all languages. It is not an innate universal but one that is hypothesised on the basis of learning several languages: it is a crosslinguistic generalization. The example selected for the 1983(b) paper was L2 loss under the influence of an L3. The item was shared by L1 and L3 and was imported into L2. The example was *a biting product* (instead of *corrosive*) where the L1 – Polish – has *grysacy* and the L3 – Dutch – has *bijtend*, both literally meaning *biting*. There is a follow-up on this story in that at the time the utterance was originally recorded, the subject was aware that this L2 item did not exist – it was borrowed consciously. At a later date, however, when the same idiom was uttered, the subject denied that it was deviant. This is an interesting example of an idea that might well be susceptible to a kind of simple regression-based explanation in that metalinguistic awareness – the last stage in Karmiloff-Smith's model – may be the first stage in attrition.

To sum up so far, a person who has, to take one hypothetical example, located a given area in a given language as psychologically proximate and who has two items, one in L1 and one in another language which is structurally similar but has another meaning is, by hypothesis, highly likely to transfer the semantic representation of the L2 item onto the L1 item, especially where a third language provides crosslinguistic support for recategorizing the item in the L1 lexicon. That, at least, is the likeliest explanation we can imagine with the factors dealt with so far.

Iconicity

Iconicity or "semantic transparency" works in L1 attrition when L1 and L2 have equivalents, but L2 has the more semantically transparent item (cf. Kellerman, 1983). An example, similar to the veterinary instance mentioned earlier, may serve to illustrate this. A speaker of standard British English may come to use *eye-doctor* under the influence of *oogarts* rather than a Latinate word whose meaning is less transparent from the form. He or she may of course get crosslinguistic or crossdialectal support if they knew of an English dialect where the word *eye-doctor* was acceptable – the dialect form would act as a fellow conspirator strengthening the chance of CLI. The *biting product* example could arguably be construed as an example of iconicity as well as crosslinguistic support.

Familiarity

Familiarity or "subjective frequency" is a fairly obvious candidate factor. Clearly, what is subjectively "frequent" will change depending on the learner's or loser's sociolinguistic environment, i.e. their particular usage of the language under investigation. However one could well imagine a rare lexical form whose rarity is compensated for by some of the other factors, i.e. iconicity. As always, these factors can only play their part in the general configuration of factors that obtain at any one time.

Coding efficiency

Coding efficiency has to do not with the communicative effect on the interlocutor but with the ease of processing experienced by the speaker: perhaps it should be renamed "encoding" efficiency. An L2, for example, may have a neater, more processible way of expressing a given concept than another language. We may therefore explain an English informant's *The coffee is up* meaning *there is no more coffee*, having been influenced by the Dutch *de koffie is op*, as opting for a more economically encoded meaning. Again, it is very difficult to find a pure example: we also have a structural similarity here since *the coffee is up* could as a non-deviant British utterance mean *the coffee has been served*. Also, in this example, we have a case of a certain type of CLI being explained. Coding efficiency could also be invoked in cases of over-generalization and regularization (cf. Preston, 1982, for example) but it is most striking in CLI-based manifestation. In a study of Spanish migrant workers in Switzerland, Bernard Py (1986) discusses what he calls "reinterpretation", where the L1 is reinterpreted structurally in terms of the L2. Thus certain oppositions that exist in L1 but not in L2 are lost in L1, e.g. Spanish verbs of location taking the preposition *a* and those indicating position taking *en* (p. 167). It may simply be more convenient for the bilingual using both languages to create more proximity in order to be able to use the same or similar processing control mechanisms for both languages. The extreme case would be an L1 that was so completely restructured that it was simply a relexified L2. Such cases have not, it would seem, yet been evidenced but advanced cases of language loss do show definite signs of this tendency. On the other hand, as Py himself points out (p. 170) there may be an enrichment of the lexicon: the new L2-like form does not lead to the erasure of the standard equivalent but is created as a complementary item with a special meaning. Py's example is *caja maladia* (by analogy with the French *caisse maladie* "health insurance office") which is reserved for the Swiss institution which functions quite differently from its Spanish counterpart.

Comprehensibility

Language losers may also opt for a divergent L1 form, one of the attractions of which is that it is comprehensible in the particular sociocultural context shared with the interlocutor. A borrowing which the speaker knows the interlocutor will understand may, after a certain period of conscious use, fall into the regular L1 repertoire and be regarded as new competence. The Spanish/French example quoted above may be a case in point. Presumably, comprehensibility is a condition for other factors to obtain and play a role in change.

Solidarity

The comprehensibility factor may be aided by the use of divergent forms amongst a community of "losers" to signal solidarity. Again the once consciously borrowed forms may pass out of metalinguistic awareness and become part of competence. On the other hand, if there is strong language loyalty exhibited by members of the community, solidarity will have the reverse effect and should serve as an inhibiting factor to either consciously creative or unthinking divergent use of the language.

Input sensitivity

Input sensitivity is most likely to be a personality variable although there may be stages in an attrition process when one is more sensitive to input than at others (cf. phase 2 in the Karmiloff-Smith model). Again, input sensitivity is probably a general condition for competence change to take place if one includes internal input i.e. CLI. I originally conceived of input sensitivity as having to do with *external* divergent input, such as would happen when the speaker was interacting with other people undergoing attrition. In terms of personality variables, it would be interesting to identify fast losers (divergers) and slow losers (divergers). Dorian (1982) has a recent discussion on this. Research reporting data from siblings shows that this is indeed a relevant distinction: that is, people from the same environment (abstracting away from possibly relevant age and sex differences) exhibit different rates of loss and acquisition of a new language.

Associative triggering

Associative triggering simply refers to the contextual effects of topics or objects in the environment which might trigger divergent use of the language. When talking about a culturally idiosyncratic phenomenon in the L2 community, for example, users of a given L1 may be tempted to increase their rate of borrowings, especially in cases similar to Py's *caja maladia*.

Semantic enrichment

This (as was suggested in Sharwood Smith, 1983b) might be grouped together with coding efficiency. A L1 user will be likely to borrow and eventually copy over a term in L2 for which there is no easy equivalent in L1, initially in order to avoid a clumsy paraphrase or circumlocution. Where the newly incorporated term does not replace anything, we can really speak in terms of an enrichment (cf. Vildomec, 1963:170; Ringbom, 1986:157). Where the divergent term replaces another term which is more difficult to manipulate in encoding, then it is easier to speak in terms of efficiency. Again, both of these terms are not names of processes but names of explanations for processes.

Ludic potential

Apart from the conscious use of divergent terms, especially those of a crosslinguistic character, to express solidarity between interlocutors, we should also mention the ludic factor, i.e. play with language, since bilinguals very often enjoy the conscious manipulation of their bilingual resources. It is, of course, possible that this "play" aspect to divergent language usage may help prolong the metalinguistic phase and delay the incorporation of given forms into the subconscious usage.

Markedness and UG

Many of the above factors relate most transparently to performance: they allow for the strategic use of (in most examples) the mother tongue in divergent ways – use that may or may not eventually come to be a reflection of tacit competence rather than of conscious strategy. However, there may well be changes that cannot possibly, at least under normal circumstances, be conscious. This is particularly the case with reference to the internal restructuring of competence according to principles of UG. The same kind of hypotheses that have been put forward in acquisition by Mazurkewich, White and others can be made for attrition (see Sharwood Smith and Van Buren, forthcoming). Does attrition involve "demarking"? People have generally suggested that it does, but not in terms of this particular linguistic theory. Here, one would try to find out if parameters of UG were reset to unmarked values, and if they were, whether this was the result of CLI, i.e. an unmarked setting in the L2 affecting the marked setting in L1, or whether it occurred irrespective of the parameter settings in L2. Do English speakers lose stranding (cf. Adjemian and Liceras, 1984; Van Buren and Sharwood Smith, 1985) and do gerund complements as in *like doing*, fall away to be replaced by the unmarked infinitive *like to do* (Mazurkewich, 1985)? Without the effect of L2 influence, it is not clear why markedness in this sense should be avoided. In acquisition terms, marked forms are resorted to when there is positive evidence. Unless divergent speakers effectively supply positive evidence to the language loser in the form of "loser talk" under the additional assumption that the loser in question is sensitive to that evidence, it is hard to see why a parameter should be automatically reset. It makes more sense if it is a question of CLI or if the marked setting entails a bothersome complication in the grammar or in processing terms which the language user would be, as it were, glad to be rid of.

Concluding remarks

Clearly, these frameworks are all pretheoretical and hence question-begging. They are pretheoretical from the purely linguistic point of view – what, for example, is the precise meaning of "marked" (cf. Kean, 1984) let alone terms like "grammar", "agrammatical", "language" etc. – and they are also pretheoretical from a psycholinguistic point of view. What is "transfer", what are the constraints on transfer and how do the various posited processes interact or "conspire" to produce observed results, and what constitutes processing, processing difficulty and so on? For this reason, as much as for any other, it is useful to take on board more developed theories from associated areas which can posit some explanations as well as a list of sites, processes and outcomes so that a productive research programme in language attrition can be set up. Probably enough observational data have been collected for us to say that a necessary pretheoretical stage is now at an end. At any rate, we can say quite confidently now that language attrition can be regarded as a type of development, often a type of enrichment, involving processes that have much in common with those posited to account for acquisition but which also differ in their manifestation in interesting ways.

References

Adjemian, C. and Liceras, J. (1984), Accounting for adult acquisition of relative clauses: universal grammar, L1, and structuring the intake. In Eckman, F., Bell, L. and Nelson, D. (eds.), _Universals of Second Language Acquisition._

Alatis, J. (ed.) (1968), _Linguistics and Language Study._ Georgetown Monograph 172. Washington D.C.

Andersen, R. W. (1979), _The Acquisition and Use of Spanish and English as First and Second Languages._ Washington, D.C.: TESOL.

   (1982), Determining the linguistic attributes of language attrition. In Lambert, R. and Freed, B. (eds.), _The Loss of Language Skills._

Berman, N. and Olshtain, E. (1983), Features of first language transfer in second language attrition. _Applied Linguistics_ **1**:222–234.

Berndt, R. and Caramazza, A. (1980), A redefinition of Broca's aphasia. _Applied Psycholinguistics_ **1**: 225–278.

Bialystok, E. and Sharwood Smith, M. (1985), Interlanguage is not a state of mind. _Applied Linguistics_ **6**:101–117.

Carroll, J. (1968), Contrastive linguistics and language study. In Alatis, J. (ed.), _Linguistics and Language Study._

Chomsky, N. (1965), _Aspects of the Theory of Syntax._ The Hague: Mouton.

Davies, A., Criper, C. and Howatt, A. (eds.) (1984), _Interlanguage._ Edinburgh University Press.

Dorian, N. (1982), Language loss and language maintenance in language contact situations. In Lambert, R. and Freed, B. (eds.), _The Loss of Language Skills._

Eckman, F., Bell, L. and Nelson, D. (eds.), _Universals of Second Language Acquisition._ Rowley, MA: Newbury House.

Felix, S. and Wode, H. (eds.) (1983), _Language Development at the Crossroads._ Tubingen: Narr.

Freed, B. (1982), Language loss: current thoughts and future directions. In Lambert, R. and Freed, B. (eds.), _The Loss of Language Skills._

Galbraith, N. (1981), _A Study of Transfer in Language Loss._ Unpublished M.A. dissertation. University of Utrecht.

Gass, S. and Selinker, L. (eds.) (1983), _Language Transfer in Language Learning._ Rowley, MA: Newbury House.

Jakobson, R. (1941, 1968), _Child Language, Aphasia and Phonological Universals._ The Hague: Mouton.

Karmiloff-Smith, A. (1985), Language and cognitive processes from a developmental point of view. _Language and Cognitive Processes_ **1**:61–85.

Kean, M-L. (1984), On the relation between grammatical markedness and L2 markedness. _Interlanguage Studies Bulletin_ **8**:5–23.

Kellerman, E. (1983), Now you see it, now you don't. In Gass, S. and Selinker, L. (eds.), _Language Transfer in Language Learning._

   (1984), The empirical evidence for the influence of L1 in interlanguage. In Davies, A., Criper, C. and Howatt, A. (eds.), _Interlanguage._

Kellerman, E. and Sharwood Smith, M. (eds.) (1986), _Crosslinguistic Influence in Second Language Acquisition._ Oxford: Pergamon.

Lambert, R. and Freed, B. (eds.) (1982), _The Loss of Language Skills._ Rowley, MA: Newbury House.

McLaughlin, B. (1980), Theory and research in second language learning: an emerging paradigm. *Language Learning* **3**:331–350.

Mazurkewich, I. (1985), Syntactic markedness and language acquisition. *Studies in Second Language Acquisition* **7**:15–36.

Obler, L. (1982), Neurolinguistic aspects of language learning as they pertain to second language attrition. In Lambert, R. and Freed, B. (eds.), *The Loss of Language Skills*.

Preston, D. (1982), How to lose a language. *Interlanguage Studies Bulletin* **6**:2, 64–87.

Py, B. (1986), Competence and attrition in the native language of immigrants. In Kellerman, E. and Sharwood Smith, M. (eds.), *Crosslinguistic Influence in Second Language Acquisition*.

Ringbom, H. (1986), The transfer of lexis. In Kellerman, E. and Sharwood Smith, M. (eds.), *Crosslinguistic Influence in Second Language Acquisition*.

Seliger, H. (1984), Primary language attrition in the context of other language loss and mixing. Unpublished manuscript, Queen's College, C.U.N.Y.

Seliger, H. and Vago, R. (forthcoming), *First Language Attrition: Structural and Theoretical Perspectives*. Cambridge University Press.

Sharwood Smith, M. (1983a), On first language loss in the second language acquirer. In Gass, S. and Selinker, L. (eds.), *Language Transfer in Language Learning*.

(1983b), On explaining language loss. In Felix, S. and Wode, H. (eds.), *Language Development at the Crossroads*.

(1986), Comprehension versus acquisition: two ways of processing linguistic input. *Applied Linguistics*. **7**:239–256.

Sharwood Smith, M. and Van Buren, P. (forthcoming), First language attrition and the parameter-setting model. In Seliger, H. and Vago, R. (eds.), *First Language Attrition*.

Tarone, E. (1980), Communication strategies, foreigner talk and repair in interlanguage. *Language Learning* **30**:417–431.

Van Buren, P. and Sharwood Smith, M. (1985), On the acquisition of preposition stranding by second language learners and parametric variation. *Second Language Research* **1**:18–46.

Van Vlerken, M. (1980), *Adverbial Placement in English: a Study of First Language Loss*. Unpublished M.A. Dissertation. University of Utrecht.

Vildomec, V. (1963), *Multilingualism*. Leiden: Sijthoff.

Weltens, B., de Bot, K. and van Els, T. (eds.) (1986), *Language Attrition in Progress*. Dordrecht: Foris.

12. Bilingualism in Alzheimer's dementia: two case studies

KENNETH HYLTENSTAM AND CHRISTOPHER STROUD

Introduction

One of the most intriguing aspects of bilingualism which has increasingly come to interest researchers is the question of how a bilingual's languages are organized and processed psycholinguistically. In exploring this question, one major approach has been to analyze the pathological speech produced by bilingual aphasics, on the assumption that the types of linguistic breakdown observed there have important implications for how healthy language is organized and processed.

Case studies of bilingual aphasics have documented differential patterns of loss and recovery for each language – along with the more frequent case where both languages are affected in a like manner. Examples of language mixing[1] in the aphasic have also been reported. Data of this type have been used to formulate neuro- and psycholinguistic models of bilingual system interaction (for reviews, see Paradis, 1983, 1977, and Albert and Obler, 1978).

In addition to bilingual aphasia, other neurological pathologies may also be used to elucidate the psycholinguistic functioning of bilinguals. Informal observations from demented bilingual speakers show that their linguistic and communicative behavior in each language may be differently affected in ways similar to that of aphasics. Specifically the demented bilingual may exhibit difficulties in choosing the appropriate language for the monolingual interlocutor, or upholding one language throughout the interaction.

Demented patients may provide particularly interesting insights into the neuro- and psycholinguistics of language mixing, in that the cognitive (set maintenance, memory, attention) and neurophysiological factors (a diffuse cerebral damage with parietal lobe involvement (Jolley and Arie, 1980)) implicated by the disease can be taken to underlie the pragmatic skills necessary for appropriate bilingual behavior. Since these patients exhibit a successive linguistic breakdown (Obler and Albert, 1985) it may be possible that the phenomena of aberrant language mixing can be correlated to specific stages in the dissolution.

To date, little interest has been accorded bilinguals suffering from dementia; no published accounts whatsoever exist.[2] In this chapter, data from bilinguals suffering from Alzheimer's dementia are used to further the discussion of how two languages interact with each other and with other cognitive systems. Specifically, the main focus in the present investigation is to examine which abilities underlie language separation and language choice, and to contribute to the discussion on the psycholinguistics of code-switching. For definitions of these notions, see pp. 208ff.

Work on such questions has to confront substantial analytical and conceptual difficulties. This is clearly illustrated by many case studies of bilingual aphasics. From an analytical point of view, for example, it has been all too usual to ascribe departures from a monolingual norm in each language to the pathology. Thus, the existence of mixed language in aphasic speech production has usually been considered a consequence of the aphasia, even though many instances of language mixing may actually comprise normal bilingual behavior (cf. Grosjean, 1985). As for conceptual, or theoretical problems, the majority of studies on bilingual aphasics seem to lack clear criteria for defining central notions such as language choice, code-switching, interference, and borrowing.

The recent research into the socio- and psycholinguistics of bilingual language processing now provides a more appropriate framework with which to approach questions of linguistic pathology in bilinguals. An increased understanding of the socio-psychological determinants of language choice (interlocutor characteristics, especially language proficiency and language preference, situation characteristics, discourse content, and function of the interaction, cf. Grosjean, 1982) puts one in a better position to specify the dimensions along which an individual's bilingualism may be disrupted. The specification of grammatical constraints suggested for normal code-switching, such as the free morpheme constraint and the equivalence constraint (Poplack, 1980), allows a precise characterization of the nature of the aberrations found in bilingual pathologies. Also, recent psycholinguistic models of bilingual language processing (Paradis, 1977; Sridhar and Sridhar, 1980; and Green, 1986) provide a framework for a treatment of notions such as differential language availability and dominant/subordinate bilingual competencies.

Present study

This chapter presents a selective analysis of the language of two bilinguals with Alzheimer's dementia. Utilizing a case study approach, we will attempt to provide the first detailed account of the types of linguistic problems encountered in these subjects.

The two subjects were selected on the basis that they had been diagnosed as exhibiting Alzheimer's dementia and that they had premorbidly been high proficiency bilinguals. Both subjects were at advanced stages of dementia and resided in dementia wards at hospitals in the Stockholm area. The diagnosis of Alzheimer's dementia was confirmed by (1) consulting the medical expertise on the wards, and (2) studying the medical records of the patients. Information on the subjects' general intellectual and emotional functioning was obtained through interviews with the ward personnel. A former high level of bilingualism was assured from interviews with the patients' close family members, where the patients' language histories were obtained.

Subject GM, a male, was 89 years old at the time of this study. He was born in Germany, lived in Latvia for a number of years, without learning Latvian, and emigrated to Sweden in 1942 at the age of 45, where he has since resided. His wife is a native speaker of German, but she also speaks Latvian, Russian, and Swedish. The language of family interaction has always been German. In Sweden, GM was first employed at a Swedish–German office of commerce before opening his own business around 1950. At that time, his proficiency in Swedish, according to his wife, was very good, although the language was spoken with a German accent. GM used only Swedish at work, both in speech and for purposes of business correspondence.

Subject KL, a female, was 83 years old at the time of the study. This subject was a member of the Swedish-speaking minority in Finland, so although she was born in Finland, her first language was Swedish. As a child, KL attended a Swedish school, but acquired Finnish through social contacts outside the home. KL married a Swedish minority speaker like herself, and Swedish was the language used in the home and in most social contacts. In 1942, when KL was 37 years of age, the family moved to Sweden, where they subsequently settled. Finnish was not used by KL after that time, except sporadically; her son is a monolingual Swedish speaker.

Neither of the two subjects has ever been a member of speech communities where code-switching was the norm and, according to the family members interviewed, no mixing occurred in either of the patients' speech to any mentionable extent premorbidly.

Data from each language were elicited in three types of production task:

(1) A 15–20 minute conversation on a set of 9 predetermined topics such as family history, immigration history, previous occupation etc. (Data type 1)
(2) elicited production, comprising a picture description task, (the Cookie Theft Picture from the Boston Diagnostic Aphasia Examination, Goodglass and Kaplan, 1972), an action naming task (from the Action Naming Test, Obler and Albert, 1979), and an automatic speech task (numbers, months of the year, days of the week) (Data type 2)
(3) a situation-contextualized interaction, where the interviewer walked with the patient around the ward, engaging him/her in conversation on immediately observable objects or actual routines. (Data type 3)

Efforts were made to make the data elicitation situation as monolingual as possible: data from each language were elicited on separate days, but at approximately the same time of the day. Each interviewer spoke only his/her native language with the patient, but did not pretend ignorance of the other language, if it was used by the patient and known to the interviewer. (The Swedish speaking interviewer of KL knew no Finnish.) All interaction was audio-recorded.

Each interaction was transcribed in normal orthography, and the transcriptions were either performed or checked by linguists who were native speakers of the languages concerned.

In order to confirm the quantitative comparability of the conversational data in each language from each patient, the number of utterances, the number of turns, and the number of words were calculated. Obviously, the word count does not give directly comparable figures for different languages. Therefore, when the amount of data in each language is compared, the most reliable measurements are those given in terms of the number of utterances and the number of turns.

To illustrate the issues involved in language choice and language separation, the number of utterances containing elements from both languages and the number of monolingual utterances in each language were determined. The patients' propensity to choose a specific language mode was correlated here to phenomena such as the interactant's communicative behavior, the type of communicative situation, topical coherence, and whether and to what extent the patient made requests for clarification.

All instances of code-switching in the patients' contributions were analyzed according to the grammatical constraints on non-pathological code-switching mentioned above.

In order to elucidate the question of differential availability of each language, the patients' contributions were scanned for expressive difficulties manifested as lexical search problems. At the pragmatic level, the patients' ability to cooperate on the conversational topic, to perform adequate turn-taking, to monitor contributions, and to produce requests for clarification were analyzed.

Table 12.1 *Base measures calculated from conversational interaction (data type 1)*

	Subject	SI	GI/FI
Turns	GM	66	80
	KL	33	28
Utterances	GM	76	76
	KL	14	13
Utterance	GM	17	11
fragments	KL	5	8
Words	GM	410	362
	KL	71	39
Words/utterance	GM	5.4	4.8
	KL	5	3

SI = Swedish interaction; GI = German interaction; FI = Finnish interaction

Results

The results are presented in four sections. The first section contains base measures on the two patients' behavior in conversational interaction (data type 1, see p. 205). The second section deals with data on language choice and language separation for the two subjects. In section three, instances of code-switching are presented and discussed. Finally, in section four, the patients' abilities in each language are compared. Sections two through four draw on data of all types, 1 – 3.

Base measures

Table 12.1 displays the amount of speech from each patient in different interactions, on measures of number of turns, number of utterances, number of utterance fragments, number of words, and average number of words per utterance. The definition of *turn* used here is that of a continuous stretch of speech by one speaker that contains at least one utterance and that is delimited either by another speaker's contribution or by being the first or last contribution in a conversation. Feedback signals (*ja, mm,* "yes, mm" etc.) are not considered to be utterances and are therefore not counted as turns.

An *utterance* is defined as a syntactically delimited category corresponding to either a full sentence in written language, an elliptical sentence, a fragment of a sentence, or an interjection such as *ja, nej, jaså, oj,* "yes, no, really, oh" that is not a feedback signal. (In other words, syntactic criteria are given precedence over prosodic criteria.) Functionally, utterances are full contributions to the content being negotiated in the conversation. In Table 12.1, only a subset of the utterances produced are included. All utterances that are interjections or requests for clarification have been excluded from the analysis here, as they are mainly one word utterances (*ja, nej, va* etc, "yes, no, pardon,") or repetitions of words produced by the interactant as in the following example.

I: Var- var är du född?	"Where- where were you born?"
GM: Född?	"Born?"

An *utterance fragment* is any utterance that is not a full sentence and that does not constitute an approprite elliptical reply. Fragments thus arise through non-completion of utterances or omission of utterance elements as in KL's contribution below.

I: Vad var detta för en sång?	"What song is this?"
KL: Det var redan...	"It was already..."

The number of *words* calculated here comprises those words contained in the subset of utterances tabulated.

We will comment on the figures in Table 12.1 for each of the two subjects in turn, beginning with GM. When considering the results from this patient, it is necessary to point out that large portions of his interaction with the Swedish interlocutor are produced not in Swedish but in German, a fact which we will come back to in section two. To take just one measure, among the 410 words he produces, only 30 are in fact Swedish.

It is interesting to note that the amount of language produced by this subject is quite similar in each interaction. Although the number of turns is larger in conversation with the German interlocutor than with the Swedish interlocutor, the number of utterances is exactly the same in both interactions. More words are produced and the number of words per utterance is consequently somewhat larger in the Swedish interaction than in the German one.

We have chosen not to display mean turn-length in Table 12.1, as such a measure would veil an interesting differential distribution in turn-length between the two interactions for GM, a difference displayed in Figure 12.1. Whereas the short turns produced by this subject in SI mainly consist of one-word utterances, in GI, turns containing 2–5 word utterances are favored. This is a striking difference. An immediate interpretation of this distribution is that the availability of syntactic structure is greater for this patient when interacting with a speaker of German. This is also supported by the differential length of turns in SI and GI in the range of 6–10 words. The longer turns (more than 11 words), however, have a similar distribution in both interactions. This result can be understood when we see that GM successively reverts to German in his long turns (see next section), seemingly ignoring the situational demands to speak Swedish.

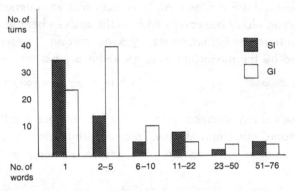

Figure 12.1. Turn-length in Swedish and German interaction for GM

GM produces more utterance fragments in SI than in GI, 22 percent and 14 percent respectively. An analysis of the utterance fragments produced in each language in SI revealed that 40 percent of the relatively few Swedish utterances and 24 percent of the many German utterances are fragments. Thus, not only do we find a larger proportion of utterance fragments when GM actually speaks his second language, Swedish, but also when he speaks in German to the Swedish interlocutor. Once again we see that the patient's speech is less proficient with the Swedish interlocutor despite the fact that most of it is in German.

For KL, there is a small difference in the number of turns between the two interactions, whereas, as was the case for GM, the number of utterances is similar. The big difference in number of words calls for a comment. As can be seen from the small amount of speech generally, KL produces very little language in both interactions. The relatively larger number of words and words per utterance in SI are a result of a sudden verbosity (57 words) in a limited segment of the Swedish interaction (in 11 turns) that is otherwise not typical of her speech. The difference in number of fragments may also be considered in this context: the verbose section just mentioned contains no fragments, which otherwise typify KL's speech. This accounts for the relatively lower proportion of fragments in the Swedish interaction.

Language choice and language separation

In this chapter, we take the notion of *language choice* to refer to a process whereby a bilingual speaker, in taking account of situational cues, selects the appropriate language. Among such cues, the monolingual or bilingual status of the interlocutor is a primary determinant of language selection. With monolingual speakers, the choice of language is obviously dictated by what

Table 12.2 *Mixing-in of the other language in SI and GI by GM.*

SI			GI		
S	M	G	G	M	S
10	16	50	76	0	0

S = Swedish utterances
M = Mixed utterances
G = German utterances

language the interlocutor speaks. If both speakers are bilingual in the same languages, the language of interaction is determined by a constellation of factors such as interlocutor characteristics, situation, topic, and purpose of discourse (Grosjean, 1982). Under specific circumstances, the bilingual may choose L1 or L2, or use L1 as a base language with mixed-in elements from L2 or vice versa.

We employ the notion of *language separation* to designate the bilingual speaker's ability to keep two languages apart *in production* when speaking in a monolingual mode. This use of the term carries no assumptions on how the languages are stored in an individual's brain (as does the notion of code differentiation, used in developmental studies on child bilingualism, see McLaughlin, 1984).

A failure to uphold a separation between two languages in production with a monolingual interactant is manifested as *involuntary code-switching*, which can range from a complete transition to the other language, to the mixing-in of isolated lexical elements. By *code-switching* we simply refer to a bilingual speaker's alternate use of two languages within the same discourse (Poplack, 1980). We have found no evidence that code-switching in our data is consciously used by the subjects for specific purposes, and we therefore designate it as involuntary in order to distinguish it from the code-switching found in healthy populations.

Both subjects considered in this study exhibit extensive problems with regard to language choice and language separation, although the nature of these problems are quite different for GM and KL. We will treat GM first as his linguistic behavior is more complex.

As shown in Table 12.2, GM's language production differs remarkably in conversation with the Swedish interlocutor and the German interlocutor. In SI, as mentioned earlier, a substantial amount of switching into German occurs throughout the interaction, whereas no switching into Swedish is found in GI, which is completely monolingual in German.

In order to determine what parameters trigger the use of German and

Swedish respectively in the Swedish interaction, the distribution of GM's utterances in each language was correlated to two candidate factors: (1) the recency of interlocutor turns, and (2) the topic content produced by the subject. The first factor was chosen in order to investigate the patients' ability to attend to the situational conditions (i.e. to keep to the language of the interlocutor). The second factor was included to discern whether specific topics would favor a certain choice of language.

With regard to the first factor, we find that a Swedish utterance on behalf of the Swedish interlocutor predisposes the subject to speak Swedish; in 9 cases out of 10, a Swedish utterance is found either immediately following the Swedish interlocutor's turn (7 cases) or in direct contingency to a prior Swedish utterance by the subject (2 cases). The remaining Swedish production, not following this distribution, has a metacommunicative function:[3]

GM: *In Riga.* (JAHA) *Ganz-*   "In Riga. (AHA) Totally-
I Riga heter det.   In Riga I mean."

Interestingly however, not all the subject's utterances immediately contingent on the interlocutor's turns are in Swedish. Only those interlocutor turns that initiate new topics and serve to secure the subject's attention trigger responses in Swedish; interlocutor turns that are contributions to ongoing topic treatment are responded to in German.

Of the 16 mixed utterances, 1 occurs directly after an interlocutor contribution, 10 occur directly after a Swedish or another mixed utterance by the subject, and 5 occur after a German utterance.

In summary so far, a typical pattern found for GM's performance with the Swedish interlocutor is the appropriate choice of Swedish turn initially, followed by one or more mixed utterances, and terminated by an expanded contribution in German. This is illustrated in the following example:

I: När kom du till Sverige?   "When did you come to Sweden?"
GM: Över huvud taget- Min far   "Generally- My father
(skratt) (JA) var-   (laughter) (YES) was
hade en- en *Offiziersposten,*   had an- an officer's post,
(JA) *in der- eh eh eh der*   (YES) in the- uh uh uh the
deutsche Marine. (JA)   German marines. (YES)
Aber für Russ- Aber für   But for Russ- But for
Russland. (JASÅ) *Das war*   Russia. (REALLY) It was
der eh eh Punkt warum sie   the uh uh point why they
haben wollten dass er kommt.   would have it that he comes.
(JAHA)…"   (AHA)…"

With regard to the second factor, viz. what type of content occurs in the Swedish and German segments of GM's turns respectively, we find that GM's German talk in SI deals exclusively with experiences he had in the earlier phases of his life, typically in his childhood and early adulthood. Not once

Table 12.3 *Mixing-in of German in the situation-contextualized data from GM.*

S	M	G
35	5	4

S = Swedish utterances
M = mixed utterances
G = German utterances

does he talk about experiences from his life in Sweden in these passages. Our subject seems to treat long-term memories in the language in which they have first been encoded, i.e. German. A parallel finding is reported in a case study by Dronkers, Koss, Friedland and Wertz (1986), who discuss such behavior in terms of the Alzheimer patient's relative superiority of long-term memory in relation to short-term memory.

So far we have seen that GM switches into German with a Swedish interlocutor, when "allowed" to talk around topics related to earlier experiences. Conversation on predetermined topics is a fairly abstract activity, cognitively demanding in its requirement that participants develop talk collaboratively. One may therefore query whether GM's switching is a general phenomenon in his Swedish interaction, or whether it is confined to certain, communicatively more demanding, situations. Data from the situation-contextualized interaction (data type 3) was thus analyzed with respect to the amount of Swedish used by the subject.

Looking at the amount of Swedish and German in this interaction, we can see that GM switches substantially less here as seen from the utterance count in Table 12.3. When GM is interacting in Swedish around heavily contextualized matters with situational support (such as the door passed by, the drinking of coffee in the next room, the time shown by the hallway clock etc.), he produces many more utterances in Swedish and succeeds better in separating his languages in relation to his interlocutor. This is shown especially clearly in the following example, where both the Swedish and the German interlocutors are by happenstance simultaneously present and address the subject in their respective languages:

German I: Bitte nehmen sie Platz!	"Please take your seat!"
Swedish I: Var så god och sitt!	"Please sit down!"
GM: Sitta här?	"Sit here?" (in Swedish)

Turning now to KL, we see that her type of language choice and language separation problem is quite different. From the two data-sets, SI and FI, KL gives only minor evidence that she experiences any problems in keeping the two languages separate (see Table 12.4): she produces Swedish in SI and

Table 12.4 *Mixing-in of the other language in SI and FI by KL.*

	SI			FI	
S	M	F	F	M	S
14	0	0	11	1	1

S = Swedish utterances
M = mixed utterances
F = Finnish utterances

Finnish in FI. In FI, there is only one utterance in Swedish, produced at the beginning of the interaction, directly after the subject had been addressed in Swedish by another speaker. In the total FI there is also only one instance of code-switching:

> KL: Se on vaan *ett halvt.*   "It is only a half."

In SI, there are no Finnish elements at all. On other occasions this subject has been recorded, she has produced small amounts of Finnish utterances in otherwise totally Swedish speech. These rare mixed-in utterances differ in type from those produced by GM, as they are invariably due to inter-sentential switches, i.e. no intra-sentential code-switches have been documented in her productions apart from the one in FI just mentioned.

KL's problems in the area of language choice and language separation are, however, more severe than these observations indicate. On the first occasion the Swedish interlocutor met the subject, KL spoke only Finnish in a 30 minute encounter. Unfortunately, no recordings were made, since this meeting was for the purpose of getting acquainted, although notes taken immediately after the encounter mention that the "subject spoke mainly in Finnish. Single phrases in Swedish, especially directly after questions." According to reports from ward personnel and family members, KL may choose Finnish or Swedish irrespective of interlocutor, and has difficulties in altering the language set she has chosen for the occasion. Surprisingly, given that her premorbid Swedish was the language most used, Finnish is the language she more often chooses.

For KL, it would appear that her problems lie mainly in the area of language choice, whereas for GM we find major difficulties in his ability to separate the languages.

Code-switching

A speaker may choose to code-switch at various points in a stretch of speech; between sentences, clauses, phrases and single lexical elements. Here, we consider only intra-sentential code-switching. For this type of switching, certain grammatical constraints have been proposed. The switch may only occur at points where the word order in each language is the same and only between free morphemes, i.e. not within words (the Equivalence Constraint and the Free Morpheme Constraint respectively, Poplack, 1980). Further, the units from each language must conform to the grammar of their respective language, that is, code-switching involves a complete change of code (the Dual Structure Principle, Sridhar and Sridhar, 1980). Code-switching is thus a distinct phenomenon not to be confused with other language contact phenomena such as borrowing, interference, or calquing, where the foreign element is more or less adapted to the grammar of the recipient language.

In the present sample from GM, there are a number of instances of intra-sentential code-switching in SI but none in GI. KL exhibits, as noted above, one single intra-sentential code-switch in FI and none in SI.

In order to see to what extent the subjects' code-switching accords with the linguistic regularities proposed for normals, a categorization of all examples of switch points (altogether twenty-one) was made, following Sankoff and Poplack (1981):

Between ADVL and preceding or following category

(1) Annars *es wär recht schön.* (GM)
   "Otherwise *it were quite beautiful*"
(2) Ja min syster *natürlich* (GM)
   "Yes my sister *of course*"
(3) Har du- du har mycket, DU (JA) säkert *hier gearbeitet.* (GM)
   "Have you- you have a lot, YOU (YES) certainly *here worked*"
(4) *Nee da kam man* först *zurück nach Kiel.* (GM)
   "*No then came one* first *back to Kiel*"
   (= "No then one came back to Kiel first")
(5) Det är jag, *in* Tysk-, Tysk- (GM)
   "I am, *in* Germ-, Germ-"

Between pred adj and preceding category

(6) Det är *merkwürdig.* (GM)
   "It is *strange*"
(7) Det är inte *weit.* (GM)
   "It is not *far*"

Between DET and N or NP

(8) Han har en *Ratstette eh,* (GM)
   "He has an *inn eh*"

(9) Min far var-, hade en-, en *Offiziersposten, in der deutsche Marine,* (GM)
"My father was-, had an-, an *officer's post, in the German marines*"

(10) Det var alltså en *paar, paar Monate schon, eh, vor dass er fest angestellt war.* (GM)
"It was thus a *couple, couple of months already, eh, before he permanently employed was*"
(="It was thus a couple of months before he was permanently employed.")

(11) *Ein* fru *war Professor.* (GM)
"*A* mrs *was professor*"

Between coordinating conjunction and preceding category

(12) *Und* därför fick jag en barn, *und* det är min moder. (GM)
"*And* therefore got I a child, *and* that is my mother"

Between subordinate conjunction and following category

(13) Ja och det var så att, eh-, mm, mm, *meine, meine, eh, Eltern drückten n'bisschen, nicht wahr,* (GM)
"Yes and it was so that, eh-, mm, mm, *my, my, eh parents forced a little, didn't they*"

Between PRED NP and preceding category

(14) Det var, det var *keine Ordnung, verstehst du.* (GM)
"There was, there was *no order, understand you*"
(=" ..., you understand.")

(15) Se on vaan *ett halvt.* (KL)
"It is only *a half*"

Between coordinate conjunction and following category

(16) *Und* därför fick jag en barn, *und* det är min moder. (GM)
"*And* therefore got I a child, *and* that is my mother"

Between PREP and following category

(17) Det är jag, *in* Tysk-, Tysk- (GM)
"I am, *in* Germ-, Germ-"

(18) I *Dienst-* (MM) *Im Dienst nicht.* (GM)
"In *duty-* (MM) *In duty no*"

Between PRON and preceding or following category

(19) Så är *das.* (GM)
"So is *it*"

(20) Det *hast du sicher.* (GM)
"That *have you certainly*"
(="I'm sure you have.")

Unlabeled

(21) Mycket lätt *möglich sein.* (GM)
"Very easy *possibly be*"

The majority of switch points follow the code-switching regularities suggested for normal subjects in the literature. Example (21) is not syntactically complete in any of the two languages; it is an utterance fragment through omission of elements, which means that its code-switching grammaticality can not be ascertained. Examples (19) and (20) are interesting because although the switches are grammatical according to the constraints proposed by Poplack (1980), they are nevertheless highly infrequent in the code-switching data that has been presented in the literature; Sankoff and Poplack (1981) give an incidence of < .1 percent in data from a larger study of a speech community where code-switching is the norm. In this perspective, the two examples we have found of 20 code-switches by GM may be considered a high proportion, indicating that this syntactic point may be more available for switching in a language pair such as German and Swedish, both of which, like English, obligatorily mark semantically empty subject positions with dummy pronouns (Hammarberg and Viberg, 1977). This is a feature that distinguishes these languages from Spanish and may explain why code-switching data from Poplack's Spanish/English speakers do not exhibit this switch point to any great extent.

Also of interest is the fact that the three most frequent intra-sentential switch-points in this data are the same as those reported by Sankoff and Poplack (1981) for Spanish/English speakers.

As we can see in the examples from GM, in most cases switching involves a transition from a Swedish utterance-initial part to a German utterance completion. There are only three exceptions to this pattern, the first two in examples (4) and (11), where a Swedish lexical unit is mixed into an utterance that is otherwise completely in German, and the third in example (16) – which is the same utterance as (12) – where GM mixes in German coordinate conjunctions in a stretch of Swedish speech.

It is important to note that many of the switches are produced after hesitations, suggesting that the switch may occur at points of higher processing load, possibly in conjunction with lexical search problems.

In summary, even though the subjects have problems in language choice or language separation, their mixing of languages is not random, but would seem to accord with the grammatical constraints and frequency hierarchy for switching points that govern code-switching for normals. This ability is obviously preserved late in dementia.

Differential availability

The measures chosen in this study to evaluate the subjects' current differential abilities in each language are necessarily limited. The selective aspects of the subjects' pragmatic abilities studied were *topic treatment*, and *turn structure* in data type 1. Data from the elicited material (data type 2) were used to estimate the extent of *lexical search problems* and abilities in *automatic speech*. All these phenomena have been shown to be sensitive to disruption in Alzheimer's dementia (Obler, 1985) and were therefore chosen for inclusion in this study.

Topic treatment In order to compare the subjects' use of the two languages with respect to how the content of conversation was treated, utterances were classified into the following 4 categories (utterances exemplifying each category are marked by #):

(1) *Topic focused contributions* (TF). A contribution which connects locally to prior utterances, and also adds to the thematic development of the talk as a whole.

I: Gerhardt hast du Geschwister?	"Gerhard do you have any brothers and sisters?"
GM: Ein, nein.	"One, no."
I: Ganz allein?	"All alone?"
GM: # Ja eine Schwester.	"Yes one sister."
I: Eine Schwester?	"One sister?"
GM: Ja.	"Yes."
I: *Jaha.* Ist die älter oder jünger als du?	"Aha. Is she older or younger than you?"
GM: # Ja, war-, sie war, jünger.	"Yes, was-, she was, younger."

(2) *Topic related contributions* (TR). An utterance with some lexical or other superficial connection to prior utterances, but where the thematic contribution to the discourse is vague, indiscernable or off-focus.

I: In welcher Stadt?	"In what town?"
GM: In welcher Stadt?	"In what town?"
I: Jaa.	"Yes."
GM: Mja, hö, eh (8 sek) Oben in Bergen.	"Mja, hö, eh (8 sek) Up in the mountains."
I: In den Bergen?	"In the mountains?"
GM: # Ja, wie eine Stadt, wo die Stadt noch, mm, m, uh, hat nicht?	"Yes, like a town, where the town still, mm, m, has, hasn't it?"

(3) *Topic digression* (TD). An utterance appearing after a TF or TR that exhibits neither local connections to prior utterances nor thematic development of the talk.

I: Har du varit i Tyskland på senare år?	"Have you been in Germany recently?"
GM: På senar år? I *Dienst?* (MM) *Im Dienst nicht aber privat war es* (PRIVAT) *angesehen-* # *Da war es-, man weiss nie im im Dienst was wird dir alles zugemutet.* (NÄ JUST DET) *Und sie, sie, erfand*	"Recently? In duty? (MM) Not in duty but privately it was (PRIVATELY) seen- Then it was-, You never know in in duty what you will all be asked. (NO I SEE) And they, they found..."

(4) *Topic change* (TC). A contribution that involves a complete change of topic framework in relation to the interviewer's prior utterance.

I: Bo- bor hon här i Stockholm också?	"Does she live here in Stockholm also?"
GM: # Det född Kiel.	"That born Kiel".

Table 12.5 *Number of utterances per topic treatment type.*

		TF	TR	TD	TC	Total
GM	SI	12	5	38	21	76
	GI	26	22	12	13	73*
KL	SI	–	2	–	12	14*
	FI	–	3	–	8	11

* The total number of utterances in GI for GM and for KL in SI is lower than that given in Table 12.1 as certain utterances initiated by the subjects could not be classified in the categories of topic treatment used here.

The number of utterances produced by the subjects for each category of topic in each interaction was tabulated as displayed in Table 12.5. For GM, there is a noticeable difference in the distribution of topical behavior in his interaction with the Swedish and German interlocutor respectively. The majority of utterances in SI are topic changes or topic digressions, 78 percent as against 22 percent for topic focused or topic related utterances. In GI, the distribution of utterances per topic category is the direct opposite, with a mere 34 percent of the utterances in topic changes or topic digressions, and 66 percent in topic focused or topic related speech. This pattern suggests that GM finds it easier to attend to the topic of discourse in GI than in SI.

KL's very limited topical contributions on the other hand do not show any comparable difference. Her contributions are more or less consistently unrelated to the topics initiated by the interlocutor. There is no evidence of monitoring for topic in either SI or FI.

Although the results for GM are suggestive, they do not confirm that his greater facility in topic treatment in GI depends on the easier availability of German. Alternative explanations are readily available when we look at the style of interaction established between the patient and the different interlocutors. There would, for example, seem to be a clear connection between the amount of topic work carried out by the interlocutor and the amount of topic focused speech on behalf of the subject.

Consequently, the interlocutors' speech was coded for number of initiations on each of the nine predetermined topics, and GM's speech was coded for the number of topic focused utterances produced on each topic. In SI, the interlocutor gave a total of 24 initiations, and GM produced 12 topic focused utterances. In GI, 40 initiations were produced by the interlocutor, and the total number of topic focused utterances by GM was 26. Furthermore, a rank correlation of the topics by number of initiations and number of topic focused utterances showed a tendency for more topic work by the interactant to result in more topic focused speech by the demented subject. We can not know, however, whether these differences in communicative behavior between interlocutors are because they were different sorts of conversationalists or whether they were responding differently to GM's different abilities in the two languages.

Another factor that may have contributed to GM's differential topic behavior in the two interactions is his degree of communicative attention on each occasion. One manifestation of greater communicative attention is a larger proportion of utterances that monitor and negotiate topics. In fact, our data show a significant difference between topic treatment when the subject monitors topic establishment, suggesting that monitoring does invariably result in more focused talk around topics (TF or TR). However, when GM's monitoring, operationalized in terms of requests for clarification produced by the subject, was examined, we found no differences in this regard between the two interactions (GI: 14 requests for clarification, SI: 14 requests for clarification).

Thus, of the two alternatives we have examined, we would argue that only the first one has any explanatory potential, although it seems unlikely that the interlocutor's communicative style alone can account for why GM produces more topic focused contributions in GI than in SI. In fact, it is quite reasonable that both the interlocutor's communicative engagement and GM's own pattern of topic treatment are a result of his finding German easier to access.

Turn structure There are significant differences between the subjects in how they handle interactional routines. GM consistently fulfills his obligation as next speaker in both SI and GI; there are no major inter-turn silences and few examples of overlapping speech. KL exhibits some difficulties in fulfilling her obligations as next speaker in both interactions. Even though she takes her turn appropriately in the majority of cases, there is a small number of instances where her turn is preceded by long inter-turn pauses; sometimes she does not take her turn at all but remains silent.

GM's turns are often not relevant second-pair parts in relation to the interactant's initiation; his utterances often have the function of "avoiding" substantial contributions to the topic. Such avoidance typically takes the following forms:

I: Kan du se vad de gör?	"Can you see what they are doing?"
GM: Ja, jaja.	"Oh yes, oh yes."
I: Uhu.	"Uhu."
GM: *Ach so, jajaja, jaja*	"Aha, oh yes, oh yes."

Interestingly, this behavior is more prevalent with the Swedish interlocutor;

in SI, 46 percent (N = 11) of the interactant's initiations are followed by avoidance utterances, and in GI the figure is 23 percent (N = 9), a considerable difference.

The greater part of KL's utterances are not relevant second-pair parts; many avoid topic treatment, being short yes/no-utterances, which may occur inappropriately even after wh–questions for example. Characteristic of a number of this subject's turns is the production of a melodic sequence, which she hums to completion.

Once again we find that the two subjects differ from each other in how they treat their two languages. GM manages interactional routines more proficiently than KL. While GM is more competent in these respects in GI than in SI, there are no detectable differences in KL's behavior with each interlocutor.

Causino, Knoefel, Obler and Albert (1985) note that pragmatic abilities, such as turn structure, otherwise resistant to deterioration, may be affected in late-stage dementia. This is something we note for KL. Interestingly, each of the two subjects performs the *mechanics* of turn-taking in the same way in both interactions, suggesting that this pragmatic parameter may be language independent and correlate well with degree of dementia.

Lexical search problems Further differences in how the subjects perform in each interaction are apparent from an analysis of the elicited production data. The data are used here only to extract information on the subjects' lexical search problems.

Cookie Theft Picture: In SI, the interlocutor introduces the picture to GM, and attempts to elicit a description of the picture from the subject through 5 initiations. GM's responses to these are different types of avoidance turns, and one comment in German that is vaguely related to the picture:

I: Vad gör den här människan?	"What is this person doing?"
GM: *Mm. Jetzt sind sie ganz hier nicht?*	"Mm. Now they are completely here,
(JA,JA) *Fest.*	aren't they? (YES) Party."

In GI, the first initiation produced by the interlocutor leads to an ontarget response by the patient:

I: Kannst du sehen was, hier passiert auf	"Can you see what happens here in
diesem Bild?	this picture?"
GM: Ja was pa-, was passiert da?	"Yes what ha-, what happens there?
Da sind Kinder.	There are children."

Further, GM correctly refers to the adult in the picture, mentioning the word *erwachsen* "adult" and refers vaguely to the cookie tin, which he describes in a circumlocution, *Das ist- das ist, fü- für Kinder nicht?* "That is- That is, fo- for children, isn't it." Otherwise, no content in the picture is described.

With the exception of a couple of unrelated utterances, KL is unresponsive to the picture description task in both SI and FI despite repeated initiations and prompting from the interlocutors. She takes her turns with *yeses* or humming. ANT: In the Action Naming Test, the subject is confronted with pictures depicting actions, and the task is to find the appropriate verb. The following examples show the strategies used by GM in each interaction.

Target	Response	Gloss
SI: sleeps	*så härligt*	"how pleasant"
eats	*sehr gut*	"very good"
skies	*das ist merkwürdig*	"that is strange"
paints	*das ist sehr schwer*	"that is very difficult"
weeps	*das ist ja hübsch*	"that is pretty, right"
smokes	*ganz hübsch*	"very pretty"
GI: eats	es un Junge	"it a boy"
skis	Sport, ist über alles, Schien	"sport, is over all, skis" (noun)
salutes	geht spazieren	"goes walking"
irons	bügelt	"irons"
drinks	trinkt	"drinks"
proposes	geben sich die Händer	"give each other the hands"
fishes	sie spielt mit ein Angel	"she is playing with a fishing-rod"
runs	läuft	"runs"

From this comparison, we see that GM produces more on-target speech in GI than in SI. In the latter interaction we find an abundance of evaluative comments on the type often used by the subject, seemingly as an avoidance strategy. Note also that most of GM's responses in SI again are in German.

KL offers a minimal amount of focused language on this as on other tasks. In FI, the elicitation session was interrupted before the ANT could be presented. The following examples illustrate the nature of the responses given by the subject in SI:

Target	Response	Gloss
SI: sleeps	(1) Det är ni. Fin.	"It is you. Fine."
	(2) Det är där.	"It is there."
	(3) sutsar	neologism, verb form
	(4) vilar	"rests"
eats	Han är snäll. Han gör-	"He is kind. He makes-"
weeps	blått	"blue" ≠ sad

Her contributions are often vague and far from the target. In this perspective, the 4 responses for *sleeps* are interesting. Her first 2 attempts to reach the target fail, whereupon she produces a neologism, phonologically similar to the Swedish verb *sussar* "dozes", and finally an appropriate verb.

KL's lexical search problems are greater than those of GM; among other things, she produces much less language when confronted with the tasks. For GM, the lexical search data suggest that his lexicon is more available in GI than in SI, whereas the data from KL do not allow any firm conclusions on this point.

Automatic speech In SI, despite many initiations and prompts on behalf of the interactant, GM does not collaborate on the tasks. In GI, on the other hand, he not only complies with the task demands, but correctly enumerates the days of the week, the months of the year, and counts from 1 to 20. However, he had to be prompted to start on weekdays and months.

KL produces no appropriate responses whatsoever on these tasks.

In summary, for GM, all our measures indicate that German is more available to him than Swedish. However, we have pointed out that caution must be exercised in the interpretation of the data, as there may be other reasons for GM's better results in GI over SI that need to be investigated more thoroughly. For KL, there is no obvious advantage in either of the two languages, although the generally limited set of data from this subject makes it difficult to be conclusive on this point.

Discussion

In our result section, three major facts are presented that need explanation; firstly the differences in linguistic and communicative behavior between the two interactions for each subject, secondly, the characteristic individual patterns of problems displayed by each subject, and thirdly, the grammaticality of the subjects' code-switches.

(1) The differences between the interactions in L1 and L2 are most obvious for GM. Data that suggest that he fares better in interaction with the German interlocutor are found in analyses of automatic speech, lexical availability, the amount of German mixed into his Swedish, and the high number of one-word turns and sentence fragments in SI. Furthermore, there are also pragmatic indications that GM copes better in GI; his topic treatment is more focused, and he has fewer avoidance turns.

In the case of KL, there is no clear evidence that she performs better in either one of her languages. There is simply not enough data. It is, however, surprising that her level of performance in Swedish and Finnish is at all similar when one considers that Swedish is her L1 and that she has only used Finnish sporadically for a period of at least 35 years. As KL shows similar behavior in each interaction, the discussion at this point will focus on GM.

A plausible hypothesis to account for GM's pattern of differential language availability would build on the following assumptions: language processing utilizes resources from the individual's limited cognitive capacities. In mature language production, linguistic material is treated largely by so called automatic processes (Bock, 1982). Many aspects of language processing which are treated automatically in an L1 require the implementation of controlled processes in an L2 (Dornic, 1978 and McLaughlin, Rossman and McLeod, 1983). We would expect subjects suffering from dementia to be impaired on language functions requiring controlled processing such as specific lexical selection, complex syntax or pragmatic functions such as topic monitoring. A demented bilingual, operating in his/her non-dominant language, should experience even greater problems with a wide range of linguistic functions.

Against this background, GM's more favorable results in GI could then be traced back to the fact that German is his L1 and thus more available to him. Greater cognitive resources would be freed for processing topical content, for monitoring output (among other things to exclude involuntary code-switching) and for selecting lexical items.

GM's relatively greater abundance of topic focused speech in the contextualized speech situation (our data type 3) fits well within such an explanatory frame. Here processing requirements are less severe than with more decontextualized content.

We have seen that GM's speech with the Swedish interlocutor consists largely of utterances in German. Although German is his better language, according to our interpretation, it is clear that his level of linguistic functioning is not as good when he speaks German in SI as when he speaks German in GI. This apparent contradiction can be resolved if it is the case that the subject experiences a greater processing load in SI, even though having switched into German. This is a feasible conjecture, as it would seem that both languages are continuously activated to some degree when GM attempts to speak his non-dominant language, Swedish. This is manifested in two ways in our data. Firstly, the subject slides into German continuously, which shows that his L1 is not inhibited in his speech production. Secondly, having switched into German, Swedish is never totally deactivated. Evidence for this comes from those mixed utterances with Swedish items in stretches of German speech. Thus, when two competing systems are available, it requires cognitive capacity to inhibit one of them (cf. Perecman, this volume); the resources to execute this are likely to be too scarce in a demented speaker. When GM speaks German in GI, however, we find no switching into Swedish whatsoever, implying that when he speaks his dominant language, his second language is never activated.

It has been suggested that a psycholinguistic requirement for code-switching is that both languages are continuously activated, which allows for their interaction at different levels in production (Sridhar and Sridhar, 1980 and

Hyltenstam and Stroud, 1985). On the basis of the results from GM, we would like to suggest that the simultaneous activation of two languages is restricted to two conditions:[4] (1) when the bilingual speaks in a bilingual mode with another bilingual, i.e. allowing normal code-switching, and (2) when the bilingual speaks his/her non-dominant language. We would argue, therefore, that it is not the case that a bilingual activates both languages for all language processing. This means that resources must be deployed to inhibit the dominant language in conversations with monolingual speakers of the non-dominant language. The matter of inhibition is not at issue when the natural choice of language is the speaker's dominant code. Here the non-dominant language is never activated. Thus the inhibition process is *unidirectional*.

Given a language production model where the notion of limited cognitive capacity plays a central role, it is likely that the types of cognitive, linguistic, and social parameters present in a specific communicative situation are essential for the successful management of bilingual functioning. We suggest that situational parameters, interlocutor characteristics and type of topic content, to all of which demented patients are especially sensitive, are of significantly greater importance for pragmatic behavior and linguistic functioning when the interaction is conducted in the demented bilingual's non-dominant language.

(2) Turning now to the second point of discussion, inter-subject variability, we find clear differences between our two subjects in their characteristic patterns of problems. Firstly, KL produces considerably less language than GM, and exhibits more severe problems both structurally and communicatively. We can therefore conclude that KL is in a more advanced stage of linguistic dissolution than GM. Secondly, GM has language separation problems although he manages language choice, while KL has problems with language choice but not language separation to any mentionable degree.

One explanation for these facts is that language choice and language separation are governed by different pragmatic abilities and that selective impairments in these abilities will appear at different points in the demented subject's linguistic regression. In a preliminary model of bilingual speech production (Hyltenstam and Stroud, 1985), it was suggested that language choice is achieved through a process that scans the speech situation, whereas language separation relies on the ability to inhibit the inappropriate language and to monitor one's own linguistic output. GM, being at a less advanced stage of dementia, still has the ability to take account of the speech situation and in particular the language of the interlocutor. KL shows no sensitivity to situational cues. This is evidenced not only in her neglect of the language of interaction but also, for example, in her turn taking problems.

GM, on the other hand, has a language separation problem, something that seems to be absent in KL's case. GM shows that he is aware on some level that the language of interaction in SI is Swedish and not German, but is unable to keep to this language set, i.e. he can not inhibit his dominant language and monitor his output as we mentioned above.

The age of acquisition and type of acquisition context may bear on the neurophysiological organization of two languages in later life, and give rise to differential ability to activate and inhibit a language (cf. Vaid, 1983). A contributing explanation for the differences between our two subjects, then, may lie in these factors. Recall that GM acquired his second language in late adulthood, while KL acquired hers at preschool age. Needless to say, such differences might conspire with the stage of dementia to produce specific types of language dissolution for different groups of bilinguals.

(3) With regard to our third point of discussion, the grammaticality of code-switching in pathological data, KL's productions are again of little interest – apart from the possibility that her lack of switches may depend on the typological incompatibility of Finnish and Swedish. For GM, we have seen that he switches between his two languages following the grammatical regularities proposed for speech communities where switching is a pervasive phenomenon (Poplack, 1980). No previous detailed comparisons have been made of the structural characteristics of switches from speakers who are members of a code-switching speech community and those who switch involuntarily (for pathological or psychological reasons). We have found, admittedly on the basis of a small sample, that the grammatical constraints followed by both types of speakers are identical. Since neither of our subjects have been members of code-switching speech communities, they can not be said to have ever *acquired* the ability to code-switch grammatically. We must conclude that the ability to code-switch, according to the constraints, appears to follow from the competence that the bilingual speaker has in each language and the simultaneous activation of both languages in production. This kind of data would thus give new support to the hypothesis proposed by various authors, for example Pfaff (1979) and Lederberg and Morales (1985), that a specific code-switching grammar does not need to be postulated. What is acquired in a code-switching community is not the grammar itself, but rather the social norms that determine when switching is appropriate, and the possible metalinguistic behavior that accompanies such switching.

Acknowledgments

This research was supported by grant Dnr 850057:2, A 1–5/1907 from The Swedish Research Council (FRN). We gratefully acknowledge the assistance of Sid Hedström, S:t Görans sjukhus, and personnel in Västra sjukvårdsdistriktet, Stockholm. The Finnish data were collected, transcribed and translated by Pirkko Bergman. Help with translation was also given by Paula Ernebo. The German data were collected by Irmgard Baumgard, and Astrid Stedje helped check the transcriptions. Don Kulick and Loraine Obler have read and commented on earlier drafts of the paper. Their comments have substantially improved this work.

Notes

1. We employ the term language mixing in a non-technical sense to cover all aspects of language contact phenomena. A more precise terminology is introduced later in this chapter to refer to specific types of language mixing.
2. The language of demented monolingual subjects, however, in particular those with Alzheimer's disease, has been substantially researched during the last fifteen years or so (see e.g. Irigaray, 1973; Obler, 1983; and Kempler and Curtis, 1983). This research shows that patients with Alzheimer's dementia exhibit a progressive deterioration in linguistic abilities, described by Obler and Albert (1985) as comprising six definable stages. Initially word finding problems predominate, but mild pragmatic disturbances, such as discourse digression and inadequate answers to questions, also occur. At this point, the patient is conscious of linguistic and communicative difficulties, which is evident from his/her metacommunicative behavior. In the middle stages, disturbances become more pervasive on the semantic and pragmatic levels, with severe topical digressions and empty speech resembling that found in patients with fluent aphasia. Certain pragmatic phenomena, such as turn-taking, may be less affected. The patient exhibits little consciousness of communicative or linguistic difficulties. Phonology, morphology and syntax remain largely intact. In the final stages, the patient's small linguistic resources for communication may render him/her completely non-communicative.
3. In this and in all following examples, the following special notational conventions are employed. Italics are used for segments produced in the "non-appropriate" language. Feedback signals are given in bracketed capitals. Hyphens signify self- or other interruptions.
4. In this discussion, it should be emphasized, that only language *production* is dealt with. For perception we assume that both languages are activated to a sufficient threshold for ready interpretation of incoming language stimuli in either language.

References

Albert, M. and Obler, L. K. (1978) *The Bilingual Brain. Neuropsychological and Neurolinguistic Aspects of Bilingualism*. New York: Academic Press.

Bock, J. K. (1982), Toward a cognitive psychology of syntax: Information processing contributions to sentence formulation. *Psychological Review* **89**, 1–47.

Causino, M., Knoefel, J., Obler, L. and Albert, M. (1985), Communication in the end-stage of Alzheimer's disease. Paper presented at the National Alzheimer's Disease Conference, Boston, November, 1985.

Dornic, S. (1978), The bilingual's performance: Language dominance, stress and individual differences. In: Gerver, D. and Sinaiko, H. (eds.), *Language, Interpretation, and Communication*. New York: Plenum Press.

Dronkers, N. F., Koss, E., Friedland, R. P. and Wertz, R. T. (1986), "Differential" language impairment and language mixing in a polyglot with probable Alzheimer's disease. Paper presented at International Neuropsychological Society meetings.

Goodglass, H. and Kaplan, E. (1972), *The Assessment of Aphasia and Related Disorders*. Philadelphia: Lea and Febiger.

Green, D. W. (1986), Control, activation, and resource: a framework and a model for the control of speech in bilinguals. *Brain and Language* **27**, 210–223.

Grosjean, F. (1982), *Life with Two Languages. An Introduction to Bilingualism*. Cambridge, MA.: Harvard University Press.

(1985), Polyglot aphasics and language mixing: a comment on Perecman (1984). *Brain and Language* **26**, 349–355.

Hammarberg, B. and Viberg, Å. (1977), The place-holder constraint, language typology, and the teaching of Swedish to immigrants. *Studia Linguistica* **31**, 106–163.

Hyltenstam, K. and Stroud, C. (1985), The psycholinguistics of language choice and code-switching in Alzheimer's dementia: some hypotheses. *Scandinavian Working Papers on Bilingualism* **4**, 26–44.

Irigaray, L. (1973), *Le langage des déments*. The Hague: Mouton.

Jolley, D. and Arie, T. (1980), Dementia in old age: an outline of current issues. *Health Trends* **12**, 1–4.

Kempler, D. and Curtiss, S. (1983), Selective preservation of syntax in Alzheimer's patients. Paper presented at the 8th Annual Boston University Conference on Language Development, Boston, October, 1983.

Lederberg, A. R. and Morales, C. (1985), Code switching by bilinguals: evidence against a third grammar. *Journal of Psycholinguistic Research* **14**, 113–136.

McLaughlin, B. (1984), *Second-Language Acquisition in Childhood*: Volume 1. *Preschool Children*. Second Edition, Hillsdale, New Jersey: Erlbaum.

McLaughlin, B., Rossman, T. and McLeod, B. (1983), Second language learning: an information-processing perspective. *Language Learning* **33**, 135–158.

Obler, L. K. (1983), Language and brain dysfunction in dementia. In: Segalowitz, S. (ed.), *Language Functions and Brain Organization*. New York: Academic Press.

(1985), Language through the life-span. In: Berko-Gleason, J. (ed.), *Language Development*. Columbus, OH: Charles Merrill.

Obler, L. K. and Albert, M. (1979), *The Action Naming Test*. Boston.

(1985), Language change with aging. In: Birren, J. and Schaie, W. (eds.), *Handbook on the Psychology of Aging*. New York: Van Nostrand Reinhold.

Paradis, M. (1977), Bilingualism in aphasia. In: Whitaker, H. and Whitaker, H. (eds.), *Studies in Neurolinguistics*, Vol. 3. New York: Academic Press.

(1983), (ed.). *Readings in Polyglot Aphasia*. Quebec: Didier.

Pfaff, C. (1979), Constraints on language mixing. *Language* **55**, 291–318.

Poplack, S. (1980), Sometimes I'll start a sentence in Spanish y termino en Español: Towards a typology of code-switching. *Linguistics* **18**, 581–618.

Sankoff, D. and Poplack, S. (1981), A formal grammar for code-switching. *Papers in Linguistics, International Journal of Human Communication* **14**, 3–45.

Sridhar, S. and Sridhar, K. (1980), The syntax and psycholinguistics of bilingual code-mixing. *Canadian Journal of Psychology* **34**, 407–416.

Vaid, J. (1983), Bilingualism and brain lateralization. In: Segalowitz, S. (ed.), *Language Functions and Brain Organization*. New York: Academic Press.

13. Language processing in the bilingual: evidence from language mixing

ELLEN PERECMAN

Introduction

One of the more important questions in the study of bilingualism is: to what extent are the bilinguals' two languages functionally independent and to what extent do they constitute a single functional system?

Evidence of interaction between systems, namely from language mixing or code mixing,[1] provides an important source of data on bilingual language processing. While such data can come from normal bilinguals as well as bilingual aphasics, language mixing in bilingual aphasia is presumed to offer a direct window on the mechanism of interaction between language systems and is therefore more valuable in modeling the neurolinguistic organization of two language systems with respect to one another.

In this chapter I will outline a neurolinguistic model of language processing in the bilingual and then propose to account for language mixing in terms of the framework of this model. According to this framework, both languages are activated when a bilingual prepares to speak and the two language systems interact via links between corresponding stages along a processing continuum. The different manifestations of language mixing reflect the interaction of language systems at different levels of language processing.

I will begin by reviewing the examples of language mixing in aphasia that have been reported in the literature. I will then discuss the relationship between language mixing in aphasia and language mixing in normals. In the final part of the chapter I will outline the model and show how various forms of language mixing may arise in terms of this model.

Language mixing in aphasia

Using words from different languages in the same utterance

There have been a number of reports of patients using words from several languages together in the same utterance. Herschman and Poetzl (1920) report mixing of Czech and German words in spontaneous speech and naming, in a Czech patient who spoke German as his primary language from the age of 14. Poetzl (1925) reports the interjection of Czech words into German utterances in a 52 year old German who had recently been studying Czech. A German patient described by Kauders (1929), who had learned English and French perfectly at the age of 16, produced German and French words together in his spontaneous speech when he became aphasic. Stengel and Zelmanowitz's (1933) patient, a Czech who learned German at the age of 35, also mixed words from both of these languages. Cases 2, 3, and 4 reported by Gloning and Gloning (1965) were found to mix words of more than one language in the same utterance. Case 2, a native Italian, spoke Serbo-Croatian, German and Spanish; case 3 was a Bulgarian who learned German at the age of 36; case 4, a 50 year old woman, used German and Hungarian words together. Finally, Mossner and Pilsche (1971) report the use of English words in predominantly German sentences, in a 36 year old German woman who had returned to Germany 4 years before, after living in Australia for 12 years. The 80 year old patient described in Perecman (1984), a German–French–English polyglot who was raised in a German speaking family in Cameroon, West Africa, produced sentences with all combinations of his languages: English and German words (e.g. *In English **das wird Bleistift genannt***); English and French words (e.g. *à la/ **I say**/ il est un peu*); and German and French (e.g. *la **Vetter***).

Combining a stem from one language with an affix from another

Some patients produce words that are themselves combinations of morphemes from more than one language. The patient of Herschman and Poetzl (1920) produced German words with Czech affixes. Kauders' (1929) patient produced English affixes on German words. Stengel and Zelmanowitz (1933) observed German words with Czech plural affixes. Schulze (1968) reports Russian words with Bulgarian affixes in a 55 year old professor of German literature, who also spoke Russian and French, in addition to having knowledge of English and Latin. An American patient fluent in German, reported in Perecman (1980), produced the German word *gelt* with the English suffix *–ing*. The polyglot aphasic reported in Perecman (1984) produced the English word *come* with the German infinitival suffix *–en*.

Blending syllables from different languages in a single word

Kauders' (1929) patient produced blends of German and English words. Gloning and Gloning's (1965) case 4 blended Hungarian and German syllables together to form words. Their case 2 also produced blends but the languages blended are not specified. In Perecman (1984), one might interpret as syllable blends (1) the translation of the English *butterfly* into French *la votre fly*; and (2) the production of "[geʃvɛldɛs] *haus*" in response to the request to interpret the English phrase *swelled head*.

Intonation of one language with vocabulary of another

The Czech–German bilingual described by Stengel and Zelmanowitz (1933) produced vocabulary from one language with intonation patterns of the other.

Using syntax of one language with vocabulary of another

Case 4 of Weisenberg and McBride (1935), a native English speaker who had eight languages at his command, including English, Spanish, French, Italian, Greek, Latin, Old French, and Arabic, used French and Spanish syntax with English vocabulary. A German–English–French polyglot described by L'Hermitte, Hecaen, Dubois, Culioli, and Tabouret-Keller (1966) used English syntax with French vocabulary. Perecman's (1984) case produced English vocabulary with German syntax in reading (i.e. *I got home from work* was produced as I [vɪl] home [kʌmɪn]). He read the year 1936 in an English sentence as 1963, suggesting that he interpreted it as the German *neunzehn sechs und dreizig*.

Responding with a phonetically similar word from the mother language

Herschman and Poetzl (1920) report that their patient sometimes produced a phonetically similar Czech counterpart to an intended German word. A number of examples of such phonological mixing are reported in Perecman (1984). This patient converted the English *door* to the French *dur*, and the English *groom* as the possible English word *broom* [bʁum] on a translation task, read an English word as a phonetically similar German word (i.e. *heard* was produced as *hund*), translated the English *wall* as the French *val*, and repeated the Spanish *como se llama usted* as the German *kommen sie immer hier*.

Responding in a language different from the language of address

When patients respond in a language other than the one in which they were addressed, I assume that this reflects interaction of languages at the conceptual level. This symptom was observed by Pick (1909) in a 74 year old man who answered Czech questions in German, and German questions in Czech. The 57 year old Slovak woman described in case 1 of Gloning and Gloning (1965), who also spoke German and Spanish, was on occasion observed to answer in Spanish when addressed in German. Their case 2, the 56 year old Italian, who also spoke Serbo-Croatian and German, answered in Italian when he was addressed in German. Perecman's (1984) patient responded to English questions with German, and to German questions with French or English.

Spontaneous translation

Spontaneous translation is the immediate and unsolicited translation of one's own (or another speaker's) utterances into a second language. Overt spontaneous translation has been reported by Kauders (1929), whose patient named objects correctly in French and/or English and then produced the German translation. Schulze's (1968) patient apparently demonstrated similar behavior. The 65 year old English aphasic described by Veyrac (1931) had spoken predominantly French from the time she was 21; she is reported to have automatically translated two commands addressed to her with an apparent lack of comprehension for the meaning of the commands. Case 4 of Weisenberg and McBride (1935) was reported to have spontaneously translated an English color term into Spanish. Goldstein (1948) describes a Swedish immigrant to the U.S. who repeated words and sentences in one language and then the other. In a self-report, Roman Jakobson (1964) tells of finding himself translating each of his utterances into four or five languages subsequent to a car accident. The patient described in Paradis, Goldblum and Abidi (1982) was noted to spontaneously translate names of objects from French into English, and Perecman's (1984) patient quite frequently spontaneously translated his utterances from German into English.

Conceivably, the occasional naming of objects in a language other than the language in which a patient is addressed, or a response to questions in a language other than that of address, are also examples of spontaneous translation, but in these cases, the translation occurs covertly, rather than overtly. This has been observed in the patients described by Kauders (1929), Stengel and Zelmanowitz (1933), Weisenberg and McBride in their case 4 (1935), Gloning and Gloning in their case 2 (1965), and L'Hermitte *et al.* (1966).

Language mixing in normals

Pfaff (1979) analyzed language-mixing in the conversational speech of normal Spanish–English bilinguals and observed a number of regularities: (1) speakers infrequently produce the determiner and noun in one language, and verb in another except in contexts where the noun functions as a technical or quasi-technical term; (2) full relative clause switching occurs very rarely except when functioning as a framing device, marking the sequence as an aside; (3) prepositions alone are never switched; (4) mixing of an entire prepositional phrase occurs infrequently; and (5) there is a tendency for function words, sentence adverbials, tags, and loosely bound interjections to be realized in the first language even in a predominantly second language sentence. "Such forms function socially as markers of ethnic identification" (p. 314).

Several general principles governing language-switching in normals, as it affects syntactic structure, have been suggested. Sridhar (1978) has proposed the "Dual Structure Principle", which states that the internal structure of the guest constituent need not conform to the constituent structure rules of the host language, so long as its placement in the host sentence obeys the rules of the host language.

Poplack (1980) analyzed 1,835 switches and concluded that: (1) a switch cannot take place between the stem of a word and its affix unless the stem has been phonologically integrated into the language of the affix (the "free-morpheme constraint"), and (2) word order immediately before and immediately after a switch point must be possible in both languages if the switch is to occur ("the equivalence of structure constraint").

"The free-morpheme constraint" also applies to idiomatic expressions and set phrases, e.g. greetings and discourse elements such as, *you know*, and *I mean*. Poplack found less than one per cent switches within idiomatic expressions and no examples of switches between the stem and its bound morpheme. "The equivalence constraint" also applies to languages that do not share the same adjective placement rules, i.e. *J'ai acheté **an American car**, but * *J'ai acheté **an American** voiture*. Poplack found that less than one per cent language-switches in her corpus violated this constraint. Sridhar and Sridhar (1980) criticize Poplack's equivalence constraint for failing to specify the internal constituency of the switched element. They point out that in Poplack's example (26) ordering rules in the verb phrases in both the main and the subordinate clause are violated in the mixed sentence though the VPs as whole constituents do map onto each other. Grosjean (1982) suggests, on the basis of the unacceptability of examples like * *they want **à venir***, that these constraints should also take into account such factors as length of phrase and semantic or pragmatic unity of the segments. It would seem to me that the example he cites may violate a syntactic constraint on breaking up a major constituent, in this case a VP (*want to come*).

Metalinguistic knowledge

Pfaff concluded from her study of Spanish–English bilinguals that speakers who switch languages are competent in the syntactic rules of both languages. While HB provided no evidence directly relevant to this claim, one might consider the following example from HB (Perecman, 1984) to be consistent with that observation: when asked to interpret the phrase *swelled head*, the patient said *geschweltes haus*. Note the appropriate neuter ending in *geschwelltes haus*, even though *kopf*, the German translation of *head*, is masculine. It would appear that even though the interaction between the English *swelled head* and the German *geswelltes haus* was at the phonological level, nonetheless, there is a syntactic check on the output of that level.

Note also the following example, where HB's utterance indicates his knowledge of the grapheme–phoneme correspondence rules of both languages: *standing that means **ständig fuhren stein ständig** you don't say the word [ʃtendig] [ʃtendiʃ] you say [iʃ]*.

Does aphasic language mixing differ from normal language mixing?

From the cases reported in the literature, one might conclude that, independent of symptoms associated with the aphasia itself, aphasic polyglots mix languages in much the same way as normal polyglots do. However, given the fact that language mixing in aphasia ofter occurs in the context of language which deviates from the standard in other ways as well, it may be difficult in principle to determine whether a particular case of language mixing in aphasia observes the constraints on normal language mixing. For example, consider again the patient HB (Perecman, 1984), in whom utterances such as the following were not uncommon: *à la/ à la/ à la/ I say/ il est il est un peu/ voulez vous un peu*, which translates as "to the to the to the I say it is it is a little do you want a little."

Though Sridhar and Sridhar (1980) found that grammatical items such as articles, quantifiers, auxiliary verbs, prepositions, and clitics are unlikely to be mixed in isolation, the utterance *la vetter* from Perecman (1984) is an example of precisely this. Notice also the error in gender. I should point out that the confusion of gender seen in *la vetter* is not unusual in semantic jargon, where we see substitution such as HER for HIM.

Poplack's (1980) "free morpheme constraint" is violated in this patient in the example *I [vII]* home *[kʌMIn]*, where the stem *come* is not phonologically integrated into the language of the affix. In another example from the same patient we see violation of Poplack's "equivalence constraint", according to which word order immediately before or after a switch point must be possible in both languages: *the dialect I used would be something that contained **ein bisschen** a little **ein bisschen deutsch** a little German*. Here, the German word order would have been *Der Dialekt den ich genutzt hatte sei etwas der ein bisschen Deutsch enthalt*. In German, the verb in the subordinate clause must follow the object, though it precedes it in English.

The mechanism of language mixing

The premise of this chapter is that the interaction of language systems at different levels of processing produces language mixing. Let me now try to show how this interaction might occur. Suppose that each language constitutes a semi-independent processing system and that the interaction of these systems is hierarchically defined in the following way:

(1) multiple languages are unified in a single system at the prelinguistic conceptual level;
(2) they are strongly linked at the lexical–semantic level;
(3) links between language systems are progressively weaker as processing moves from the lexical–semantic to the articulatory phonetic level.

The notion that there are progressively weaker links between language systems is supported by evidence that language mixes are more common at the lexical than at the phonological level of processing, both in aphasia and in normals.

It has been claimed that in most cases, apart from the predominantly sociolinguistic and paralinguistic symptoms associated with the cerebral insult causing an aphasia, aphasic polyglots mix languages in much the same way as normal polyglots do (Grosjean, 1985). This result is predicted by the view that the aphasic polyglot has an intact language system but imperfect control of the system (Green, 1986) and that the damaged brain processes language according to the same general principles as the non-damaged brain (Brown and Perecman, 1986).

The threshold hypothesis

Green (1986) assumes that language-switching in aphasia operates in terms of the same mechanism Luria proposes to explain normal naming. Luria (1973:45) argues that naming processes are dictated by the "law of strength", according to which every strong (or biologically significant) stimulus evokes a strong response, while every weak stimulus evokes a weak response. He writes that

> when affected by a pathological lesion, the cerebral cortex is usually in an abnormal inhibitory or "phasic" state in which "the law of strength" is upset and weak stimuli begin to evoke the same reactions as strong. Naturally under these conditions a well stabilized and dominant value will no longer be distinguished from irrelevant and weaker connections, and these irrelevant connections will start to appear just as easily as the required name ... The appearance of a flood of equally probable possibilities prevents the discovery of the required dominant word. (Luria, 1973:157)

Taking a similar view with respect to language switching, Green agrees that a word must reach a certain level of activation to become available as a response, and "that the appropriate name comes to dominate other possible candidate names by reducing their level of activation [and] speakers can output whichever expression first achieves threshold."

Green argues that in some cases of polyglot aphasia, a bilingual speaker calls up L2 instead of L1 not because L1 is inactive, but because there is insufficient suppression of activation in the L2 system. Grosjean (1982) appears to hold the same view where he refers to language-switching as taking advantage of "the most available word."

He remarks that this phenomenon is extremely frequent in bilingual speech and occurs when speakers are "tired, lazy or angry," suggesting too that a failure to actively, perhaps consciously, regulate the systems is at issue.

As an alternative to "the threshold hypothesis", consider that altered brain states – altered by brain damage, drowsiness, fatigue, or laziness – might effect a change in the rate of flow of neural activity from one stage in the language processing continuum to another, and that as a consequence of this change in rate of processing, the period of activation of a given pre-terminal stage in the processing continuum is lengthened. Language mixing would then be explained by the hypothesis that a disruption of the normal rate of processing, i.e. an abnormal lengthening of a period of activation, upsets the functional unity of a language system and disturbs the automaticity of a processing routine, thus facilitating a linkage with the other system. In other words, under these conditions, a unit being processed in one system may suddenly be shunted over to the next level of processing in the other system.

The notion that changes in the threshold of activation account for language mixing and switching is compatible with this conceptualization insofar as a change in the rate of flow of activity may affect a change in the threshold of activation necessary to go from one level of language processing to another.

A microgenetic model of language processing

Language is on a continuum with prelinguistic conceptual thought, and the goal of the language processing mechanism is to translate prelinguistic concepts into linguistic forms, and vice versa. Aphasic errors, "slips-of-the-tongue" in normals, and language mixing phenomena in both populations suggest that on the microgenetic time-scale, the translation from prelinguistic conceptual thought to linguistic form is an emergent process, which occurs sequentially over a series of stages.

Brown's (1977 and 1979) microgenetic theory of language speculates that these stages are levels of processing which are mediated by evolutionarily distinct levels of brain structure, and that linguistic deviations reflect functional changes in the fabric of the language processing system at different stages in the emergence of language. The aphasic symptom thus represents in macrocosm the preconscious processing activity which in normal language is mediated by the lesioned area. The linguistic output produced by the altered flow of activity identifies the contribution of that stage of language production which has been directly affected by the alteration, a contribution which can be identified only indirectly in the error-free language of normal speakers under optimal conditions.

From a microgenetic point of view, the stages at which errors occur may be interpreted as levels of linguistic representation. Representations are conceived of as static "photographs" of different points along the processing continuum, as artificially frozen segments in a naturally dynamic processing system.

In this view, an utterance (let us consider a single word) originates at the conceptual level, where non-linguistic properties of the utterance relating to spatial, causal, temporal, quantitative, etc. relations, are encoded (see Garrett's (1980) discussion of message level). Once this conceptual representation is sufficiently specified, it assumes lexical–semantic features. When this representation achieves a sufficient degree of specificity in terms of lexical–semantic features, phonological features are assigned. There are at least two stages of phonological processing; a level at which language is represented in terms of units larger than the phoneme, phonological gestalts, and another level at which the elementary unit of representation (and processing) is the phonemic segment.

Language processing in the bilingual

In modeling bilingualism, the functional independence of the prelinguistic conceptual level from the lexical–semantic level becomes crucial. The prelinguistic conceptual level reflects properties of the human mind and is therefore common to both of the language systems of the bilingual. The lexical–semantic level, on the other hand, differs for each language. That the two levels are functionally independent is both theoretically motivated and empirically supported (Zurif and Blumstein, 1978, and Caramazza, Gordon, Zurif and Deluca, 1976).

The distinction between a prelinguistic conceptual representation and a properly linguistic representation is particularly relevant in accounting for the ability to translate from one language to another. For, certainly, translations must make reference to a common level of information processing, and the conceptual level is the only plausible candidate.

Paradis (1985) comes to the same conclusion. He argues for a "a distinction between a conceptual memory store of multisensory images independent of language (and hence of languages) and a linguistically-constrained semantic memory for lexical meanings" (p. 9) and proposes that bilinguals have one "conceptual memory store," and two distinct "semantic stores," and that "units of meaning in each language combine conceptual features in different ways" (p. 9). The following example from Paradis (1985:9) makes this notion quite clear:

> Thus, the English unit of meaning "ball" is connected with conceptual features such as "spheric", "bouncy", "play", etc. The French unit of meaning that corresponds to *balle* shares these features but is also connected to "small". If it is too large to hold in one hand, it is no longer *une balle* but becomes *un ballon*, a distinction which is irrelevant in English.

That language processing systems diverge beyond the conceptual level of processing follows from the fact that each level of language processing is characterized by a uniquely defined network of relations among items at that level. Since our discussion is focused at the single word level, we will be concerned here with the lexical–semantic and phonological levels, ignoring the issue of syntactic processing. For the lexical–semantic system this uniquely defined network of relations is a set of language-specific semantic fields; each lexical item in a given language is only meaningful in terms of its semantic field, that is, within the network of relations that define its semantic field. In terms of Paradis' example above, what this suggests is that the meaning of the French word *ballon* is defined by the relation between, or more precisely, the contrast between, *ballon* and *balle*. Given that no such contrast is provided for in the semantic field for the English word *ball*, the translation of French *balle* as English *ball* is not entirely accurate.

At the phonological level, phonological units are language-specific in that here, too, a unit is uniquely defined by its relation to the other units in the network. At this level, there is a network defined by linguistically significant contrasts in the language, i.e. minimal pairs.

Since the conceptual system of the monolingual feeds into only one linguistic system, it is probably fair to assume that in monolinguals, the processing routines from conceptual to phonological forms have become automatized. Each level of representation emerges from the next in a continuous, uninterrupted fashion, and the distinction between pairs of representatives is likely to be poorly defined.

In contrast, the conceptual system of the bilingual has two options with respect to lexical–semantic processing. It can be encoded in the features of either one or two linguistic systems. As a consequence, the processing routines from conceptual to phonological form are likely to be less automatic for the bilingual than for the monolingual, and the distinction between levels of representation will be more marked.

Are languages tagged at the level of mental representation?

It is reasonable to assume that at some point in the processing continuum words are tagged to identify the language as well as register and style (Green, 1986) of output. Presumably, this language tagging occurs at, or near, the lexical–semantic level, where language systems begin to function independently. We might then speculate that overt tagging behavior points to a lengthened period of activation of the lexical–semantic level of processing.

In the case described in Perecman (1984) overt language tagging, that is, identifying the language in which an utterance is spoken, was not uncommon. Indeed, one had the impression that the patient was preoccupied with the identity of the languages he spoke. Often he would identify the language being addressed to him while at the same time being unable to respond appropriately to the question asked of him in that language. For example, when asked in German to subtract four from twelve, he responded "zwölf weniger weniger weniger vier ist Deutsch." Thus instead of performing the calculation, he simply defined the language of the question. It is also tempting to conclude that when HB was asked to translate into French the German word *Seife* and produced *französische Auskunft* (French information), he succeeded in accessing the French "tag" on the lexical representation for *Seife*, but failed to access the linguistic features necessary to translate the word into French.

Spontaneous translation

In the normal literature, translation either at the point of language mixing or in the neighborhood of a mix, is interpreted as a cue indicating the speaker's perception of the foreignness of a word (or words), and mixing is seen as "principally a stylistic device denoting change in affect, addressee, mode, etc." (Pfaff, 1979:298). Grosjean (1985:351) argues that spontaneous translation is "a well-known communicative strategy which is used to emphasize or clarify a point." This is an unlikely explanation for the occurrence of spontaneous translation in aphasia. If spontaneous translation reflects a lesion-induced lengthening of the period of activation of the prelinguistic conceptual level – the level of processing at which multiple languages are unified in a single system – perhaps the speaker utters these translations because the increase in activation at this level causes the processing routines for both languages to be activated.

Evidence from experiments with normal bilinguals

There is experimental evidence that in normal bilinguals, although only one language may be selected, the other is nonetheless active at least when both languages are in regular use (Preston and Lambert, 1969 and Altenberg and Cairns, 1983). In particular, it has been shown that bilingual children take longer to name an object than monolinguals (Mägiste, 1979; but see Obler, Albert and Lozowick, 1986). These findings are consistent with any one of several logical possibilities for the organization of the two language systems with respect to one another:

(1) the two systems are entirely integrated;
(2) the systems are entirely independent of each other and all processing is conducted separately;
(3) the systems are integrated at some level of processing but other processing is conducted separately.

There are other studies, however, which specifically support the notion that the conceptual level is common to both systems, while the lexical level is language-specific.

Shanon (1982) used as subjects 16 university students, half of whom were native English speakers and half of whom were native Hebrew speakers, but all were reported to have perfect mastery of the non-native language. Shanon found that for all subject groups, latencies for naming drawings of objects in the non-native language were not significantly longer than latencies for naming them in the native language, and furthermore that across groups the total time to make overt categorization responses to drawings and written words in either language was not affected by whether the response was uttered in the native or non-native language. Together these results suggest that both languages were processed via a single system. But the finding that the different language groups had different response times to reading written words in the two languages suggests that the early stages in reading, and possibly subsequent stages in lexical access are language dependent, implying separate language systems. Semantic processing, on the other hand, is language independent, implying a shared level of processing. I would argue that this shared level of processing is the conceptual level.

Support for this specific claim comes from a study by Guenther (1984), in which Persian–English bilingual subjects read and then answered questions about a series of short texts written in either Persian or English. Subjects were native speakers of Persian but fluent in both languages. The experimental paradigm required subjects to judge whether probe sentences, written either in the same language as the text or in the other language, were true or false in terms of the previously read texts. Probes were either explicitly presented or only implied; false probes were related but not strictly implied. Guenther found a non-significant difference between reaction time to same- and different- language versions for the implicit and false probes. He concludes that this result is consistent with the hypothesis that the conceptual representation produced by reading an English text has essentially the same form as the conceptual representation produced by reading a Persian text.

Similarly, Lopez and Young (1974) found that on a list learning task, equivalents in a second language produce the same effect of interference as observed in a unilingual task. Sixty-four Mexican–American high school students, bilingual in English and Spanish, were first given a 16-word list to read, either in Spanish or English, and then asked to learn a list of 16 words presented on audio-tape, which included either the same words or a translation of the words on the original list. English-dominant bilinguals showed an equivalent facilitation effect of Spanish words on English words and English words on Spanish words. The authors conclude that this argues against the notion that the words from one language must be translated into the other in order for the facilitation effect to occur. They reason that a translation hypothesis would have predicted that since subjects were English-dominant, they would spontaneously translate from Spanish to English and would therefore be facilitated more when the learning list was in English than when it was in Spanish. Similar findings are reported by Kolers (1966) and Glanzer and Duarte (1971).

The distinction between unitary conceptual processing and dichotomous lexical processing is brought to bear in comparing the Lopez and Young study with the study carried out by Costermans and Galland (1980). Costermans and

Galland investigated reading in semantically related word pairs when one member of the pair was in French and one in Dutch. Subjects were native Dutch speakers bilingual in Dutch and French. The authors predicted that if the two lexicons form an integrated structure, then both *couteau* and *mes* (Dutch for knife) should facilitate *fourchette* to an equal extent. They found that latencies of response were longer when reading an item preceded by an item from a different language, and conclude that the structures are not integrated.

On the basis of the model outlined above, one would expect a difference in latency of response for the subjects in the two studies. In the Costermans and Galland study, subjects were comparing two words where one was presented immediately after the other, and one can therefore assume that subjects were comparing phonological representations from two separate systems. In Lopez and Young, on the other hand, subjects were making comparisons over a longer time delay, and with the consequent decay of phonological information in the memory representation, it is likely that they were comparing representations from a single conceptual memory store.

Aphasia treatment studies as evidence

Treatment studies have also been considered when addressing the question of whether the multiple languages of a polyglot are organized within a single system or whether they constitute separate systems. It has been argued that if a speech/language therapy program targeted at L-a^2 is also effective in remediating L-b, it might suggest that both languages are part of the same system in this patient. It is also possible, however, that if the languages are hierarchically organized with respect to one another, and are unified at precisely that level at which the therapy is targeted, the false conclusion will be drawn that these languages constitute a single system. It is therefore not clear in principle how to interpret the generalization of treatment for language/speech disturbance from one language to another, with respect to the question of single versus multiple language systems. The actual data are even more confusing. Watamori and Sasanuma (1978) found that recovery was comparable for both treated and untreated languages of a Broca's aphasic, but favored the treated language in the case of a Wernicke's aphasic.

Differential impairment in polyglot aphasia as evidence

It has been suggested that differential linguistic impairment in polyglot aphasia indicates a multisystem hypothesis. In this regard, Vaid and Genesee (1980) conclude on the basis of their review of studies of unselected cases that "differential language impairment and restitution is probably an exception to the more frequent parallel pattern, and by implication, therefore both or all languages are usually processed by common neuropsychological mechanisms." While I do not agree with their conclusion, I think they make an important point in arguing that what may appear as differential language impairment may actually reflect the fact that different languages may require different perceptuo-cognitive analysers, and that a non-linguistic impairment in one of those analysers may be interpreted as a differential language impairment. In particular they point out that because acoustic analysers, which underlie processing of phonetic writing systems, are found in the temporal cortex, temporal lesions are associated with greater impairment in reading and/or writing of phonetically-based scripts. Similarly, lesions in posterior occipito-parietal cortical areas are associated with greater impairment in reading and/or writing of scripts with ideographic or irregular phonetic bases, because these areas mediate the processing of ideographic scripts which involve visuo-spatial analysis.

Concluding remarks

Though one would have to concur with Vaid and Genesee (1980) that "the most striking feature of the findings to emerge from studies of bilingual/polyglot aphasia is their extreme variety and complexity," it is precisely this variety and complexity of case studies which will eventually shed light on the nature of multilingualism, and it is only in the context of case studies that we will approach an understanding of why that variety and complexity exists. (See Caramazza, 1986 and Shallice, 1979 for discussions of the case study approach.)

In view of the claim that language mixing is so common among normal bilinguals (Grosjean, 1982), one might wonder why it is reported to be so rare (7 per cent) in multilingual aphasics (Albert and Obler, 1978). One possibility is that it is indeed rarer among aphasics than among normals. Another possibility is that it is in fact, not rare, but that (1) many cases of language mixing are interpreted as jargon and therefore go unreported; or (2) poor delineation of the bilingual population accounts for an inflated total number of cases of bilingual aphasia. In other words, it may be the case that at least some of the reportedly bilingual aphasics would not be considered bilingual if more stringent criteria for bilingualism were applied to them (see Albert and Obler, 1978).

In the early literature, mastery of classical languages like Latin and Greek met the criteria for bilingualism, and very broad definitions of bilingualism continue to be the rule. In a study by Collison (1974) the bilingual population was defined by "the parallel usage of two languages, ranging from the ability to use a few functional words of a foreign language to being equally fluent in the two languages," a definition as useless as it is broad. More commonly, the term is used in Weinreich's (1967) sense, as the practice of alternately using two languages; here the definition is somewhat more circumscribed, but still vague.

Another problem relates to the definition of bilingualism. Although, technically, the word *bilingual* refers to a person who speaks two languages, and the word *polyglot* refers to the speaker of more than two languages, some authors do not distinguish between bilinguals and polyglots in defining their populations. Whether this is a necessary or even useful distinction with respect to psycholinguistic and/or neurolinguistic processing is an empirical issue, and the relevance of the distinction cannot be ruled out.

Still, as poor as it is in definition, bilingualism is rich in the potential it holds for the study of language and the language processing system.

Notes

1. The terms language mixing and code mixing refer to the same phenomena. I prefer the term language mixing.
2. Since the abbreviations L1, L2, etc. have come to be associated with order of acquisition, I have chosen the abbreviations L-a, L-b, etc as a designation of the languages of a polyglot which is neutral with respect to order of acquisition.

References

Albert, M. and Obler, L. (1978), *The Bilingual Brain*. New York: Academic Press.

Altenberg, E. and Cairns, H. (1983), The effects of phonotactic constraints on lexical processing in bilingual and monolingual subjects. *Journal of Verbal Learning and Verbal Behavior*, **22**, 174–188.

Brown, J. W. (1972), *Aphasia, Apraxia and Agnosia: Clinical and Theoretical Aspects*. Springfield, IL.: Charles C. Thomas.

(1977), *Mind, Brain and Consciousness*. New York: Academic Press.

(1979), Language representation in the brain. In Steklis, H. and Raleigh, M. (eds.), *Neurobiology of Social Communication in Primates; An Evolutionary Perspective*. New York: Academic Press, 133–195.

Brown, J. W. and Perecman, E. (1986), The neurological basis of language processing. In Chapey, R. (ed.), *Language Intervention Strategies in Adult Aphasia* (2nd Edition). Baltimore: Williams & Wilkins.

Caramazza, A. (1986), On drawing inferences about the structure of normal cognitive systems from the analysis of patterns of impaired performance: The case for single-patient studies. *Brain and Cognition*, **5**, 41–66.

Caramazza, A., Gordon, J., Zurif, E. W. and DeLuca, D. (1976), Right hemisphere damage and verbal problem solving behaviour. *Brain and Language*, **3**, 41–46.

Collison, G. O. (1974), Concept formation in a second language: a study of Ghanaian school children. *Harvard Educational Review*, **44**, 441–457.

Costermans, J. and Galland, J. (1980), On the accessibility of lexical terms in bilinguals. *Canadian Journal of Psychology*, **34**, 381–387.

Garrett, M. (1980), Levels of processing in sentence production. In Butterworth, B. (ed.), *Language Production*, Vol. 1, New York: Academic Press.

Glanzer, M. and Duarte, A. (1971), Repetition between and within languages in free recall. *Journal of Verbal Learning and Verbal Behavior*, **10**, 625–630.

Gloning, I. and Gloning, K. (1965), Aphasien bei Polyglotten: Beitrag zur Dynamik des Sprachabbaus sowie zur Lokalizations Frage dieser Störungen. *Wiener Zeitschrift für Nervenheilkunde und deren Grenzgebiete*, **22**, 362–397.

Goldstein, K. (1948), *Language and Language Disturbances*. New York: Grune and Stratton.

Green, D. W. (1986), Control, activation, and resource: a framework and a model for the control of speech in bilinguals. *Brain and Language*, **27**, 210–223.

Grosjean, F. (1982), *Life with Two Languages*. Cambridge, MA: Harvard University Press.

(1985), Polyglot aphasics and language mixing: a comment on Perecman (1984). *Brain and Language*, **26**, 349–355.

Guenther, R. K. (1984), Bilingual representation of discourse. *Psychological Reports*, **54**, 83–90.

Herschmann, H. and Poetzl, O. (1920), Bemerkungen über die Aphasie der Polyglotten. *Neurologisches Zentralblatt*, **39**, 114–120.

Jakobson, R. (1964), Discussion. In DeReuck, A. V. S. and O'Conner, M. (eds.), *Disorders of Language*. Boston: Little, Brown, p. 120.

Kauders, O. (1929), Über polyglotte Reaktionen bei einer sensorien Aphasie. *Zeitschrift für die Gesamte Neurologie und Psychiatrie*, **122**, 651–666.

Kolers, P. (1966), Reading and talking bilingually. *American Journal of Psychology*, **3**, 357–376.

L'Hermitte, R., Hecaen, H., Dubois, J., Culioli, A. and Tabouret-Keller, A. (1966), Le problème de l'aphasie des polyglottes: Remarques sur quelques observations. *Neuropsychologia*, **4**, 315–329.

Lopez, M. and Young, R. K. (1974), The linguistic interdependence of bilinguals. *Journal of Experimental Psychology*, **102**, 981–983.

Luria, A. R. (1973), *The Working Brain: An introduction to neuropsychology*. New York: Basic Books.

Mägiste, E. (1979), The competing language systems of the multilingual: a developmental study of decoding and encoding processes. *Journal of Verbal Learning and Verbal Behavior*, **18**, 79–89.

Mossner, A. and Pilsche, H. (1971), Phonematisch-syntaktisch Aphasie: Ein sonderfall motorischer Aphasie bei einer zweisprachigen Patientin. *Folia Linguistica*, **5**, 394–409.

Obler, L., Albert, M. and Lozowick, S. (1986), The aging bilingual. In Vaid, J. (ed.), *Language Processing in Bilinguals: Psycholinguistic and Neuropsychological Perspectives*. Hillsdale, N. J.: Erlbaum.

Paradis, M. (1985), On the representation of two languages in one brain. *Language Sciences*, **7**, 1–40.

Paradis, M. Goldblum, M.-C. and Abidi, R. (1982), Alternate antagonism with paradoxical translation behavior in two bilingual aphasic patients. *Brain and Language*, **15**, 55–69.

Perecman, E. (1980), Semantic jargon over time. Paper presented at International Neuro-psychological Society Meeting, San Francisco.

(1984), Spontaneous translation and language mixing in a polyglot aphasic. *Brain and Language*, **23**, 43–63.

Perecman, E. and Brown, J. W. (1985), Varieties of aphasic jargon. *Language Sciences*, **7**, 176–215.

Pfaff, C. (1979), Constraints on language mixing: intrasentential code-switching and borrowing in Spanish/English. *Language*, **55**, 291–318.

Pick, A. (1909), Forgesetzte Beiträge zur Pathologie des sensorischen Aphasie. *Archiv für Psychiatrie und Nervenkrankheiten*, **37**, 216–241.

Poetzl, O. (1925), Über die parietal bedingte Aphasie und ihren Einfluss auf die Sprechen mehreren Sprachen. *Zeitschrift für die Gesamte Neurologie und Psychiatrie*, **96**, 100–124.

Poplack, S. (1980), Sometimes I'll start a sentence in Spanish y termino en Español: towards a typology of code-switching. *Linguistics*, **18**, 581–618.

Preston, M. and Lambert, W. (1969), Interlingual interference in a bilingual version of the Stroop Color-Word task. *Journal of Verbal Learning and Verbal Behavior,* **8**, 295–301.

Schultze, H. A. F. (1968), Unterschiedliche Rückbildung einer sensorischen und einer ideokinetischen motorischen Aphasie bei einem Polyglotten. *Psychiatrie, Neurologie und Medizinische Psychologie,* **20**, 441–445.

Shallice, T. (1979), Case study approach in neuropsychological research. *Journal of Clinical Neuropsychology,* **1**, 183–211.

Shanon, B. (1982), Identification and classification of words and drawings in two languages. *Quarterly Journal of Experimental Psychology,* **34**, 135–152.

Sridhar, S. (1978), On the functions of code-mixing in Kanada. In Kachru, B. B. and Sridhar, S. (eds.), *Aspects of Sociolinguistics in South Asia* (Special Issue, vol. 16, of *International Journal of Sociology and Language.*) The Hague: Mouton, 109–117.

Sridhar, S. and Sridhar, K. (1980), The syntax and psycholinguistics of bilingual code-mixing. *Canadian Journal of Psychology,* **34**, 407–416.

Stengel, E. and Zelmanowitz, J. (1933), Über polyglotte motorische Aphasie. *Zeitschrift für die Gesamte Neurologie und Psychiatrie,* **149**, 291–301.

Vaid, J. and Genesee, F. (1980), Neuropsychological approaches to bilingualism. *Canadian Journal of Psychology,* **24**, 417–445.

Veyrac, G. J. (1931), Etude de l'aphasie chez les sujets polyglottes. Thèse pour le Doctorat en Médecine, Paris. Translated by A. Conway. In Paradis, M. (ed.), *Readings on Aphasia in Bilinguals and Polyglots* (1983). Montreal: Didier.

Watamori, T. and Sasanuma, S. (1978), The recovery process of two English–Japanese bilingual aphasics. *Brain and Language,* **6**, 127–140.

Weinreich, U. (1967), *Languages in Contact.* The Hague: Mouton.

Weisenberg, T. and McBride, K. (1935), *Aphasia: A clinical and psychological study.* New York: Hafner.

Zurif, E. and Blumstein, S. (1978), Language and the Brain. In Halle, M., Bresnan, J. and Miller, G. (eds.), *Linguistic Theory and Psychological Reality.* Cambridge, MA: MIT Press.

Index